Hans D. Jarass

Neue Dimensionen der Tabakproduktregulierung
und Grundrechte sowie Grundfreiheiten

*New Dimensions of Tobacco Regulation and
Fundamental Rights and Freedoms*

Hans D. Jarass

Neue Dimensionen der Tabakproduktregulierung und Grundrechte sowie Grundfreiheiten

New Dimensions of Tobacco Regulation and Fundamental Rights and Freedoms

Grundfragen des Schutzes von Markenverpackungen, der Produktpräsentation in Verkaufseinrichtungen und der Produktzusammensetzung

Basic Questions of Brand Packaging, Product Display and Product Ingredients

Der Juristische Verlag
lexxion
Berlin

Bibliografische Informationen der Deutschen Nationalbibliothek

Die Deutsche Nationalbibliothek verzeichnet diese Publikation in der Deutschen National-bibliografie; detaillierte bibliografische Daten sind im Internet über <http://dnb.d-nb.de> abrufbar.

Das Werk ist urheberrechtlich geschützt. Die dadurch begründeten Rechte, insbesondere die der Übersetzung, des Nachdrucks, der Entnahme von Abbildungen, der Funksendung, der Wiedergabe auf fotomechanischem oder ähnlichem Wege und der Speicherung in Datenverarbeitungsanlagen, bleiben vorbehalten.

Verlag und Herausgeber übernehmen keine Haftung für inhaltliche und drucktechnisch bedingte Fehler.

A catalogue record for this book is available from the German National Libray, detailed bilbiographical data can be found on the internet at: http://dnb.d-nb.de.

All rights reserved. No part of this publication may be reproduced, stored in a retrieval system, or transmitted in any form by any means, electronic, mechanical, photocopying, recording or otherwise, without prior written permission of the publisher.

The publisher expressly disclaims all responsibility and liability with regard to the topicality, correctness, completeness or quality of the information provided.

ISBN Print: 978-3-869 65-222-1
ISBN E-Book: 978-3-869 65-223-8

© 2012 Lexxion Publisher · Berlin
www.lexxion.de

Cover & Typeset: G.K.W. Kuhle Werbung GmbH, Michael Bellenbaum

Vorwort

Die aktuelle Diskussion um die Verschärfung der Tabakproduktregulierung wirft interessante Fragen auf, die weit über den Bereich der Tabakprodukte hinaus in allen Bereichen der Wirtschaft von Bedeutung sind, in denen Produkte veräußert werden, bei denen die Prägung durch eine Marke von entscheidendem Gewicht ist. Bei diesen Fragen geht es insbesondere um die Reichweite des Schutzes, den die EU-Grundrechte und die deutschen Grundrechte in diesem Bereich vermitteln. Zudem sind die Grundfreiheiten, v.a. die Warenverkehrsfreiheit, von Bedeutung. Mit diesen Fragen befasst sich die folgende Untersuchung, die auf ein Gutachten zurückgeht, das für einen führenden Hersteller von Tabakprodukten erstellt wurde.

Preface

The current discussion on stricter regulation of tobacco products raises interesting questions which are of relevance to all sectors of economic activity with particular value put on the image of the brand of sold products, going far beyond the segment of tobacco products. These questions especially concern the scope of protection offered in this context by both the fundamental rights of the European Union and the basic rights under German Basic Law. The basic freedoms, especially the free movement of goods, are of additional relevance. These questions will be examined in the following study, based upon an expert opinion that was developed at the request of a leading manufacturer of tobacco products.

# Inhaltsverzeichnis – *Table of Contents*

Deutsche Version

A. Ausgangslage und Problemstellung 15
   I. Regulierung der Tabakherstellung und des Tabakverkaufs 15
      1. Tabakproduktregulierung auf nationaler, europäischer und internationaler Ebene 15
         a) Regelungen des deutschen Rechts 15
         b) Regelungen des europäischen Rechts 16
         c) Internationale Regelungen 16
      2. Neue Dimensionen der Tabakproduktregulierung als Untersuchungsgegenstand 17
      3. Die Marke als grundlegendes Element der Wettbewerbsordnung 19
         a) Markenrecht und Markenbegriff 19
         b) Bedeutung und Funktion von Marken 20
   II. Problemstellung und Untersuchungsgang 21
      1. Problemstellung 21
         a) Regulierungsebenen 21
         b) Probleme der Grundrechte und Grundfreiheiten sowie sonstige Probleme 22
      2. Untersuchungsgang 22

B. Grundrechte der Europäischen Union 24
   I. Allgemeines 24
      1. Grundlagen der EU-Grundrechte 24
      2. Verpflichtete und Grundrechtsträger 25
         a) Verpflichtete der EU-Grundrechte (Anwendungsbereich) 25
         b) Träger der EU-Grundrechte 26
   II. Beeinträchtigte Grundrechte 27
      1. Meinungsäußerungs- und Informationsfreiheit 27
         a) Grundlagen 27
         b) Schutzbereich 27
         c) Beeinträchtigung 28
      2. Eigentumsrecht 29
         a) Grundlagen 29
         b) Schutzbereich 29
         c) Beeinträchtigung 31
      3. Unternehmerische Freiheit 31
         a) Grundlagen 31
         b) Schutzbereich 32
         c) Beeinträchtigung 33

III. Rechtfertigung der Beeinträchtigungen...34
   1. Grundlagen...34
      a) Meinungsäußerungs- und Informationsfreiheit...34
      b) Eigentumsrecht...35
      c) Unternehmerische Freiheit...37
   2. Verhältnismäßigkeit...38
      a) Allgemeine und grundrechtliche Verhältnismäßigkeit...38
      b) Teileelemente der Verhältnismäßigkeit...39
      c) Übergangs- und Ausnahmeregelungen sowie Entschädigung...40
   3. Kontrolldichte...41
      a) Meinungs- und Informationsfreiheit...41
      b) Eigentumsrecht und unternehmerische Freiheit...41
IV. Verhältnismäßigkeit im vorliegenden Zusammenhang...42
   1. Verbot der Markenverpackung...42
      a) Beeinträchtigte Grundrechte und Gewicht des Eingriffs...42
      b) Verhältnismäßigkeit der Maßnahme...43
      c) Sondersituation der Hersteller mit vielfältigem Angebot...45
   2. Verbot der Produktpräsentation in Verkaufseinrichtungen...45
      a) Betroffene Grundrechte und Gewicht des Eingriffs...45
      b) Verhältnismäßigkeit der Maßnahme...46
   3. Verbot von Geruchs- und Geschmacksstoffen...47
      a) Betroffene Grundrechte und Gewicht des Eingriffs...47
      b) Verhältnismäßigkeit der Maßnahme...48
   4. Bedeutung additiver Grundrechtseingriffe...49
      a) Grundlagen...49
      b) Anwendung im vorliegenden Zusammenhang...49

C. Warenverkehrsfreiheit...51
I. Allgemeines...51
   1. Verbot der Maßnahmen gleicher Wirkung...51
   2. Verpflichtete...51
II. Anforderungen...52
   1. Anwendungs- bzw. Schutzbereich und Beschränkung...52
      a) Grenzüberschreitender Warenverkehr...52
      b) Maßnahmen gleicher Wirkung (Grundlagen)...52
      c) Maßnahme gleicher Wirkung im vorliegenden Zusammenhang...53
   2. Rechtfertigung...54
      a) Zulässige Gründe...54
      b) Verhältnismäßigkeit...55
      c) Verhältnis zu den Grundrechten...56
      d) Anwendung im vorliegenden Zusammenhang...57

D. Grundrechte des Grundgesetzes 59
   I. Grundlagen und beeinträchtigte Grundrechte 59
      1. Grundrechtsverpflichtung und Grundrechtsträger 59
         a) Grundrechtsverpflichtung von EU-Stellen 59
         b) Grundrechtsverpflichtung deutscher Stellen 60
         c) Grundrechtsträger 61
      2. Berufsfreiheit 61
         a) Schutzbereich 61
         b) Eingriff 62
      3. Eigentumsgarantie 63
         a) Schutzfähige Positionen 63
         b) Eingriff 64
      4. Meinungsfreiheit 64
   II. Rechtfertigung der Beeinträchtigungen 65
      1. Berufsfreiheit 65
         a) Gesetzliche Grundlage und Regelungsstufe 65
         b) Verhältnismäßigkeit 66
      2. Eigentumsgarantie 68
         a) Inhalts- und Schrankenbestimmung, gesetzliche Grundlage, sonstiges Verfassungsrecht 68
         b) Verhältnismäßigkeit 69
         c) Sachlicher sowie finanzieller Ausgleich 70
   III. Verhältnismäßigkeit im vorliegenden Zusammenhang 70
      1. Verbot der Markenverpackung 70
         a) Betroffene Grundrechte und Gewicht des Eingriffs 70
         b) Verhältnismäßigkeit der Maßnahme 71
      2. Verbot der Produktpräsentation in Verkaufseinrichtungen 73
         a) Betroffene Grundrechte und Gewicht des Eingriffs 73
         b) Verhältnismäßigkeit der Maßnahme 73
      3. Verbot von Geruchs- und Geschmacksstoffen 73
         a) Betroffene Grundrechte und Gewicht des Eingriffs 73
         b) Verhältnismäßigkeit der Maßnahme 74
      4. Bedeutung additiver Grundrechtseingriffe 75
         a) Grundlagen 75
         b) Anwendung im vorliegenden Zusammenhang 75

E. Zusammenfassung 77
   I. Ausgangslage 77
   II. Grundrechte der Europäischen Union 77
   III. Warenverkehrsfreiheit 79
   IV. Grundrechte des Grundgesetzes 80

English Version

A. Initial situation and Problem Definition................................83
    I. Regulation of tobacco production and the sale of tobacco 83
        1. Tobacco product regulation on national, European and
           international levels...83
           a) German law provisions....................................83
           b) Provisions under European law............................84
           c) International provisions...................................84
        2. New dimensions of tobacco product regulation as the subject
           of this study..85
        3. The brand as a basic element of competition....................87
           a) Trademark law and the concept of a brand..................87
           b) The meaning and function of trademarks....................88
    II. The problem definition and method of examination..................89
        1. Problem definition..89
           a) Levels of regulation.......................................89
           b) Problems concerning fundamental rights and freedoms as well
             as other issues 89
        2. Method of examination.......................................90

B. Fundamental Rights of the European Union.........................92
    I. General..92
        1. Principles of the fundamental rights of the European Union 92
        2. The parties bound and those entitled to fundamental rights........93
           a) The parties bound by the EU fundamental rights
             (scope of application) 93
           b) Parties entitled to the fundamental rights of the
             European Union 94
    II. Infringement of fundamental rights 95
        1. Freedom of expression and information........................95
           a) Principles 95
           b) Scope of protection 95
           c) Infringement 96
        2. Right to property 97
           a) Basic principles 97
           b) Scope of protection 97
           c) Infringement 99
        3. Freedom to conduct a business 99
           a) Principles 99

       b) Scope of protection 100
       c) Infringement 101
  III. Justification of the infringements................................ 101
    1. Basic principles... 101
       a) Freedom of expression and information 101
       b) Right to property.. 102
       c) Freedom to conduct a business 104
    2. Proportionality... 105
       a) Proportionality in general and with regard to
          fundamental rights 105
       b) Elements of proportionality................................ 106
       c) Transitional regulations, exceptions and compensation.......... 107
    3. Intensity (standard) of control 108
       a) Freedom of expression and information 108
       b) Right to property and freedom to conduct a business 108
  IV. Proportionality in the present context........................... 110
    1. Prohibition of brand packaging 110
       a) Infringement of fundamental rights and severity of the
          infringement 110
       b) The proportionality of the measure 111
       c) Special situation of manufacturers with a wide assortment 112
    2. Prohibition of product display in retail facilities 113
       a) Fundamental rights affected and the severity of the
          encroachment 113
       b) Proportionality of the measure 113
    3. Prohibition of odorous substances and flavouring agents 114
       a) Fundamental rights affected and severity of the infringement..... 114
       b) Proportionality of the measure 115
    4. Consequences of cumulative infringements of fundamental rights .. 116
       a) Principles 116
       b) Applicability in the present context 116

C. Free movement of goods 117
  I. General... 117
    1. Prohibition of measures having equivalent effect 117
    2. Parties bound 117
  II. Requirements 118
    1. Scope of protection and restrictions 118
       a) Cross-border movement of goods 118
       b) Measures with equivalent effect (principles).................. 118
       c) Measures having equivalent effect in the present context........ 119

  2. Justification...120
   a) Permissible grounds 120
   b) Proportionality 121
   c) In relation to fundamental rights 122
   d) Applicability in the present context 122
D. Basic rights under German Basic Law................................124
 I. Principles and infringed basic rights................................124
  1. Parties bound by the Basic Law and those entitled to basic rights ...124
   a) Obligations of EU bodies under the basic rights................124
   b) Obligation of German institutions based on basic rights.........125
   c) Those entitled to basic rights..................................125
  2. Freedom of profession...126
   a) Scope of protection..126
   b) Infringement 127
  3. Right to property 127
   a) Positions worthy of protection..................................127
   b) Infringement 128
  4. Freedom of expression 129
 II. Justification of the infringements..................................130
  1. Freedom of profession..130
   a) Statutory basis and level of regulation 130
   b) Proportionality 131
  2. Right to property 132
   a) Determining content and limits, legal basis, other
    constitutional law 132
   b) Proportionality 133
   c) Factual and financial compensation............................134
 III. Proportionality in the present context..............................135
  1. Prohibition of brand packaging 135
   a) Fundamental rights affected and severity of the infringement....135
   b) The proportionality of the measures 135
  2. Prohibition of product display in retail facilities 137
   a) Basic rights affected and severity of the infringement..........137
   b) The proportionality of the measure 137
  3. Prohibition of odorous substances and flavouring agents 138
   a) Fundamental rights affected and severity of the infringement....138
   b) The proportionality of the measure 138
  4. The relevance of cumulative infringements of basic rights 139
   a) Principles 139
   b) Applicability in the present context 140

E. Summary..141
  I. Initial situation 141
  II. Fundamental Rights of the European Union......................141
  III. Free movement of goods.......................................143
  IV. Basic rights under German Basic Constitutional Law 144

A. Ausgangslage und Problemstellung

I. Regulierung der Tabakherstellung und des Tabakverkaufs

1. Tabakproduktregulierung auf nationaler, europäischer und internationaler Ebene

a) Regelungen des deutschen Rechts

Die Regulierung von Tabakerzeugnissen erfolgt in Deutschland durch das *„Vorläufige Tabakgesetz"* (VTG), das ursprünglich als Lebensmittel- und Bedarfsgegenständegesetz ergangen ist.[1] Das Gesetz legt für die in §3 VTG definierten Tabakerzeugnisse eine Vielzahl von Anforderungen fest. Insbesondere enthält §21a VTG, in Umsetzung der Richtlinie 2003/33/EG über Werbung und Sponsoring von Tabakerzeugnissen,[2] weit reichende Verbote der Tabakwerbung und des Tabaksponsoring.

Im vorliegenden Zusammenhang wichtiger sind die Regelungen in den auf der Grundlage des „Vorläufigen Tabakgesetzes" erlassenen Rechtsverordnungen. Zu nennen ist zunächst die *Tabakprodukt-Verordnung* vom 20.11.2002.[3] Sie dient der Umsetzung der Richtlinie 2001/37/EG vom 5.6.2001.[4] Inhaltlich regelt die Verordnung in §§2–4 den zulässigen Teer-, Nikotin- und Kohlenmonoxydgehalt von Zigaretten. §5 betrifft Mitteilungspflichten zu den Zusatzstoffen. In §§6–9 werden Anforderungen an die Angaben und Hinweise auf den Packungen getroffen.

Weiter ist die Verordnung über Tabakerzeugnisse (*Tabakverordnung*) vom 20.12.1977 von Bedeutung.[5] Sie regelt in detaillierter Weise die Zulassung von Zusatzstoffen bei der Herstellung von Tabakerzeugnissen. Dazu enthält §1 eine Positivliste der zugelassenen Stoffe bzw. Stoffgruppen. §2 schließt bestimmte

---

1   Vom 15.8.1974, neu gefasst am 9.9.1997 (BGBl I 2296), zuletzt geändert am 9.12.2010 (BGBl I 1934). Das ursprüngliche Lebensmittel- und Bedarfsgegenständegesetz wurde durch das Gesetz vom 1.9.2005 (BGBl I 2618) weitgehend durch das Lebensmittel-, Bedarfsgegenstände- und Futtermittelgesetzbuch ersetzt. Lediglich die tabakbezogenen Regelungen blieben bestehen; das Gesetz wurde gleichzeitig in Vorläufiges Tabakgesetz umbenannt.
2   Zu dieser Richtlinie unten A I 1 b.
3   BGBl I 4434; zuletzt geändert durch Art. 360 der Verordnung vom 31.10.2006 (BGBl I 2407). Näher zur Auslegung der Verordnung vgl. die Amtliche Begründung zum Entwurf vom 9.10.2002 (BR-Drs. 758/02).
4   Näher zu dieser Richtlinie unten A I 1 b.
5   BGBl I 2831, zuletzt geändert durch Art. 1 der Verordnung vom 28.6.2010 (BGBl I 851). Näher zur Auslegung der Verordnung vgl. die Amtliche Begründung zum Entwurf v. 13.10.1977 (BR-Drs. 479/77).

Geruchs- und Geschmacksstoffe generell aus.[6] Für andere Stoffe werden in § 3a Höchstmengen festgelegt. Hinzu treten weitere Regelungen, die zum Teil über die zulässigen Zusatzstoffe hinausgehen. So trifft § 5a Regelungen zur Verwendung von Tabakerzeugnissen.

b) Regelungen des europäischen Rechts

Auf europäischer Ebene erfolgt die Regulierung von Tabakerzeugnissen durch die Richtlinie 2001/37/EG über die Herstellung, die Aufmachung und den Verkauf von Tabakerzeugnissen (Tabakerzeugnis-Richtlinie) vom 5.6.2001.[7] Die Richtlinie wurde auf den EG-Vertrag, insbesondere auf Art. 95 EGV (heute Art. 114 AEUV) und Art. 133 EGV (heute Art. 207 AEUV) gestützt. Inhaltlich dient die Richtlinie gem. Art. 1 der Rechtsangleichung in dem hier interessierenden Bereich, unter Beachtung eines „hohen Gesundheitsschutzniveaus". Art. 3, 4 treffen Vorgaben zum Teer-, Nikotin- und Kohlenmonoxidhöchstgehalt von Zigaretten. Art. 5 regelt die Etikettierung der Packungen von Tabakerzeugnissen. Art. 6 betrifft die Bereitstellung von Produktinformationen durch die Hersteller und Importeure von Tabakerzeugnissen. Anforderungen an die Produktbezeichnung finden sich in Art. 7. Hinzu kommen weitere Vorgaben in Regelungen in Art. 8–12. Andererseits wird der freie Warenverkehr im Bereich der Tabakerzeugnisse durch Art. 13 sichergestellt, wenn die Erzeugnisse den Anforderungen der Richtlinie entsprechen.

Den Vertrieb von Tabakprodukten betrifft die Richtlinie 2003/33/EG über Werbung und Sponsoring von Tabakerzeugnissen vom 26.5.2003.[8] Die Richtlinie sieht weit reichende Einschränkungen der Werbung und des Sponsoring in Druckerzeugnissen, im Rundfunk, im Internet und bei Veranstaltungen vor.[9] Hinzu treten spezielle Regelungen zu den Verbrauchssteuern auf Tabakwaren.[10]

c) Internationale Regelungen

Auf internationaler Ebene ist das WHO-Rahmenübereinkommen zur Eindämmung des Tabakgebrauchs zu nennen, das durch die 56. Weltgesundheitsversamm-

---

6 Wie der Amtlichen Begründung zum Entwurf der Verordnung zu entnehmen ist, dient die Vorschrift dem Gesundheitsschutz (BR-Drs. 479/77, S. 23 f.).
7 ABl L 194/26; geändert durch die Verordnung (EG) Nr. 596/2009 (ABl L 188/14). Zur Richtlinie *Hardach/Ludwigs*, DÖV 2007, 288; *Marwitz*, K & R 2004, 214; *Riessen u.a.*, Assessing the Impacts of Revising the Tobacco Products Directive, Rand, 2010, 3 f.
8 ABl L 152/16, ber. am 5.3.2004 (ABl L 67/34).
9 Dazu *Marwitz*, K & R 2004, 214.
10 Vgl. die jüngste Änderung dieser Richtlinien durch die Richtlinie 2010/12/EU (ABl L 50/1).

lung am 21.5.2003 angenommen wurde.[11] Das Abkommen wurde von fast allen Staaten unterzeichnet, auch von Deutschland. In Deutschland gilt es aber nur, soweit ein innerstaatlicher Akt dies anordnet.[12] Das Übereinkommen enthält weitgehende Verpflichtungen zur Produktion, zum Verkauf, zum Vertrieb, zur Werbung und zur Besteuerung von Tabakprodukten.[13]

2. Neue Dimensionen der Tabakproduktregulierung als Untersuchungsgegenstand

Derzeit findet insbesondere auf der Ebene der Europäischen Union eine umfangreiche Diskussion darüber statt, ob und gegebenenfalls auf welche Weise die Regelungen zur Tabakherstellung und zum Tabakverkauf verschärft werden sollen, um die negativen Wirkungen des Rauchens zu reduzieren und damit den Schutz der Gesundheit zu fördern.[14] Die Generaldirektion Gesundheit und Verbraucher der Europäischen Kommission hat dazu eine öffentliche Konsultation zur möglichen Überarbeitung der Tabakerzeugnis-Richtlinie 2001/37/EG in englischer Sprache durchgeführt. Die Befragung betraf sechs Gebiete:
1. Scope of the Directive
2. Smokeless tobacco products
3. Consumer information
4. Reporting and registration of ingredients
5. Regulation of ingredients
6. Access to tobacco products

Die Konsultation hat eine ungewöhnlich hohe Resonanz gefunden. Die Ergebnisse der Konsultation wurden von der Generaldirektion in ihrem „Report on the public consultation on the possible revision of the Tobacco Products Directive (2001/37/EC)" vom 27.7.2011 zusammengefasst.

In der Konsultation wurden zahlreiche Politikoptionen präsentiert, zu denen die Öffentlichkeit Stellung nehmen konnte.[15] Darunter waren auch sehr weit reichende Änderungen des geltenden Rechts, die den Gegenstand dieser Untersuchung bilden

---

11 WHO Framework Convention on Tabacco Control.
12 *BVerfGE* 73, 339/375; *Jarass*, in: drs./Pieroth, Grundgesetz, 11. Aufl. 2011, Art. 25 Rn. 1a; Art. 59 Rn. 17.
13 Dazu *Pauling*, VuR 2010, 444 f.
14 Soweit der Rechtsakt auf Art. 114 AEUV gestützt wird, muss die Rechtsangleichung das primäre Ziel sein. Daneben können aber auch Gesundheitsbelange verfolgt werden.
15 Dazu *Pauling*, VuR 2010, 443 f.

und die als „neue Dimensionen" der Tabakproduktregulierung bezeichnet werden können. Gemeint sind damit folgende Vorschläge (im Folgenden als zu untersuchende Regulierungsvorschläge bezeichnet):

(1) Verbot von Markenverpackungen

Im ersten Vorschlag geht es um das „Plain packaging"; auch von „Standardized packaging" ist die Rede.[16] Im Deutschen könnte man von schlichter oder standardisierter Verpackung oder Einheitsverpackung sprechen. Dabei geht es um das Verbot der Verwendung von Markenemblemen, markenspezifischen Farben und Ähnlichem als Gestaltungsmerkmale der Verpackung von Tabakprodukten, mit Ausnahme des Firmen- bzw. Produktnamens.[17] Auch sollen die Verpackungen einheitlich gestaltet und eingefärbt werden, etwa schwarz-weiß.[18] Da der Verbraucher eine Marke nicht allein als Wort wahrnimmt, sondern ganz wesentlich auch durch die Figuren und Farben, wie noch zu erörtern sein wird,[19] handelt es sich praktisch um ein Verbot von Markenverpackungen. Die Bezeichnung als Verpflichtung zu schlichter oder standardisierter Verpackung ist euphemistisch und kennzeichnet Gewicht und Bedeutung der Maßnahme nur unzureichend. Daher wird im Folgenden vom „Verbot von Markenverpackungen" gesprochen.

(2) Verbot der Produktpräsentation in Verkaufseinrichtungen

Ein weiterer Vorschlag wird als „Retail display ban" bezeichnet.[20] Hier geht es darum, die Auslage und Sichtbarkeit von Tabakprodukten in den Verkaufsstellen des Einzelhandels zu untersagen. Es geht um ein Verbot der Produktpräsentation in Verkaufseinrichtungen. Der Käufer soll die Produkte nur auf Verlangen sehen können; die Produkte werden „unter der Theke" gehalten. Das Verbot schließt ein Verbot der Werbung für Tabakprodukte in Einzelhandelsverkaufseinrichtungen ein.

(3) Verbot von Geruchs- und Geschmacksstoffen

Der dritte Vorschlag, der in dieser Untersuchung näher geprüft werden soll, besteht darin, den Einsatz von Geruchs- und Geschmacksstoffen vollständig zu verbieten, um auf diese Weise die „attractiveness" (Attraktivität) der Produkte zu

---

16 Etwa Report on the public consultation on the possible revision of the Tobacco Products Directive (2001/37/EC)" vom 27.7.2011, S. 14.
17 *Kunz-Hallstein*, in: Bender/Schülke/Winterfeldt (Hg.), 50 Jahre Bundespatentgericht, 2011, 661.
18 KOM (2007) 754 endg., S. 12; *Pauling*, VuR 2010, 443; *Ziegenaus*, GRUR Prax 2010, 475.
19 Unten A I 3 a.
20 Etwa Report on the public consultation on the possible revision of the Tobacco Products Directive (2001/37/EC)" vom 27.7.2011, S. 20.

reduzieren.[21] Ein Verbot von Geruchs- und Geschmacksstoffen hat für die betroffenen Hersteller weit reichende Folgen, da das Produkt, das der Verbraucher erwartet, durch diese Stoffe geprägt wird.[22]

3. Die Marke als grundlegendes Element der Wettbewerbsordnung

a) Markenrecht und Markenbegriff

Die zu untersuchenden Vorschläge der Regelung der Tabakherstellung und des Tabakverkaufs haben insbesondere gravierende Auswirkungen auf die einzelnen Tabakmarken und deren Nutzung. Beim Verbot der Markenverpackung ist das offenkundig, geht es doch dabei um ein zentrales, wenn nicht das zentrale Instrument für die Nutzung der mit einer Marke aufgebauten Möglichkeiten durch den Hersteller. Wie sich noch zeigen wird, ist die Art und Weise der Verpackung markenfähig.[23] Auch beim Verbot der Produktpräsentation in Einzelhandelsverkaufseinrichtungen geht es wesentlich um eine Markennutzung.[24]

Angesichts des Stellenwerts des Markenrechts im vorliegenden Zusammenhang ist es vorweg angebracht, einen kurzen Blick auf die Bedeutung und die Funktionen von Marken und deren rechtlichen Schutz zu werfen. Dabei werden einerseits die entsprechenden Vorgaben des EU-Markenrechts zugrunde gelegt, also der Richtlinie 2008/95/EG über die Marken (Marken-Richtlinie; MarkenRL)[25] und der Verordnung EG Nr. 207/2009 über die Gemeinschaftsmarke (GMVO).[26] Zugleich wird auf das deutsche Markenrecht abgehoben, also auf das Gesetz über den Schutz von Marken und sonstigen Kennzeichen (MarkenG).[27]

Als Marke können, wie Art. 2 MarkenRL und § 3 Abs. 1, § 8 Abs. 1 MarkenG zu entnehmen ist, alle Zeichen fungieren, die sich graphisch darstellen lassen und die geeignet sind, Waren[28] eines Unternehmens von denjenigen anderer Unternehmen

---

21   Vgl. Report on the public consultation on the possible revision of the Tobacco Products Directive (2001/37/EC)" vom 27.7.2011, S. 18. Eine vorsichtigere Lösung besteht in einer Positiv- und einer Negativliste.
22   Dementsprechend hat *EuGH*, Rs. 273/00, Slg. 2002, I-11737 Rn. 44 ff., 69 ff. einen Geruch sogar als markenfähiges Zeichen, das ein Produkt kennzeichnet, in Erwägung gezogen und ihn nur an der fehlenden Visualisierbarkeit scheitern lassen.
23   Näher unten A I 3 a.
24   Unten B II 2 b bb.
25   Vom 22.10.2008 (ABl L 299/25).
26   Vom 20.2.2009 (ABl L 78/1).
27   Vom 25.10.1994 (BGBl I, 3082), zuletzt geänd. durch Art. 17 des Gesetzes vom 22.12.2010 (GBGl I, 2253).
28   Gleiches gilt für Dienstleistungen, worauf es im Folgenden aber nicht ankommt.

zu unterscheiden, wie Worte (insbesondere Namen), Abbildungen, Buchstaben, Zahlen und die Form sowie Aufmachung einer Ware. Erfasst werden, wie insbesondere der Europäische Gerichtshof herausgestellt hat, auch Farben und Farbkombinationen und die Verpackung einer Ware, insbesondere deren graphische und farbliche Gestaltung.[29]

b) Bedeutung und Funktion von Marken

Marken bilden in modernen Wirtschaftssystemen eine höchst bedeutsame Größe. In einem soeben erschienenen Lehrbuch zum deutschen und europäischen Markenrecht findet sich dazu folgende Aussage: „Marken haben in hoch entwickelten Wirtschaftssystemen eine überragende Bedeutung. Sie sind zentrale Instrumente im unternehmerischen Marketing. Sie ermöglichen die Kommunikation mit dem Verbraucher und prägen nicht selten das Erscheinungsbild des Unternehmens in der Öffentlichkeit. Marken können sehr wertvoll sein und in vielen Fällen das wertvollste Wirtschaftsgut eines Unternehmens darstellen".[30]

Die Gründe für diesen Befund lassen sich der Funktion von Marken entnehmen, die insbesondere der Europäische Gerichtshof herausgearbeitet hat: In einer Wettbewerbswirtschaft muss ein Unternehmen in der Lage sein, die Kunden durch die Qualität seiner Waren an sich zu binden, was Kennzeichen voraussetzt, die eine Identifizierung der Waren ermöglichen.[31] Die Marke soll dem Endabnehmer die Ursprungsidentität der Ware gewährleisten, indem sie ihm ermöglicht, die Ware ohne Verwechslungsgefahr von Waren anderer Herkunft zu unterscheiden.[32] Die Marke soll sicherstellen, dass alle Waren, die sie kennzeichnet, unter der Kontrolle eines einzigen, für die Qualität verantwortlichen Unternehmens hergestellt worden sind.[33] Dabei wird auch das Interesse des Markeninhabers berücksichtigt, den besonderen Ruf seiner Erzeugnisse zu schützen.[34]

Zu dieser Herkunftsfunktion der Marke, die nach der Rechtsprechung des Europäischen Gerichtshofs deren Hauptfunktion bildet, kommen weitere Funktionen,

---

29 *EuGH*, Rs. 218/01, Slg. 2004, I-1725 Rn. 37, 44; Rs. 49/02, Slg. 2004, I-6129 Rn. 22; *Lange*, Marken- und Kennzeichenrecht, 2006, § 1 Rn. 8.
30 *Sosnitza*, Deutsches und europäisches Markenrecht, 2010, § 3 Rn. 13.
31 *EuGH*, Rs. 517/99, Slg. 2001, I-6959 Rn. 21 f.; Rs. 206/01, Slg. 2002, I-10273 Rn. 47 f.; Rs. 228/03, Slg. 2005, I-2337 Rn. 25 f.; *Lange*, Marken- und Kennzeichenrecht, 2006, § 1 Rn. 11.
32 *EuGH*, Rs. 143/00, Slg. 2002, I-3759 Rn. 12; Rs. 329/02, Slg. 2004, I-8317 Rn. 23; Rs. 304/06, Slg. 2009, I-3297 Rn. 66; Rs. 265/09 v. 9.10.2010, Rn. 31.
33 *EuGH*, Rs. 299/99, Slg. 2002, I-5475 Rn. 30; Rs. 273/00, Slg. 2002, I-11737 Rn. 35; Rs. 371/02, Slg. 2004, I-5791 Rn. 20; *Lange*, Marken- und Kennzeichenrecht, 2006, § 1 Rn. 11; *Fezer*, Handbuch der Markenpraxis, Bd. 1, 2007, Einl. 66.
34 *EuGH*, Rs. 349/95, Slg. 1997, I-6227 Rn. 22; Rs. 63/97, Slg. 1999, I-905 Rn. 52.

wie deren Werbewirkung, die Vertrauens- oder Qualitätsfunktion, die Hinweisfunktion und die Kommunikationsfunktion.[35] Das Bundesverfassungsgericht hat neben der Herkunftsfunktion die Garantiefunktion, also die Bekundung einer bestimmten Beschaffenheit, und die Werbefunktion herausgestellt.[36] Nimmt man das alles zusammen, kann die eingangs angesprochene Bedeutung der Marken nicht überraschen. Auch belegt das die These des Europäischen Gerichtshofs, dass die Marke einen wesentlichen, ja unverzichtbaren Bestandteil des Systems unverfälschten Wettbewerbs darstellt, das durch das EU-Primärrecht errichtet wird.[37]

II. Problemstellung und Untersuchungsgang

1. Problemstellung

a) Regulierungsebenen

Die Regulierung von Tabakprodukten kann auf verschiedenen Ebenen erfolgen, wie das auch schon bisher geschehen ist. Sie kann zum einen auf europäischer Ebene stattfinden, wobei zwei unterschiedliche Möglichkeiten bestehen: Die europäische Union kann einerseits unmittelbar geltende Verordnungen erlassen, die gem. Art. 288 Abs. 2 S. 2 AEUV in den Mitgliedstaaten ohne Umsetzung gelten. Andererseits kann sie Richtlinien gem. Art. 288 Abs. 3 AEUV einsetzen, die von den Mitgliedstaaten in nationales Recht umgesetzt werden müssen, um geltendes Recht in den Mitgliedstaaten zu bilden.[38] Regelungen können daneben auch auf der nationalen Ebene, also durch deutsche Gesetze getroffen werden, auch wenn keine EU-rechtliche Verpflichtung besteht, sofern dem EU-Recht nicht entgegensteht.

Bei den dargelegten Vorschlägen einer drastischen Verschärfung der Tabakproduktregulierung ist offen, ob sie umgesetzt werden und ggf. auf welcher Ebene das geschehen soll. Aus diesem Grunde soll im Folgenden sowohl eine Regelung auf europäischer Ebene wie auf deutscher Ebene untersucht werden.

---

35 *Lange*, Marken- und Kennzeichenrecht, 2006, §1 Rn. 12; *Ingere/Rohnke*, Markengesetz, 3. Aufl. 2010, Einl. 72; *Fezer*, Handbuch der Markenpraxis, Bd. 1, 2007, Einl. 69 ff.
36 BVerfGE 51, 193/216.
37 *EuGH*, Rs. 39/97, Slg. 1998, I-5507 Rn. 28; Rs. 299/99, Slg. 2002, I-5475 Rn. 78; Rs. 104/01, Slg. 2003, I-3797 Rn. 48; *Fezer*, Handbuch der Markenpraxis, Bd. 1, 2007, Einl. 65 f.
38 Im Falle der unmittelbaren Wirkung sind allerdings Richtlinien in den Mitgliedstaaten auch ohne Umsetzung anzuwenden.

b) Probleme der Grundrechte und Grundfreiheiten sowie sonstige Probleme

Die dargelegten Vorschläge einer gravierenden Verschärfung der Tabakproduktregulierung könnten nur dann geltendes Recht werden, wenn sie mit den Grundrechten vereinbar sind. Soweit es um EU-rechtliche Regelungen geht, sind insoweit die Grundrechte der Europäischen Union bedeutsam. Vorschriften des sekundären EU-Rechts können nur dann als rechtens anerkannt werden, wenn sie den Anforderungen der im primären Recht verankerten Grundrechte entsprechen.[39] Ein gegen die Grundrechte verstoßender Rechtsakt ist ungültig.[40] Deutsche Regelungen sind an den Grundrechten des Grundgesetzes zu messen. Auch insoweit gilt, dass Gesetze nur wirksam sind, wenn die Grundrechte beachtet werden.[41] Regelungen auf beiden Stufen müssen zudem den Anforderungen der Grundfreiheiten des AEU-Vertrags gerecht werden. Angesichts der weit reichenden Wirkungen der genannten Vorschläge ist die Vereinbarkeit mit Grundrechten wie mit Grundfreiheiten durchaus unsicher. Daher wird dem im Folgenden näher nachgegangen.

Daneben werfen die genannten Vorschläge, soweit sie auf europäischer Ebene vorgenommen werden, nicht unerhebliche Kompetenzprobleme auf.[42] Diesen Fragen kann im Folgenden nicht nachgegangen werden. Die kompetenziellen Grenzen gilt es aber zusätzlich neben den materiellen Grenzen zu beachten.

2. Untersuchungsgang

Die folgende Untersuchung wird in einem ersten Teil der Vereinbarkeit der aufgeführten Vorschläge zur Tabakproduktregulierung mit den EU-Grundrechten nachgehen. Dazu wird zunächst auf die rechtlichen Grundlagen der EU-Grundrechte und deren Verpflichtungsadressaten eingegangen (unten B I). Dann wird geklärt, in welche Grundrechte eingegriffen wird (unten B II), um darauf aufbauend zu erörtern, welche Anforderungen an die Rechtfertigung von Eingriffen zu stellen sind

---

39 *EuGH*, Rs. 112/00, Slg. 2003, I-5659 Rn. 73; Rs. 402/05, Slg. 2008, I-6513 Rn. 284; Rs. 45/08, Slg. 2009, I-12073 Rn. 41.
40 *EuGH*, Rs. 92/09 v. 9.11.2010, Rn. 45 f.
41 BVerfGE 84, 9/20; Schulze-Fielitz, in: Dreier (Hg.), Grundgesetz, Bd. II, 2. Aufl. 2006, Art. 20 Rn. 84; *Jarass*, in: drs./Pieroth, Grundgesetz, 11. Aufl. 2011, Art. 20 Rn. 33; *Sommermann*, in: v.Mangoldt/Klein/Starck, Grundgesetz, 6. Aufl., Bd. II 2010, Art. 20 Rn. 256.
42 Allgemein zu den Kompetenzproblemen der Tabakregulierung *Pache*, in: Pache/Schwarz/Sosnitza, Aktuelle Rechtsfragen der Tabakregulierung in Europa, 2012, 21 ff.; *Pauling*, VuR 2010, 444; *Stein/Rauber*, Rechtliche Grenzen der Bekämpfung des Tabakkonsums im Mehrebenensystem, 2011, 15 ff.; *Koenig/Kühling*, EWS 2002, 17 ff.

Ausgangslage und Problemstellung

(unten B III). Schließlich wird die zentrale Voraussetzung der Verhältnismäßigkeit im vorliegenden Zusammenhang näher zu untersuchen sein (unten B IV).

In einem weiteren Teil der Untersuchung wird auf die Vereinbarkeit der Vorschläge zur Tabakproduktregulierung mit der einschlägigen Grundfreiheit, der Warenverkehrsfreiheit, eingegangen. Dazu wird zunächst das Verbot der Maßnahmen gleicher Wirkung skizziert und untersucht, wer durch die Warenverkehrsfreiheit verpflichtet wird (unten C I). Sodann werden die Anforderungen untersucht, die sich aus dem Verbot der Maßnahmen gleicher Wirkung im vorliegenden Zusammenhang ergeben (unten C II).

Im letzten Teil der Untersuchung geht es um die Vereinbarkeit der genannten Vorschläge zur Tabakproduktregulierung mit den Grundrechten des Grundgesetzes. Dazu wird zunächst geprüft, wer durch diese Grundrechte gebunden und in welche Grundrechte eingegriffen wird (unten D I). Sodann wird herausgearbeitet, welchen Anforderungen die Grundrechtseingriffe entsprechen müssen, damit sie gerechtfertigt sind (unten D II). Schließlich wird die zentrale Voraussetzung der auch im Rahmen der deutschen Grundrechte bedeutsamen Verhältnismäßigkeit im vorliegenden Zusammenhang näher untersucht (unten D III).

B. Grundrechte der Europäischen Union

I. Allgemeines

1. Grundlagen der EU-Grundrechte

aa) Die Prüfung der Vereinbarkeit der zu untersuchenden Regulierungsvorschläge mit den Grundrechten der Europäischen Union muss sich zwangsläufig mit den einzelnen betroffenen Grundrechten beschäftigen. Vorweg sind aber einige Fragen zu behandeln, die übergreifender Natur und die für alle betroffenen Grundrechte relevant sind. Das gilt zunächst für die Frage, woraus sich die EU-Grundrechte ergeben.

Seit dem 1.12.2009 ist die „Charta der Grundrechte der Europäischen Union" gem. Art. 6 Abs. 1 EUV verbindliches Recht, und zwar im Rang der Verträge, also des primären EU-Rechts. Daneben sind weiterhin die vom Europäischen Gerichtshof als allgemeine Rechtsgrundsätze entwickelten Grundrechte gem. Art. 6 Abs. 3 EUV geltendes Unionsrecht. Da andererseits die Charta, wie etwa Abs. 4 der Präambel zur Charta zu entnehmen ist, vor allem den Schutz der Grundrechte, wie sie durch den Europäischen Gerichtshof entwickelt wurden, „sichtbarer" machen soll, liegt es nahe, die Grundrechte der beiden Quellen aufeinander abgestimmt bzw. harmonisierend zu interpretieren.[43] Vielleicht handelt es sich sogar nur um zwei verschiedene Quellen der gleichen Grundrechte.[44] Im Folgenden werden dementsprechend die Vorgaben der Charta und der Rechtsprechung des Europäischen Gerichtshofs zusammen behandelt.

bb) Eine wichtige Erkenntnisquelle der Unionsgrundrechte bildet die „Europäische Konvention zum Schutze der Menschenrechte und Grundfreiheiten" (EMRK). Ein Teil der in der Charta enthaltenen Grundrechte wurde ähnlich wie in der Konvention geregelt.[45] Dazu schreibt Art. 52 Abs. 3 S. 1 GRCh vor, dass diese Charta-Rechte die gleiche Bedeutung und Tragweite wie die entsprechenden Rechte der Konvention haben. Allerdings kann die Charta gem. Art. 52 Abs. 3 S. 2 GRCh einen weitergehenden Schutz gewähren. Daraus folgt, dass die Grundrechte der Charta in keinem Punkt hinter den Anforderungen der Konvention zurückbleiben (dürfen).[46]

---

43 *Jarass*, Charta der Grundrechte, 2010, Einl. 33.
44 *Skouris*, in: Merten/Papier (Hg.), Handbuch der Grundrechte, Bd. VI/1, 2010, § 157 Rn. 45.
45 Im vorliegenden Zusammenhang betrifft das die Meinungsäußerungs- und Informationsfreiheit und das Eigentumsrecht.
46 Charta-Erläuterungen, ABl 2007 C 303/33; *Heringa/Verhey*, MJ 2001, 17; *Jarass*, Charta der Grundrechte, 2010, Art. 52 Rn. 63; *Hilf*, in: Merten/Papier (Hg.), Handbuch der Grundrechte, Bd. VI/1, § 164 Rn. 46.

Das gilt auch für die Konkretisierung der Konvention durch die Rechtsprechung des Europäischen Gerichtshofs für Menschenrechte (EGMR).[47]

Schließlich ergeben sich aus den vom Präsidium des Grundrechte- bzw. Verfassungskonvents erarbeiteten „Erläuterungen zur Charta der Grundrechte" wichtige Anhaltspunkte für die Auslegung der Charta. Gem. Art. 6 Abs. 1 UAbs. 3 EUV wie gem. Art. 52 Abs. 7 GRCh sind die Erläuterungen bei der Charta-Auslegung gebührend zu berücksichtigen. Sie sind damit nicht verbindlich, stellen aber eine wichtige Erkenntnisquelle dar.[48]

2. Verpflichtete und Grundrechtsträger

a) Verpflichtete der EU-Grundrechte (Anwendungsbereich)

aa) Übergreifender Natur ist des Weiteren die Frage, wer durch die EU-Grundrechte verpflichtet wird. Sie wird in Art. 51 GRCh unter der Überschrift „Anwendungsbereich" behandelt. Nach dieser Vorschrift verpflichten die Unionsgrundrechte zunächst die *Organe, Einrichtungen* und *sonstigen Stellen der Union*. Dies gilt für sämtliche Aktivitäten der Union und ihrer Stellen.[49] Insbesondere wird der Erlass von Sekundärrecht erfasst, was im vorliegenden Zusammenhang bedeutsam ist.

bb) Des Weiteren werden durch die EU-Grundrechte die *Mitgliedstaaten* verpflichtet. Allerdings gilt das gem. Art. 51 Abs. 1 S. 1 GRCh nur dann, wenn sie EU-Recht durchführen.[50] Der Begriff der „Durchführung" ist dabei sehr weit zu verstehen und umfasst die Umsetzung wie den Vollzug des EU-Rechts durch die Mitgliedstaaten, insbesondere die Umsetzung von Richtlinien[51] und der Vollzug von EU-Recht durch Verwaltungsaktivitäten.[52] Weiter sind die EU-Grundrechte beim Erlass nationaler Vorschriften zu beachten, soweit sie zu einer Einschränkung von Grundfreiheiten führen.[53] Erfasst wird darüber hinaus die Anwendung nationalen Rechts, das in Umsetzung von Unionsrecht, insbesondere von Richtlinien, ergangen ist (mittelba-

---

47 *EuGH*, Rs. 400/10 v. 5.10.2010, Rn. 53; Rs. 279/09 v. 22.10.2010, Rn. 35; *Jarass*, Charta der Grundrechte, 2010, Art. 52 Rn. 65.

48 Dazu *Jarass*, Charta der Grundrechte, 2010, Art. 52 Rn. 87; *Scheuing*, EuR 2005, 185.

49 *Borowski*, in: Meyer (Hg.), Charta der Grundrechte, 3. Aufl. 2011, Art. 51 Rn. 21; *Jarass*, Charta der Grundrechte, 2010, Art. 51 Rn. 4.

50 Ähnlich hat der EuGH schon früher die Grundrechte nur im Anwendungsbereich des EU-Rechts angewandt.

51 *EuGH*, Rs. 74/95 Slg. 1996, I-6609 Rn. 25; Rs. 275/06, Slg. 2008, I-271 Rn. 68; Borowski, in: Meyer (Hg.), Charta der Grundrechte, 3. Aufl. 2011, Art. 51 Rn. 27.

52 *Jarass*, Charta der Grundrechte, 2010, Art. 51 Rn. 17.

53 *EuGH*, Rs. 260/89, Slg. 1991, I-2925 Rn. 43 f; Rs. 368/95, Slg. 1997, I-3689 Rn. 24 f Rs. 60/00, Slg. 2002, I-6279 Rn. 40.

rer Vollzug).⁵⁴ Soweit die EU-Grundrechte die Mitgliedstaaten binden, werden nicht nur diese selbst, sondern als Folge der unmittelbaren Geltung der Grundrechte, auch alle ihre Organe, Einrichtungen und sonstigen Stellen verpflichtet.⁵⁵

Im vorliegenden Zusammenhang ergibt sich daraus, dass der deutsche Gesetzgeber an die EU-Grundrechte gebunden ist, wenn er Richtlinien zur Tabakregulierung in deutsches Recht umsetzt. Und die deutsche Verwaltung und Rechtsprechung haben die Grundrechte zu beachten, wenn sie EU-Vorschriften oder die zu ihrer Umsetzung ergangenen deutschen Vorschriften auslegen und anwenden.

b) Träger der EU-Grundrechte

Träger der Unionsgrundrechte sind zunächst alle natürlichen Personen, soweit das Grundrecht nicht ausdrücklich auf Unionsbürger beschränkt ist. Daneben stehen die Grundrechte auch juristischen Personen zu, obgleich das nur bei einzelnen Grundrechten explizit gesagt wird.⁵⁶ Entsprechendes lässt sich der Rechtsprechung des Europäischen Gerichtshofs für die Grundrechte (als allgemeine Rechtsgrundsätze) entnehmen.⁵⁷ Allerdings gilt das nicht für alle Grundrechte; manche sind ihrem Wesen nach allein auf natürliche Personen anwendbar. Bei den hier einschlägigen Grundrechten bestehen aber insoweit keine Zweifel: Auf die Meinungs- und Informationsfreiheit können sich juristische Personen berufen.⁵⁸ Gleiches gilt für das Eigentumsrecht⁵⁹ und für die unternehmerische Freiheit bzw. die Berufsfreiheit.⁶⁰ Daher können im vorliegenden Zusammenhang auch als juristische Personen verfasste Unternehmen der Tabakherstellung oder des Einzelhandels die relevanten Grundrechte geltend machen.

---

54 *EuGH*, Rs. 74/95, Slg. 1996, I-6609 Rn. 25; Rs. 275/06, Slg. 2008, I-271 Rn. 68; *Borowski*, in: Meyer (Hg.), Charta der Grundrechte, 3. Aufl. 2011, Art. 51 Rn. 28; *Jarass*, Charta der Grundrechte, 2010, Art. 51 Rn. 17.

55 *Rengeling/Szczekalla*, Grundrechte in der EU, 2004, § 4 Rn. 330; *Jarass*, Charta der Grundrechte, 2010, Art. 51 Rn. 12.

56 Insoweit ist kein Umkehrschluss zu ziehen; etwa *Tettinger*, in: Merten/Papier (Hg.), Handbuch der Grundrechte, Bd. II, 2006, § 51 Rn. 76; *Ladenburger*, in: Tettinger/Stern (Hg.), Europ. Grundrechte-Charta, 2006, Art. 51 Rn. 3.

57 *EuGH*, Rs. 11/70, Slg. 1970, 1125 Rn. 4 ff.; Rs. 265/87, Slg. 1989, I- Rn. 2237 Rn. 15.

58 *Calliess*, in: Calliess/Ruffert (Hg.), EUV/AEUV, 4. Aufl. 2011, Art. 11 Rn. 9; *Jarass*, Charta der Grundrechte, 2010, Art. 11 Rn. 13.

59 *Duschanek*, in: Duschanek/Griller (Hg.), Grundrechte für Europa, 2002, 64; vgl. *EuGH*, Rs. 200/96, Slg. 1998, I-1953 Rn. 21 ff; Rs. 368/96, Slg. 1998, I-7967 Rn. 61 ff, 79 ff; Rs. 20/00, Slg. 2003, I-7411 Rn. 2, 66 ff.

60 *Ruffert*, in: Calliess/Ruffert (Hg.), EUV/AEUV, 4. Aufl. 2011, Art. 16 Rn. 3; *Schwarze*, EuZW 2001, 518; *Streinz*, in: Streinz (Hg.), EUV/EGV, 2003, Art. 16 Rn. 7.

II. Beeinträchtigte Grundrechte

1. Meinungsäußerungs- und Informationsfreiheit

a) Grundlagen

In Art. 11 Abs. 1 GRCh wird das Recht auf freie Meinungsäußerung im weitesten Sinne gewährleistet. Wie die Vorschrift ausdrücklich sagt, wird neben der Meinungsfreiheit auch die Freiheit gesichert, Informationen und Ideen ohne behördliche Eingriffe zu empfangen und weiterzugeben. Schon vor Inkrafttreten der Charta hat der Europäische Gerichtshof die Meinungsäußerungsfreiheit als allgemeinen Rechtsgrundsatz des Gemeinschafts- bzw. Unionsrechts anerkannt,[61] unter Einbeziehung der Informationsfreiheit.[62] Wie dargelegt, ist diese Rechtsprechung auch bei der Auslegung von Art. 11 GRCh heranzuziehen.[63]

Darüber hinaus entspricht dem Grundrecht des Art. 11 GRCh, wie die Charta-Erläuterungen festhalten, das in Art. 10 EMRK verankerte Grundrecht.[64] Gem. Art. 52 Abs. 3 GRCh darf daher Art. 11 GRCh nicht hinter den Vorgaben dieses Rechts, einschließlich seiner Konkretisierung durch den Europäischen Gerichtshof für Menschenrechte zurückbleiben.

b) Schutzbereich

Die Gewährleistung des Art. 11 Abs. 1 GRCh bezieht sich auf Meinungen sowie auf Informationen und Ideen. Das macht deutlich, dass alle Kommunikationsinhalte erfasst werden, welcher Art sie auch immer sind. Insbesondere ist der Inhalt und die Qualität der Inhalte ohne Bedeutung.[65] Das Grundrecht gilt „nicht nur für Informationen und Ideen, die Zustimmung erfahren oder die als harmlos oder unerheblich betrachtet werden".[66] Geschützt werden auch die Form und die Darstellung der Inhalte.[67]

Die Meinungsäußerungs- und Informationsfreiheit, wie sie auf europäischer Ebene gewährleistet wird, hat auch und gerade im wirtschaftlichen Bereich besonderes Gewicht. In den Schutzbereich fällt insbesondere jede Art von Werbung, insbeson-

---

61 Etwa *EuGH*, Rs. 112/00, Slg. 2003, I-5659 Rn. 79; Rs. 380/03, Slg. 2006, I-11573 Rn. 154; Rs. 421/07, Slg. 2009, I-2629 Rn. 26.
62 *EuGH*, Rs. 479/04, Slg. 2006, I-8089 Rn. 64.
63 Oben B I 1.
64 Charta-Erläuterungen
65 *Calliess*, in: Calliess/Ruffert (Hg.), EUV/AEUV, 4. Aufl. 2011, Art. 11 Rn. 6.
66 *EuGH*, Rs. 274/99, Slg. 2001, I-1611 Rn. 39; *Kugelmann*, EuGRZ 2003, 20.
67 *Jarass*, Charta der Grundrechte, 2010, Art. 11 Rn. 10.

dere wirtschaftlicher Natur.⁶⁸ Das muss auch für die Nutzung einer Marke gelten. Wie dargelegt, bildet die Marke das zentrale Instrument des unternehmerischen Marketing und damit der Kommunikation vom Hersteller zum Verbraucher.⁶⁹ Es geht um Hinweise und Auffassungen des Herstellers und damit um durch Art. 11 GRCh geschützte Tätigkeiten.

Die Situation unterscheidet sich insoweit etwas von den deutschen Grundrechten, bei denen das Bundesverfassungsgericht, wie sich noch zeigen wird, teilweise von einem Vorrang der Berufsfreiheit ausgeht.⁷⁰ Auf europäischer Ebene umfasst das Grundrecht, anders als im deutschen Bereich, von vornherein auch sämtliche Tatsachenäußerungen. Dementsprechend lautet die amtliche Überschrift des Art. 11 GRCh auch „Freiheit der Meinungsäußerung und Informationsfreiheit".⁷¹ Angesichts dieses Befundes sind Art und Gestaltung von Markenverpackungen sowie deren Einsatz als Vermittlung von Meinungen bzw. Informationen und Ideen im Sinne des Art. 11 GRCh einzustufen.

c) Beeinträchtigung

Werden Markenverpackungen verboten oder in ihren Wirkungen gravierend beschränkt, liegt darin gegenüber dem Hersteller als dem Urheber der entsprechenden Informationen und Meinungen ein Grundrechtseingriff.⁷² Das muss weiter für das Verbot der Produktpräsentation in Einzelhandelseinrichtungen gelten, da damit ein wichtiger Weg zur Verbreitung der auf der Verpackung angebrachten Informationen bzw. Symbole versperrt wird. Daneben beeinträchtigt das Verbot der Produktpräsentation auch den Verbraucher in seinem Grundrecht aus Art. 11 GRCh, weil er an der Aufnahme der mit der Präsentation der Produkte verbunde-

---

68 *GA Fenelly*, Rs. 376/98, Slg. 2000, I-8419 Tz. 153; *GA Trstenjak*, Rs. 316/09 v. 24.11. 2010, Tz. 77; *Stern*, in: Tettinger/Stern (Hg.), Europ. Grundrechte-Charta, 2006, Art. 11 Rn. 25; implizit *EuGH*, Rs. 245/01, Slg. 2003, I-12489 Rn. 72 f.; Rs. 71/02, Slg. 2004, I-3025 Rn. 72 f.
69 Oben A I 3 b.
70 Unten D I 4.
71 Zudem lässt der Europäische Gerichtshof für Menschenrechte das Grundrecht gerade im wirtschaftlichen Bereich zum Tragen kommen, wohl auch deshalb, weil die EMRK kein Grundrecht der Berufsfreiheit oder der unternehmerischen Freiheit kennt.
72 *Pache*, in: Pache/Schwarz/Sosnitza, Aktuelle Rechtsfragen der Tabakregulierung in Europa, 2012, 112; *Schroeder*, ZLR 2012, 416 f. Wenn im Hinblick auf Warnhinweise ein Verstoß abgelehnt wird, weil die negative Meinungsfreiheit nicht geschützt sei (so *Wachovius*, BayVBl 2005, 620 f.), ist das im vorliegenden Zusammenhang unerheblich, weil es um die positive Meinungsäußerungs- und Informationsfreiheit geht. Zudem schützt Art. 11 GRCh auch die negative Meinungsäußerungs- und Informationsfreiheit (*Jarass*, Charta der Grundrechte, 2010, Art. 11 Rn. 10; *Koenig/Kühling*, EWS 2002, 13 f.; *Kühling*, in: Heselhaus/Nowak, Handbuch der europ. Grundrechte, 2006, § 23 Rn. 23).

nen Informationen gehindert wird.[73] Art. 11 GRCh schützt anerkanntermaßen auch die Informationsaufnahme durch die Verbraucher.[74] Insgesamt ist festzuhalten, dass sowohl das Verbot von Tabak-Markenverpackungen wie das Verbot der Präsentation von Tabakwaren in Einzelhandelseinrichtungen eine Beeinträchtigung des Grundrechts des Art. 11 GRCh darstellen. Noch mehr: Werbeverbote betreffen sogar „primär" die Meinungs- und Informationsfreiheit.[75] Für Beschränkungen der Markennutzung kann nichts anderes gelten.

2. Eigentumsrecht

a) Grundlagen

Art. 17 GRCh gewährleistet das Recht, Eigentum zu besitzen, zu nutzen, darüber zu verfügen und es zu vererben. Es wird in der Überschrift als „Eigentumsrecht" bezeichnet. Der Europäische Gerichtshof hat dieses Grundrecht seit langem als allgemeinen Rechtsgrundsatz und damit als verbindliches Primärrecht eingestuft.[76] Weiter entspricht das Eigentumsrecht ausweislich der gem. Art. 52 Abs. 7 GRCh bedeutsamen Charta-Erläuterungen dem Grundrecht des Art. 1 EMRK-ZP.[77] Daher vermittelt es gem. Art. 52 Abs. 3 GRCh mindestens den gleichen Schutz wie Art. 1 EMRK-ZP, unter Berücksichtigung der Auslegung und Anwendung des Grundrechts durch den Europäischen Gerichtshof für Menschenrechte.[78]

b) Schutzbereich

aa) Der Eigentumsbegriff des Art. 17 GRCh ist in einem weiten Sinne zu verstehen und beschränkt sich keineswegs auf Rechtspositionen, die nach dem Recht der Mitgliedstaaten als „Eigentum" bezeichnet werden, wie insbesondere die französische und die englische Fassung verdeutlichen („ses biens"/„his possessions"). Erfasst wird *jedes vermögenswerte Recht*,[79] das von substantieller Bedeutung und dem Einzelnen zu eigenverantwortlicher Nutzung zugewiesen ist.[80] Auch das *„geistige Eigentum"*

---

73 *Schroeder*, ZLR 2012, 417 f.
74 *GA Trstenjak*, Rs. 316/09 v. 24.11.2010, Tz. 85.
75 *GA Trstenjak*, Rs. 316/09 v. 24.11.2010, Tz. 76.
76 *EuGH*, Rs. 293/97, Slg. 1999, I-2603 Rn. 54; Rs. 491/01, Slg. 2002, I-11453 Rn. 149; Rs. 154/04, Slg. 2005, I-6451 Rn. 126.
77 *Charta-Erläuterungen*, ABl 2007 C 303/23.
78 *EuGH*, Rs. 402/05, Slg. 2008, I-6513, Rn. 356; *Charta-Erläuterungen*, ABl 2007 C 303/23.
79 Vgl. *EGMR*, Nr. 15375/89 v. 23. 2. 1995, Rn. 53; *Meyer-Ladewig*, EMRK, 3. Aufl. 2011, Art. 1 ZP Rn. 8.
80 Vgl. *EGMR*, Nr. 73049/01 v. 11. 1. 2007, Rn. 63, 76.

wird geschützt, worauf Art. 17 Abs. 2 GRCh wegen dessen zunehmender Bedeutung ausdrücklich hinweist[81] und wie das bereits vor Inkrafttreten der Charta angenommen wurde.[82]

Darunter fallen insbesondere Markenrechte sowie verwandte Schutzrechte.[83] In den Charta-Erläuterungen wurde der Schutz des Markenrechts ausdrücklich als ein Fall des in Art. 17 Abs. 2 GRCh geregelten Schutzes des geistigen Eigentums aufgeführt.[84] Bedenkt man den Wert von Markenrechten und die Investitionen zum Aufbau einer Marke, kann das auch gar nicht anders sein. Als Eigentum i.S.d. Art. 17 GRCh ist des Weiteren das Verfügungsrecht eines Unternehmens über vermögenswerte *Geschäftsgeheimnisse* einzustufen, insbesondere soweit sie seine Produkte betreffen.[85] Davon ist auch der Europäische Gerichtshof ausgegangen.[86] Solche Geschäftsgeheimnisse mit Vermögenswert fallen in den Schutzbereich des Eigentumsrechts, jedenfalls wenn sie durch das Unionsrecht oder das Recht des betreffenden Mitgliedstaats als Rechtsposition geschützt werden.

bb) Was die geschützten Aspekte angeht, so wird insbesondere die Nutzung von Eigentumspositionen erfasst, wie Art. 17 GRCh ausdrücklich klarstellt. Das gilt für jede Art der Nutzung.[87] Unter den Schutz des Art. 17 GRCh fällt folglich auch die Nutzung eines Markenrechts, insbesondere der Einsatz der Marke auf Verpackungen oder in Einzelhandelsverkaufseinrichtungen. Damit betrifft das Verbot der Markenverpackungen wie das Verbot der Produktpräsentation in Einzelhandelsverkaufseinrichtungen von Art. 17 GRCh geschützte Aspekte.[88]

Komplizierter stellt sich die Situation beim Einsatz von Geruchs- und Geschmacksstoffen dar. Nach der Rechtsprechung des Europäischen Gerichtshofs betrifft ein Vermarktungsverbot für bestimmte Produkte, etwa für oral benutzte Tabakerzeugnisse, nur den Marktanteil eines Unternehmens, der durch das Eigen-

---

81   *Charta-Erläuterungen*, ABl 2007 C 303/23.
82   *EuGH*, Rs. 479/04, Slg. 2006, I-8089 Rn. 65; Rs. 275/06, Slg. 2008, I-271 Rn. 62.
83   *Charta-Erläuterungen*, ABl 2007 C 303/23; *Depenheuer*, in: Tettinger/Stern (Hg.), Europ. Grundrechte-Charta, 2006,, Art. 17 Rn. 30; *Calliess*, in: Ehlers (Hg.), Europ. Grundrechte und Grundfreiheiten, 3. Aufl. 2009, § 16.4 Rn. 17; auch *EGMR*, Nr. 19247/03 v. 29. 1. 2008, Rn. 34 ff; vgl. *EuGH*, Rs. 368/96, Slg. 1998, I-7967 Rn. 78.
84   Charta-Erläuterungen, ABl 2007 C 303/23.
85   *Heselhaus*, in: Heselhaus/Nowak (Hg.), Handbuch der europäischen Grundrechte, 2006, § 32 Rn. 50; *Jarass*, Charta der Grundrechte, 2010, Art. 17 Rn. 9.
86   *EuGH*, Rs. 368/96, Slg. 1998, I-7967 Rn. 81 ff; Rs. 453/03, Slg. 2005, I-10423 Rn. 82, 87.
87   *Jarass*, Charta der Grundrechte, 2010, Art. 17 Rn. 13.
88   *Pache*, in: Pache/Schwarz/Sosnitza, Aktuelle Rechtsfragen der Tabakregulierung in Europa, 2012, 99 f.

tumsrecht nicht geschützt wird.[89] Dies dürfte auch für ein Verbot von Geruchs- und Geschmacksstoffen gelten. Anders stellt sich die Situation jedoch dar, soweit die Rezeptur für die Geruchs- und Geschmacksstoffe ein Geschäftsgeheimnis bildet, das sorgfältig gegenüber Dritten geschützt wird und einen klaren Vermögenswert aufweist. In diesem Falle bildet das Geschäftsgeheimnis eine durch Art. 17 GRCh geschützte Position.[90] Schließlich wird der Schutz der Geschäftsgeheimnisse ausdrücklich in Art. 6 Abs. 2 S. 2 RL2001/37 angesprochen. Auf die umstrittene Frage, ob Art. 17 GRCh auch das Recht am eingerichteten und ausgeübten Gewerbebetrieb schützt,[91] kommt es damit im vorliegenden Zusammenhang nicht an.

c) Beeinträchtigung

Eine Beeinträchtigung des Eigentumsrechts liegt insbesondere dann vor, wenn die Nutzung einer geschützten Position durch eine Regelung behindert wird. Das Verbot von Markenverpackungen schränkt die Möglichkeiten der Nutzung einer Marke gravierend ein. Da die Marke eine durch Art. 17 GRCh geschützte Position ist, liegt in dem Verbot ein Eingriff in das dem Markeninhaber zustehende Eigentumsrecht.[92] Des Weiteren behindert auch das Verbot der Produktpräsentation in Einzelhandelsverkaufseinrichtungen die Nutzung der Marke, sodass insoweit ebenfalls ein Eigentumseingriff vorliegt. Schließlich stellt das Verbot von Geruchs- und Geschmacksstoffen in Tabakprodukten eine Eigentumsbeeinträchtigung dar, wenn und soweit die Stoffe die Produktformel betreffen und die Formel ein Geschäftsgeheimnis darstellt. Hinzu kommt, dass ein solches Verbot möglicherweise die Markennutzung beeinträchtigt, sofern die Geruchs- und Geschmacksstoffe ein essentielles Element der Marke bilden.

3. Unternehmerische Freiheit

a) Grundlagen

Die Grundrechte-Charta gewährleistet in Art. 15 Abs. 1 GRCh die Berufsfreiheit sowie das Recht zu arbeiten und in Art. 16 GRCh die unternehmerische Freiheit. Zur Abgrenzung der beiden Grundrechte enthält die Charta keine näheren Aussagen.

---

89 *EuGH*, Rs. 210/03, Slg. 2004, I-11893 Rn. 73; ebenso *EuGH*, Rs. 295/03, Slg. 2005, I-5673 Rn. 88; Rs. 120/06, Slg. 2008, I-6513 Rn. 185.
90 Dafür spricht auch der Umstand, dass die Entwicklung der Rezeptur mit den relevanten Geruchs- und Geschmacksstoffen und deren Vermittlung an den Konsumenten nicht unerheblicher Investitionen bedurfte.
91 Dazu *Jarass*, Charta der Grundrechte, 2010, Art. 17 Rn. 12.
92 *Schroeder*, ZLR 2012, 412 f.

Überwiegend wird zu Recht davon ausgegangen, dass der Schutz der unternehmerischen Betätigung allein in Art. 16 GRCh geregelt wird und die Berufsfreiheit des Art. 15 GRCh insoweit zurücktritt.[93] Wo dabei die Grenze genau verläuft, ist unsicher. Die Abgrenzung hängt wesentlich davon ab, was als unternehmerische Betätigung einzustufen ist. Zum Teil wird das verneint, wenn persönliche Belange bei der entsprechenden Tätigkeit dominieren.[94] Allerdings führt das zu großen Abgrenzungsproblemen. Doch kann die genaue Abgrenzung der unternehmerischen Tätigkeit dahinstehen. Im vorliegenden Zusammenhang besteht kein Zweifel, dass Tabakhersteller eine solche Tätigkeit im Sinne des Art. 16 GRCh ausüben. Aber auch bei Einzelhändlern wird man das zu bejahen haben.

In der Rechtsprechung des Europäischen Gerichtshofs ist die Berufsfreiheit bzw. die unternehmerische Freiheit in zahlreichen Entscheidungen als allgemeiner Rechtsgrundsatz eingestuft worden; vielfach sprach der Gerichtshof vom Recht der freien Berufsausübung.[95] In den meisten Fällen ging es dabei um unternehmerische Tätigkeiten. Daher ist die Rechtsprechung des Europäischen Gerichtshofs zur freien Berufsausübung auch im Rahmen des Art. 16 GRCh von größter Bedeutung. Der Schutz des Art. 16 GRCh kann schwerlich geringer ausfallen, da man anderenfalls auf das vom Gerichtshof als allgemeinen Rechtsgrundsatz entwickelte Grundrecht zurückgreifen müsste.[96]

b) Schutzbereich

Art. 16 GRCh schützt die *unternehmerische Betätigung*, also Wirtschafts- oder Geschäftstätigkeiten.[97] Erfasst wird jede dem Erwerb dienende Aktivität, die auf eine gewisse Dauer angelegt ist.[98] Weiter muss es sich um eine *selbständige* Tätigkeit handeln.[99] Nur dann kann man von einer unternehmerischen Betätigung sprechen.

---

93 *GA Trstenjak*, Rs. 316/09 v. 24.11.2010, Rn. 83; *Nowak*, in: Heselhaus/Nowak (Hg.), Handbuch der europäischen Grundrechte, 2006, §30 Rn. 58; Jarass, EuZW 2011, 360 f.
94 So *Bernsdorff*, in: Meyer (Hg.), Charta der Grundrechte, 3. Aufl. 2011, Art. 16 Rn. 10; *Nowak*, in: Heselhaus/Nowak (Hg.), Handbuch der europäischen Grundrechte, 2006, §30 Rn. 32.
95 *EuGH*, Rs. 210/03, Slg. 2004, I-11883 Rn. 72; Rs. 295/03, Slg. 2005, I-5673 Rn. 86; Rs. 120/06, Slg. 2008, I-6513 Rn. 183.
96 Vgl. die Ausführungen zu Art. 6 Abs. 3 EUV oben B I 1.
97 *Bernsdorff*, in: Meyer (Hg.), Charta der Grundrechte, 3. Aufl. 2011, Art. 16 Rn. 11; *Frenz*, Handbuch Europarecht, Bd. 4, 2009, Rn. 2679.
98 *Nowak*, in: Heselhaus/Nowak (Hg.), Handbuch der europäischen Grundrechte, 2006, §30 Rn. 38; *Frenz*, Handbuch Europarecht, Bd. 4, 2009, Rn. 2684.
99 *Ruffert*, in: Calliess/Ruffert (Hg.), EUV/AEUV, 4. Aufl. 2011, Art. 16 Rn. 3; *Frenz*, Handbuch Europarecht, Bd. 4, 2009, Rn. 2686.

Zu den geschützten Tätigkeiten gehören die Aufnahme und die Beendigung der unternehmerischen Betätigung sowie alle Aspekte ihrer Durchführung.[100] Geschützt wird die Art und Weise, wie man sein Unternehmen betreibt.[101] In den Schutzbereich fallen insbesondere Werbung und Sponsoring.[102] Erfasst wird auch die Wettbewerbsstellung des Wirtschaftsteilnehmers, zumal in den Charta-Erläuterungen auf den freien Wettbewerb hingewiesen wird.[103]

Im vorliegenden Zusammenhang besteht kein Zweifel, dass der Einsatz von Markenverpackungen von Art. 16 GRCh geschützt wird. Gleiches gilt für die Produktpräsentation in Einzelhandelsverkaufseinrichtungen. Schließlich fällt die Rezeptur von Tabakprodukten und damit der Einsatz von Geruchs- und Geschmacksstoffen in den Schutzbereich der unternehmerischen Freiheit.

c) Beeinträchtigung

Ein Eingriff in das Grundrecht des Art. 16 GRCh liegt zunächst vor, wenn ein Grundrechtsverpflichteter eine Regelung trifft, die für den Grundrechtsinhaber im Hinblick auf die unternehmerischen Aktivitäten einen Nachteil bezweckt oder *unmittelbar bewirkt*.[104] Entscheidend ist, ob die Maßnahme „hinreichend direkte und bedeutsame Auswirkungen auf die freie Berufsausübung" hat.[105] Das ist insbesondere der Fall, wenn bestimmte unternehmerische Aktivitäten verboten werden. Daher lässt sich festhalten, dass das Verbot von Markenverpackungen in das Grundrecht des Art. 16 GRCh eingreift.[106] Gleiches gilt für das Verbot der Produktpräsentation in Einzelhandelsverkaufseinrichtungen und das Verbot von Geruchs- und Geschmacksstoffen. Was speziell das Verbot der Produktpräsentation angeht, so richtet es sich primär an die Einzelhändler. Da aber das Verbot die Hersteller von Tabakprodukten in sehr gewichtiger Weise belastet, muss auch deren mittelbare Betroffenheit für die Annahme eines Eingriffs genügen.[107]

---

100 *Frenz*, Handbuch Europarecht, Bd. 4, 2009, Rn. 2693 f.
101 *EuGH*, Rs. 116/82, Slg. 1986, 2519 Rn. 27; *Ruffert*, in: Ehlers (Hg.), Europ. Grundrechte und Grundfreiheiten, 3. Aufl. 2009, § 16.3 Rn. 13; *Jarass*, Charta der Grundrechte, 2010, Art. 16 Rn. 10.
102 *GA Trstenjak*, Rs. 316/09 v. 24.11.2010, Tz. 83.
103 *EuGH*, Rs. 280/93, Slg. 1994, I-4973 Rn. 81; *Charta-Erläuterungen*, ABl 2007 C 303/23.
104 *EuGH*, Rs. 200/96, Slg. 1998, I-1953 Rn. 28; *Jarass*, Charta der Grundrechte, 2010, Art. 17 Rn. 12; *Frenz*, Handbuch Europarecht, Bd. 4, 2009, Rn. 2734.
105 *EuGH*, Rs. 435/02, Slg. 2004, I-8663 Rn. 49.
106 Ebenso *Schroeder*, ZLR 2012, 417; *Pache*, in: Pache/Schwarz/Sosnitza, Aktuelle Rechtsfragen der Tabakregulierung in Europa, 2012, 107.
107 Vgl. dazu *Jarass*, Charta der Grundrechte, 2010, Art. 16 Rn. 13 mit Nachw. und unten D I 2 b.

III. Rechtfertigung der Beeinträchtigungen

1. Grundlagen

a) Meinungsäußerungs- und Informationsfreiheit

Einschränkungen der Meinungsäußerungs- und Informationsfreiheit können gerechtfertigt sein. Einschlägig ist insoweit nicht, jedenfalls nicht primär, die allgemeine Einschränkungsregelung des Art. 52 Abs. 1 GRCh. Vielmehr kommt, wie auch den Charta-Erläuterungen zu entnehmen ist, über Art. 52 Abs. 3 GRCh der Vorbehalt des Art. 10 Abs. 2 EMRK zum Tragen.[108] Notwendig ist zunächst eine ausreichend bestimmte gesetzliche Grundlage,[109] im Unionsrecht oder im nationalen Recht. Weiter muss die Einschränkung den in Art. 10 Abs. 2 EMRK aufgeführten Zielen dienen. Im vorliegenden Zusammenhang ist insoweit bedeutsam, dass zu diesen Zielen auch der „Schutz der Gesundheit" gehört.[110]

Schließlich muss jede Beschränkung gem. Art. 10 Abs. 2 EMRK in einer demokratischen Gesellschaft notwendig, d. h. durch ein dringendes gesellschaftliches Bedürfnis gerechtfertigt sein und in einem angemessenen Verhältnis zum verfolgten Ziel stehen.[111] Damit kommt der Grundsatz der Verhältnismäßigkeit zum Tragen. Insbesondere muss die Beschränkung im Hinblick auf das verfolgte Ziel geeignet sein.[112] Weiter darf kein milderes Mittel zur Verfügung stehen;[113] Art. 10 Abs. 2 EMRK setzt voraus, dass die Beschränkung „unentbehrlich" ist. Schließlich muss die Grundrechtseinschränkung „in einem angemessenen Verhältnis zu dem verfolgten berechtigten Ziel stehen".[114] Die Maßnahme darf nicht zu einem „unverhältnismäßigen, nicht tragbaren Eingriff" führen.[115] Handelt es sich um einen höchst einschneidenden Eingriff wie ein Werbeverbot, sind die Anforderungen an

---

108 *EuGH*, Rs. 479/04, Slg. 2006, I-8089 Rn. 64; *Charta-Erläuterungen*, ABl 2007 C 303/21.
109 *EuGH*, Rs. 274/99, Slg. 2001, I-1611 Rn. 42; Rs. 380/03, Slg. 2006, I-11573 Rn. 154.
110 *EuGH*, Rs. 491/01, Slg. 2002, I-11453 Rn. 150.
111 *EuGH*, Rs. 112/00, Slg. 2003, I-5659 Rn. 79; Rs. 71/02, Slg. 2004, I-3025 Rn. 50; Rs. 421/07, Slg. 2009, I-2629 Rn. 26.
112 *EuGH*, Rs. 112/00, Slg. 2003, I-5659 Rn. 80; *Kühling*, in: Heselhaus/Nowak (Hg.), Handbuch der europäischen Grundrechte, 2006, 23 Rn. 49.
113 *Kühling*, in: Heselhaus/Nowak (Hg.), Handbuch der europäischen Grundrechte, 2006, § 23 Rn. 50.
114 *EuGH*, Rs. 380/03, Slg. 2006, I-11573 Rn. 154 f; ebenso *EuGH*, Rs. 71/02, Slg. 2004, I-3025 Rn. 50; *Kühling*, in: Heselhaus/Nowak (Hg.), Handbuch der europäischen Grundrechte, 2006, § 23 Rn. 51 ff.
115 *EuGH*, Rs. 112/00, Slg. 2003, I-5659 Rn. 80.

die Rechtmäßigkeit besonders hoch.[116] Was das im vorliegenden Zusammenhang bedeutet, wird noch näher zu untersuchen sein.[117]

b) *Eigentumsrecht*

aa) Die Rechtmäßigkeit von Beeinträchtigungen des Eigentumsrechts des Art. 17 GRCh hängt davon ab, ob es um eine Eigentumsentziehung oder um eine Nutzungsregelung geht. Die Rechtfertigung von Eigentumsentziehungen ist in Art. 17 Abs. 1 S. 2 GRCh geregelt, die der Nutzungsregelungen in Art. 17 Abs. 1 S. 3 GRCh.[118] Die Abgrenzung der beiden Formen der Eigentumsbeeinträchtigung ist mit nicht unerheblichen Unsicherheiten verbunden. Als Eigentumsentziehung ist zunächst jede förmliche Enteignung einzustufen. Hinzu tritt die sog. *de-facto-Enteignung*,[119] die zwar die formale Eigentümerstellung unberührt lässt, dem Eigentümer aber alle damit verbundenen Rechte nimmt und er faktisch wie bei einer Enteignung gestellt wird.[120] Voraussetzung ist, dass der Eigentümer von *jeder* „sinnvollen Art" der Nutzung und Verfügung ausgeschlossen ist.[121] Dementsprechend hat der Europäische Gerichtshof bei einer weit reichenden Nutzungsbeschränkung eine Entziehung abgelehnt, weil der Eigentümer noch verfügen konnte, wenn auch zu einem deutlich niedrigeren Preis.[122] Wo dabei genau die Grenzen verlaufen, ist allerdings unsicher.[123]

Im vorliegenden Zusammenhang führt das Verbot der Markenverpackung zu einem schweren Eingriff in das Markenrecht, der dem Markenrecht einen wesentlichen Teil seiner Bedeutung nimmt. Erst recht gilt das, wenn das Verbot der Produktpräsentation in Einzelhandelsverkaufseinrichtungen hinzutritt. Andererseits verbleiben dem Markeninhaber noch gewisse, wenn auch geringe Nutzungsmöglichkeiten. Es handelt sich somit erkennbar um einen Grenzfall. Angesichts der

---

116 *GA Trstenjak*, Rs. 316/09 v. 24.11.2010, Tz. 80.
117 Unten B IV.
118 Der Hauptunterschied in den Rechtsfolgen besteht darin, dass die Entziehung immer einer Entschädigung bedarf, während das bei Nutzungsregelungen nur in besonders schweren Fällen der Fall ist; vgl. unten B III 2 c.
119 *Bernsdorff*, in: Meyer (Hg.), Charta der Grundrechte, 3. Aufl. 2011, Art. 17 Rn. 20.
120 *EGMR*, Nr. 7151/75 v. 23. 9. 1982, Rn. 63; *Cremer*, in: Grote/Marauhn (Hg.), EMRK/GG, 2006, Kap. 22 Rn. 92.
121 *EuGH*, Rs. 347/03, Slg. 2005, I-3785 Rn. 122; auch *EGMR*, Nr. 14556/89 v. 24. 6. 1993, Rn. 43 f; *Cremer*, in: Grote/Marauhn (Hg.), EMRK/GG, 2006, Kap. 22 Rn. 95.
122 *EuGH*, Rs. 44/79, Slg. 1979, 3727 Rn. 19. Dem *EuGH* wird daher eine formale Betrachtung attestiert; *Grabenwarter*, EuR 2001, 15 f; *Calliess*, in: Ehlers (Hg.), Europ. Grundrechte und Grundfreiheiten, 3. Aufl. 2009, § 16.4 Rn. 20.
123 *Calliess*, in: Ehlers (Hg.), Europ. Grundrechte und Grundfreiheiten, 3. Aufl. 2009, § 16.4 Rn. 29.

Unklarheiten in der Rechtsprechung des Gerichtshofs wird im Folgenden von einer bloßen Nutzungsregelung ausgegangen,[124] allerdings einer Nutzungsregelung, die einer Entziehung vergleichbar schwer in das Eigentumsrecht eingreift. Ähnliches gilt für das Geschäftsgeheimnis an der Rezeptur für die Geruchs- und Geschmacksstoffe.

bb) Nutzungsregelungen sind zulässig, wenn sie den Vorgaben des Art. 17 Abs. 1 S. 3 GRCh gerecht werden, die in der Sache den über Art. 52 Abs. 3 S. 1 GRCh anzuwendenden Anforderungen des Art. 1 Abs. 2 EMRK-ZP entsprechen. Voraussetzung ist zunächst eine ausreichend bestimmte gesetzliche Grundlage des Unionsrechts oder des nationalen Rechts.[125] Weiter muss die Nutzungsregelung gem. Art. 17 Abs. 1 S. 3 GRCh dem „Wohl der Allgemeinheit" dienen. Darunter fällt auch der Schutz der Gesundheit.

Schließlich muss die Nutzungsregelung verhältnismäßig sein.[126] Sie muss in Anlehnung an Art. 52 Abs. 1 S. 2 GRCh dem verfolgten Zweck „tatsächlich entsprechen" bzw. dienen, also geeignet sein.[127] Das Ziel der Regelung muss gefördert werden. Weiter darf kein milderes, aber mindestens gleich wirksames Mittel zur Verfügung stehen.[128] Schließlich „müssen die eingesetzten Mittel in einem angemessenen Verhältnis zu den angestrebten Zielen stehen".[129] Sie dürfen „nicht einen im Hinblick auf die verfolgten Ziele unverhältnismäßigen, nicht tragbaren Eingriff darstellen".[130] Notwendig ist ein „gerechter Ausgleich" zwischen den Erfordernissen des Allgemeinwohls und der Wahrung der Grundrechte des Einzelnen.[131]

---

[124] Ebenso Stein/Rauber, Rechtliche Grenzen der Bekämpfung des Tabakkonsums im Mehrebenensystem, 2011, 47; für Enteignung hingegen *Pache*, in: Pache/Schwarz/Sosnitza, Aktuelle Rechtsfragen der Tabakregulierung in Europa, 2012, 103; *Schroeder*, ZLR 2012, 412 f.

[125] *EuGH*, Rs. 347/03, Slg. 2005, I-3785 Rn. 125; *Heselhaus*, in: Heselhaus/Nowak (Hg.), Handbuch der europäischen Grundrechte, 2006, § 32 Rn. 78.

[126] *EuGH*, Rs. 491/01, Slg. 2002, I-11453 Rn. 149; Rs. 347/03, Slg. 2005, I-3785 Rn. 125; Rs. 402/05, Slg. 2008, I-6351 Rn. 355; *Heselhaus*, in: Heselhaus/Nowak (Hg.), Handbuch der europäischen Grundrechte, 2006, § 32 Rn. 82.

[127] *EuGH*, Rs. 379/08, Slg. 2010, I-0000, Rn. 86; *v. Danwitz*, in: v. Danwitz/Depenheuer/Engel (Hg.), Bericht zur Lage des Eigentums, 2002, 253.

[128] *EuGH*, Rs. 379/08, Slg. 2010, I-2007, Rn. 86; *Depenheuer*, in: Tettinger/Stern (Hg.), Europ. Grundrechte-Charta, 2006, Art. 17 Rn. 53.

[129] *EuGH*, Rs. 402/05, Slg. 2008, I-6351 Rn. 360; *Heselhaus*, in: Heselhaus/Nowak (Hg.), Handbuch der europäischen Grundrechte, 2006, § 32 Rn. 84; *Frenz*, Handbuch Europarecht, Bd. 4, 2009, Rn. 2981 f.

[130] *EuGH*, Rs. 44/94, Slg. 1995, I-3115 Rn. 55; Rs. 368/96, Slg. 1998, I-7967 Rn. 79; Rs. 20/00, Slg. 2003, I-7411 Rn. 68; Rs. 154/04, Slg. 2005, I-6451 Rn. 126.

[131] *EGMR*, Nr. 7151/75 v. 23. 9.1982, Rn. 69; Nr. 21151/04 v. 8.4.08 Rn. 79; *v. Danwitz*, in: v. Danwitz/Depenheuer/Engel (Hg.), Bericht zur Lage des Eigentums, 2002, 253 f; *Cremer*, in: Grote/Marauhn (Hg.), EMRK/GG, 2006, Kap. 22 Rn. 116.

c) Unternehmerische Freiheit

Die unternehmerische Freiheit wird kraft ausdrücklicher Aussage (nur) „nach dem Unionsrecht und den einzelstaatlichen Rechtsvorschriften und Gepflogenheiten anerkannt". Darin kann schwerlich eine Begrenzung des Schutzbereichs liegen, da dann Art. 16 GRCh hinter der unternehmerischen Berufsfreiheit zurückbleiben würde, wie sie vom Europäischen Gerichtshof als allgemeiner Rechtsgrundsatz entwickelt wurde und bei der der Schutzbereich regelmäßig die gesamte unternehmerische Betätigung erfasste. Vielmehr dürfte die Beschränkung als *Ausgestaltungs- und Regelungsvorbehalt* zu verstehen sein, der dem Gesetzgeber weit reichende Regelungen ermöglicht.[132]

Damit sind Einschränkungen der unternehmerischen Freiheit auf einer ausreichend bestimmten Grundlage des Unionsrechts oder des nationalen Rechts möglich. Die zulässigen Einschränkungsziele sind bei einem Ausgestaltungs- und Regelungsvorbehalt besonders weit gesteckt und umfassen auf jeden Fall den Schutz der Gesundheit. Andererseits muss die Einschränkung, trotz des Ausgestaltungs- und Regelungsvorbehalts, verhältnismäßig sein.[133] Andernfalls käme es zu einem Widerspruch zur Rechtsprechung des Europäischen Gerichtshofs zur unternehmerischen Berufsfreiheit. Der Gerichtshof hat in seinen Entscheidungen zur Berufsfreiheit generell Einschränkungen an der Verhältnismäßigkeit gemessen, auch wenn es, wie meist, um Unternehmen ging. Würde man das im Übrigen bei Art. 16 GRCh anders sehen, käme gem. Art. 6 Abs. 3 EUV die vom Gerichtshof als allgemeinen Rechtsgrundsatz entwickelte unternehmerische Berufsfreiheit zum Tragen. Schließlich gilt es bei der Abwägung zu berücksichtigen, dass Art. 16 GRCh in den Charta-Erläuterungen auf die Vorschrift des Art. 119 Abs. 1, 3 AEUV (ex Art. 4 Abs. 1, 3 EGV) gestützt wurde, wonach die Union (und die Mitgliedstaaten) auf den freien Wettbewerb verpflichtet sind.[134] Beeinträchtigungen von Markenrechten sind aber in einer Wettbewerbsordnung besonders problematisch.[135]

---

132 Vgl. *Bernsdorff*, in: Meyer (Hg.), Charta der Grundrechte, 3. Aufl. 2011, Art. 16 Rn. 15; *Durner*, in: Merten/Papier(Hg.), Handbuch der Grundrechte, § 162 Rn. 38.

133 *GA Tizzano*, Rs. 453/03, Slg. 2005, I-10423 Tz. 75; *GA Trstenjak*, Rs. 316/09 v. 24.11.2010, Tz. 84; *Durner*, in: Merten/Papier(Hg.), Handbuch der Grundrechte, Bd. VI/1, 2010, § 162 Rn. 38; *Frenz*, Handbuch Europarecht, Bd. 4, 2009, Rn. 2758.

134 Charta-Erläuterungen, ABl 2007 C 303/23: dazu Jarass, EuGRZ 2011, 360.

135 Zur Funktion von Marken in einer Wettbewerbsordnung oben A I 3 b.

2. Verhältnismäßigkeit

a) Allgemeine und grundrechtliche Verhältnismäßigkeit

Die bisherigen Überlegungen zeigten, dass die Rechtfertigung von Beeinträchtigungen bei allen betroffenen Grundrechten wesentlich davon abhängt, ob die fragliche Grundrechtseinschränkung verhältnismäßig ist. Damit gewinnt der Umstand entscheidende Bedeutung, wie der Europäische Gerichtshof den Grundsatz der Verhältnismäßigkeit versteht und konkretisiert. Für diese Frage ist nicht nur die Rechtsprechung des Gerichtshofs zur Einschränkung von Grundrechten bedeutsam. Vielmehr darf nicht übersehen werden, dass der Gerichtshof in ständiger Rechtsprechung dem Gemeinschafts- bzw. Unionsrecht einen eigenständigen Grundsatz der Verhältnismäßigkeit als allgemeinen Rechtsgrundsatz entnimmt,[136] der seinen Niederschlag auch in Art. 5 Abs. 4 UAbs. 1 EUV gefunden hat.[137] Der Gerichtshof prüft dann ohne Anknüpfung an ein bestimmtes Grundrecht, ob die Belastungen, gemessen an den durch die Maßnahme gesteckten Zielen, unverhältnismäßig sind.[138]

Dieser Ansatz unterscheidet sich wesentlich von dem für den deutschen Betrachter üblichen Einsatz der Verhältnismäßigkeit als Schranken-Schranke innerhalb der Prüfung eines Grundrechts, der in der Rechtsprechung des Europäischen Gerichtshofs ebenfalls anzutreffen ist.[139] Zum Teil finden sich beide Prüfungen innerhalb *einer* Entscheidung, eventuell sogar mit Verweisungen.[140] Die Anforderungen unterscheiden sich dabei nicht, wie die Verweisungen verdeutlichen. Daher lassen sich die Entscheidungen des Gerichtshofs zum allgemeinen Grundsatz der Verhältnismäßigkeit auch im Rahmen der Grundrechtsprüfung nutzen. Das ist deshalb bedeutsam, weil insoweit zum Teil genauere Aussagen des Gerichtshofs vorliegen. In der Sache können denn auch die Vorgaben der grundrechtlichen Verhältnismäßigkeit schwerlich hinter denen der allgemeinen Verhältnismäßigkeit zurückbleiben.

---

136 Etwa *EuGH*, Rs. 133/93, Slg. 1994, I-4863 Rn. 41; Rs. 296/93, Slg. 1996, I-795 Rn. 30; Rs. 210/00, Slg. 2002, I-6453 Rn. 59; Rs. 380/03, Slg. 2006, I-11573 Rn. 144. Er kommt zum Tragen, wenn die fragliche Maßnahme selbst in geschützte Interessen eingreift; *EuGH*, Rs. 329/01, Slg. 2004, I-1899, Rn. 59.

137 Art. 4 Abs. 5 EUV betrifft v.a. das Verhältnis zu den Mitgliedstaaten; vgl. *EuGH*, Rs. 165/09 v. 26.5.2011, Rn. 89.

138 *EuGH*, Rs. 157/96, Slg. 1998, I-2211 Rn. 47 ff; Rs. 180/96, Slg. 1998, I-2265 Rn. 96–11; Rs. 60/00, Slg. 2002, I-6279 Rn. 43 ff; vgl. *Penski/Elsner*, DÖV 2001, 273.

139 Etwa *EuGH*, Rs. 296/93, Slg. 1996, I-795 Rn. 25–45, 63–65; Rs. 418/97, Slg. 1997, I-4475 Rn. 66–75; Rs. 368/96, Slg. 1998, I-7967 Rn. 66–86; *EuG*, Rs. 65/98, Slg. 2003, II-4653 Rn. 170–173, 201–205.

140 Vgl. *EuGH*, Rs. 368/96, Slg. 1998, I-7967 Rn. 83; Rs. 293/97, Slg. 1999, I-2603 Rn. 57; Rs. 453/03, Slg. 2005, I-10423 Rn. 88; *Koch*, Der Grundsatz der Verhältnismäßigkeit in der Rechtsprechung des EuGH, 2003, 255 ff.

b) Teilelemente der Verhältnismäßigkeit

Bei der Konkretisierung des Grundsatzes der Verhältnismäßigkeit setzt der Europäischen Gerichtshof meist zweistufig an:[141] Zunächst verlangt er, dass die „eingesetzten Mittel zur Erreichung des angestrebten Ziels geeignet sein müssen".[142] Insbesondere müssen die angeführten Gründe „zutreffend" sein.[143]

Weiter dürfen die eingesetzten Mittel nicht über das „zur Erreichung des angestrebten Ziels ... Erforderliche hinausgehen".[144] Das bedeutet zunächst, dass die ergriffene Maßnahme nur soweit gehen darf, wie das zur Zielerreichung wirklich notwendig ist. Dies gilt in sachlicher und in zeitlicher Hinsicht wie im Hinblick auf den persönlichen Anwendungsbereich.[145] Weiter darf es kein anderes Mittel geben, mit dem das verfolgte Ziel ebenso gut erreicht werden kann und das weniger in das Grundrecht eingreift.[146] „Wenn mehrere geeignete Maßnahmen zur Auswahl stehen, ist die am wenigsten belastende zu wählen".[147]

Die Erforderlichkeit des eingesetzten Mittels setzt nach der Rechtsprechung des Europäischen Gerichtshofs zudem eine ausgewogene Gewichtung der betroffenen Interessen voraus.[148] Die damit gebotene Angemessenheit kann man auch, wie das im deutschen Verfassungsrecht geschieht, als ein eigenständiges Teilelement der Verhältnismäßigkeit ansehen und nicht als zweites Teil der Erforderlichkeit. Unabhängig von dieser dogmatischen Frage ist in der Sache eine „ausgewogene Gewichtung des Interesses der Union" bzw. des Mitgliedstaats auf der einen und des Grundrechtsträgers auf der anderen Seite geboten.[149] Es sind die gegenläufigen „Interessen abzuwägen, und es ist anhand sämtlicher Umstände des jeweiligen Einzelfalls festzustellen, ob das rechtliche Gleichgewicht zwischen diesen Interessen gewahrt ist".[150] Die verursachten Nachteile müssen „in angemessenem Verhältnis

---

141 Etwa *EuGH*, Rs. 58/08 v. 8.6.2010, Rn. 51; Rs. 92/09 v. 9.11.10, Rn. 74.
142 So zur allg. Verhältnismäßigkeit *EuGH*, Rs. 28/05, Slg. 2006, I-5431 Rn. 72; Rs. 368/96, Slg. 1998, I-7967 Rn. 66; Rs. 171/03, Slg. 2004, I-10945 Rn. 51.
143 *EuGH*, Rs. 274/99, Slg. 2001, I-1611 Rn. 41.
144 So zur allg. Verhältnismäßigkeit *EuGH*, Rs. 28/05, Slg. 2006, I-5431 Rn. 72; Rs. 171/03, Slg. 2004, I-10945 Rn. 51; Rs. 37/06 v. 17. 1. 2008 Rn. 35.
145 Vgl. *EuGH*, Rs. 265/08 v. 20.4.10, Rn. 35–38.
146 Vgl. *EuGH*, Rs. 265/87, Slg. 1989, 2237 Rn. 21; Rs. 254/94, Slg. 1996, I-4235 Rn. 55.
147 So zur allgemeinen Verhältnismäßigkeit *EuGH*, Rs. 375/96, Slg. 1998, I-6629 Rn. 63; ganz ähnlich *EuGH*, Rs. 296/93, Slg. 1996, I-795 Rn. 30; Rs. 171/03, Slg. 2004, I-10945 Rn. 51.
148 Besonders deutlich *EuGH*, Rs. 92/09 v. 9.11.10, Rn. 76 f.
149 *EuGH*, Rs. 402/05, Slg. 2008, I-6351 Rn. 360; Rs. 92/09 v. 9.11.10, Rn. 77, 80.
150 *EuGH*, Rs. 112/00, Slg. 2003, I-5659 Rn. 81; *Kingreen*, in: Calliess/Ruffert (Hg.), EUV/AEUV, 4. Aufl. 2011, Art. 52 Rn. 70.

zu dem verfolgten berechtigten Ziel stehen".[151] Der Europäische Gerichtshof für Menschenrechte verlangt, in der Sache ganz ähnlich, einen „gerechten Ausgleich" zwischen den Belangen des Allgemeinwohls und den Erfordernissen des Schutzes der Grundrechte des Einzelnen.[152]

c) Übergangs- und Ausnahmeregelungen sowie Entschädigung

Der Grundsatz der Verhältnismäßigkeit ist unter Umständen nur gewahrt, wenn der Gesetzgeber *Übergangsregelungen* vorsieht.[153] Auch kann der Grundsatz in Härtefällen *Ausnahmeregelungen* verlangen; dementsprechend hat der Europäische Gerichtshof die Verhältnismäßigkeit wegen der Möglichkeit von Ausnahmen bejaht.[154] Werden Teilgruppen typischerweise sehr viel härter betroffen, können Sonderregelungen geboten sein. So gibt es bei bestimmten Tabakprodukten spezielle Verpackungsformen, die Sonderregelungen notwendig machen, um nur ein Beispiel zu nennen.

Aus ähnlichen Überlegungen kann die Verhältnismäßigkeit einer Grundrechtseinschränkung davon abhängen, ob eine *Entschädigung* gewährt wird. Das hat der Europäische Gerichtshof zunächst bei Eigentumseingriffen (auch in Form von Nutzungsregelungen) festgehalten, weil „Beschränkungen des Eigentums bei Fehlen einer Entschädigung einen im Hinblick auf den verfolgten Zweck unverhältnismäßigen, nicht tragbaren Eingriff darstellen".[155] Aber auch bei Beeinträchtigungen der unternehmerischen Berufsfreiheit und damit bei der unternehmerischen Freiheit hat er ein solches Erfordernis angesprochen.[156] Für Beeinträchtigungen der Meinungsäußerungs- und Informationsfreiheit kann dann nichts anderes gelten, obgleich es insoweit noch an entsprechenden Aussagen des Gerichtshofs fehlt.

---

151 *EuGH*, Rs. 112/00, Slg. 2003, I-5659 Rn. 79; ähnlich *EuGH*, Rs. 60/00, Slg. 2002, I-6279 Rn. 42; Rs. 482/01, Slg. 2004, I-5257 Rn. 99; ebenso zur allgemeinen Verhältnismäßigkeit *EuGH*, Rs. 37/06 v. 17.1.08 Rn. 35; Rs. 171/03, Slg. 2004, I-10945 Rn. 51.
152 *EGMR*, Nr. 12033/86 v. 18.2.91, Rn. 51; Nr. 15375/89 v. 23. 2. 1995, Rn. 62; Nr. 25404/94 v. 21.10.1997, Rn. 43; *Grabenwarter*, EMRK, 4. Aufl. 2009, § 18 Rn. 16.
153 *EuGH*, Rs. 68/95, Slg. 1996, I-6085 Rn. 40; vgl. *EuGH*, Rs. 306/93, Slg. 1994, I-5555 Rn. 28; Rs. 347/03, Slg. 2005, I-3785 Rn. 133.
154 *EuGH*, Rs. 68/95, Slg. 1996, I-6085 Rn. 40, 42 f.
155 *EuGH*, Rs. 20/00, Slg. 2003, I-7411 Rn. 79; Rs. 120/06, Slg. 2008, I-6513 Rn. 184; *Frenz*, Handbuch Europarecht, Bd. 4, 2009, Rn. 2985 f.
156 *EuGH*, Rs. 120/06, Slg. 2008, I-6513 Rn. 184.

3. Kontrolldichte

a) Meinungs- und Informationsfreiheit

Die Wirkungen des Gebots der Verhältnismäßigkeit stellen sich unterschiedlich dar, je nachdem, welche Dichte die gerichtliche Kontrolle aufweisen muss. Die Aussagen des Europäischen Gerichtshofs differieren insoweit bei den verschiedenen Grundrechten:

Eine deutliche Betonung der gerichtlichen Kontrolle findet sich im Bereich der Meinungs- und Informationsfreiheit des Art. 11 GRCh. Zwar wird den Grundrechtsverpflichteten auf der Stufe der Angemessenheit bzw. der ausgewogenen Gewichtung ein gewisser Beurteilungsspielraum zugestanden.[157] Insbesondere fällt die Kontrolldichte bei Äußerungen im Geschäftsverkehr bzw. zur Verfolgung kommerzieller Interessen, insbesondere bei der Werbung, geringer aus.[158] Andererseits muss die Kontrolle umso genauer erfolgen, je gewichtiger in die Meinungsäußerungsfreiheit eingegriffen wird.[159] Das hat auch im kommerziellen Bereich Bedeutung. Dementsprechend wurden erst jüngst bei einschneidenden Eingriffen wie einem Werbeverbot hohe Anforderungen an die Rechtfertigung gestellt.[160]

b) Eigentumsrecht und unternehmerische Freiheit

Deutlich zurückhaltender fällt die gerichtliche Kontrolldichte in der Rechtsprechung des Europäischen Gerichtshofs im Bereich des Eigentumsrechts aus. Gegenüber dem Gesetzgeber ist die Kontrolldichte grundsätzlich reduziert.[161] Die zu prüfende Maßnahme ist in solchen Fällen nur dann unzulässig, wenn sie „offensichtlich ungeeignet" ist.[162] Und die Beurteilung der Erforderlichkeit wird nur dann als korrekturbedürftig angesehen, wenn sie „offensichtlich" unzutreffend ist.[163] Auf eine nähere Prüfung der Angemessenheit wird vielfach verzichtet.[164]

---

157 *EuGH,* Rs. 274/99, Slg. 2001, I-1611 Rn. 49; Rs. 112/00, Slg. 2003, I-5659 Rn. 81 f.
158 *EuGH,* Rs. 71/02, Slg. 2004, I-3025 Rn. 51; Rs. 380/03, Slg. 2006, I-11573 Rn. 155; Rs. 421/07, Slg. 2009, I-2629 Rn. 27.
159 *EuGH,* Rs. 340/00, Slg. 2001, I-10269 Rn. 18.
160 *GA Trstenjak,* Rs. 316/09 v. 24.11.2010, Tz. 80.
161 *EuGH,* Rs. 402/05, Slg. 2008, I-6351 Rn. 360.
162 *EuGH,* Rs. 306/93, Slg. 1994, I-5555 Rn. 21; Rs. 296/93, Slg. 1996, I-795 Rn. 31; *EuG,* Rs. 13/99, Slg. 2002, II-3305 Rn. 166.
163 *EuGH,* Rs. 280/93, Slg. 1994, I-4973 Rn. 94.
164 *Calliess,* in: Ehlers (Hg.), Europ. Grundrechte und Grundfreiheiten, 3. Aufl. 2009, § 16.4 Rn. 47.

Ähnliches gilt für die unternehmerische Berufsfreiheit. Den Grundrechtsverpflichteten kommt hier ein Beurteilungsspielraum zu.[165] Eine Maßnahme muss dann offensichtlich ungeeignet oder offensichtlich nicht erforderlich sein.[166] Muss der Grundrechtsverpflichtete die künftigen Auswirkungen einer Maßnahme beurteilen, darf seine Beurteilung nur dann beanstandet werden, wenn sie im Hinblick auf die Erkenntnisse, über die er im Beurteilungszeitpunkt verfügt, offensichtlich irrig erscheint.[167]

Im Schrifttum wird diese generelle Zurücknahme der gerichtlichen Kontrolldichte im Bereich des Eigentumsrechts wie der unternehmerischen Freiheit zu Recht als defizitär kritisiert,[168] vor allem weil der Europäische Gerichtshof die Verhältnismäßigkeit ohne detaillierte Prüfung bejaht. Das ist jedenfalls dann fragwürdig, wenn der Grundrechtsträger in seiner Freiheit gravierend beeinträchtigt wird. Andererseits sollte nicht übersehen werden, dass sich die bisherige Rechtsprechung primär auf Bereiche wie die Agrarpolitik und ähnliche Felder bezog, die durch Marktordnungen und zum Teil durch eine hohe Subventionierung geprägt sind;[169] hier sind die grundrechtlichen Spielräume nicht zu Unrecht größer.

IV. Verhältnismäßigkeit im vorliegenden Zusammenhang

1. Verbot der Markenverpackung

a) Beeinträchtigte Grundrechte und Gewicht des Eingriffs

aa) Die bisher gewonnenen Befunde können nunmehr auf die hier zu untersuchenden Verbote angewandt werden. Zunächst ist zu klären, ob das Verbot von Markenverpackungen verhältnismäßig ist. Dieses Verbot greift in die Meinungs- und Informationsfreiheit des Art. 11 Abs. 1 GRCh ein.[170] Weiter liegt darin eine

---

165 *EuGH,* Rs. 44/94, Slg. 1995, I-3115 Rn. 57; Rs. 296/93, Slg. 1996, I-795 Rn. 31; *Penski/Elsner,* DÖV 2001, 273.
166 *EuGH,* Rs. 280/93, Slg. 1994, I-4973 Rn. 90; Rs. 306/93, Slg. 1994, I-5555 Rn. 21, 27; Rs. 44/94, Slg. 1995, I-3115 Rn. 58.
167 *EuGH,* Rs. 280/93, Slg. 1994, I-4973 Rn. 90.
168 *Streinz,* in: Streinz (Hg.), EUV/EGV, 2003, Art. 16 Rn. 4; *Bernsdorff,* in: Meyer (Hg.), Charta der Grundrechte, 3. Aufl. 2011, Art. 15 Rn. 18; *Ruffert,* in: Ehlers (Hg.), Europ. Grundrechte und Grundfreiheiten, 3. Aufl. 2009, § 16.3 Rn. 39; *Koch,* Der Grundsatz der Verhältnismäßigkeit in der Rechtsprechung des Gerichtshofs, 2003, 399 ff; a.A. *Kischel,* EuR 2000, 395 ff.
169 *Streinz,* in: Streinz (Hg.), EUV/EGV, 2003, Art. 15 Rn. 6, Art. 16 GC Rn. 4; *Ruffert,* in: Ehlers (Hg.), Europ. Grundrechte und Grundfreiheiten, 3. Aufl. 2009, § 16.3 Rn. 3.
170 Oben B II 1 c.

Beeinträchtigung des Eigentumsrechts des Art. 17 GRCh.[171] Schließlich führt das Verbot von Markenverpackungen zu einem Eingriff in die unternehmerische Freiheit des Art. 16 GRCh.[172]

bb) Was das Gewicht dieser Eingriffe betrifft, so führt ein Verbot von Markenverpackungen zu einer weitgehenden Entwertung des Markenrechts.[173] Ohne entsprechende Verpackung kann der Verbraucher „seine" Marke kaum mehr erkennen. Allein der Name der Marke dürfte schwerlich ausreichend sein. Die Marke soll, wie dargelegt, dem Endabnehmer ermöglichen, die Ware ohne Verwechslungsgefahr von Waren anderer Herkunft zu unterscheiden; sie soll sicherstellen, dass alle Waren, die sie kennzeichnet, unter der Kontrolle eines einzigen, für die Qualität verantwortlichen Unternehmens hergestellt oder erbracht worden sind.[174] All das wird praktisch unmöglich, wenn Markenverpackungen nicht mehr zulässig sind, die sich farblich und graphisch von anderen Verpackungen abheben. Daher muss ein Verbot von Markenverpackungen als ein sehr schwerer Eingriff in die Rechtsstellung des Markeninhabers und damit in die Grundrechte eingestuft werden, die das Verbot beeinträchtigt.

Das gilt umso mehr, als Marken, wie dargelegt, zentrale Instrumente des unternehmerischen Marketings bilden und gerade in hoch entwickelten Wirtschaftssystemen eine überragende Bedeutung besitzen.[175] Das Verbot von Markenverpackungen würde unter Einsatz erheblicher Mittel über Jahrzehnte aufgebaute und bilanzierte Markenwerte zerstören.

b) Verhältnismäßigkeit der Maßnahme

aa) Wieweit ein Verbot von Markenverpackungen zum Gesundheitsschutz beiträgt, lässt sich nur schwer abschätzen,[176] zumal diese Radikalmaßnahme bislang nirgends zum Einsatz kam. Allerdings genügt für die Voraussetzung der Geeignetheit, dass die Zielerreichung gefördert wird.[177] Daher lässt sich die Geeignetheit der

---

171 Oben B II 2 c.
172 Dazu oben B II 3 c.
173 Näher *Sosnitza*, in: Pache/Schwarz/Sosnitza, Aktuelle Rechtsfragen der Tabakregulierung in Europa, 2012, 133 f.
174 Oben A I 3 b mit Nachweisen aus der Rechtsprechung des *EuGH*.
175 Näher oben A I 3 b.
176 Vgl. *Riessen* u.a., Assessing the Impacts of Revising the Tobacco Products Directive, Rand, 2010, 131, 134; *Deloitte*, Tobacco Packaging regulation, 2011, 24 ff.
177 Oben B II 2 b.

Maßnahme nicht ausschließen, jedenfalls wenn man dem Gesetzgeber angesichts der Unsicherheiten insoweit einen weiten Beurteilungsspielraum zuerkennt.[178]

bb) Starken Bedenken ist aber die Erforderlichkeit eines Verbots von Markenverpackungen und deren ausgewogene Gewichtung ausgesetzt. Zwar besteht auch insoweit ein nicht unerheblicher Beurteilungsspielraum des Gesetzgebers, nicht nur im Bereich des Eigentumsrechts und der unternehmerischen Freiheit, sondern auch im Bereich der Meinungs- und Informationsfreiheit, da es um geschäftliche Meinungsäußerungen geht. Auch hat der Schutz der Gesundheit hohes Gewicht.[179]

Doch darf nicht übersehen werden, dass, wie ausgeführt, ein Verbot von Markenverpackungen einen sehr schweren Grundrechtseingriff darstellt.[180] Zudem gilt es zu beachten, dass Marken, wie der Europäische Gerichtshof festgehalten hat, einen wesentlichen, ja unverzichtbaren Bestandteil des Systems unverfälschten Wettbewerbs darstellen, wie er durch das EU-Primärrecht sichergestellt werden soll.[181] Mit einem Verbot von Markenverpackungen würde der Markt zementiert; künftige Veränderungen auf dem Markt, insbesondere Marktzutritte wären nur noch schwer möglich.[182] Schließlich ist zu berücksichtigen, dass Einheitsverpackungen zu einem Anstieg von Produktfälschungen führen werden.[183]

Angesichts dieser Befunde sind an eine Rechtfertigung des Verbots von Markenverpackungen strenge Anforderungen zu stellen, jedenfalls im Bereich der Meinungs- und Informationsfreiheit. Hier ist eine „ausgewogene Gewichtung" des Interesses der Union bzw. des Mitgliedstaats auf der einen und des Grundrechtsträgers auf der anderen Seite geboten.[184] Es sind die gegenläufigen „Interessen abzuwägen, und es ist anhand sämtlicher Umstände des jeweiligen Einzelfalls festzustellen, ob das rechtliche Gleichgewicht zwischen diesen Interessen gewahrt ist".[185] Angesichts der Unsicherheiten, die hinsichtlich des Nutzens des Verbots von Markenverpackungen für die Gesundheit bestehen, kann bei einem so schweren

---

178 Zweifelnd *Schroeder*, ZLR 2012, 414. Der zuständige Minister in Großbritannien war darüber hinaus 2009 der Auffassung, dass es keine genügenden Belege gibt; vgl. *Kunz-Hallstein*, in: Bender/ Schülke/ Winterfeldt (Hg.), 50 Jahre Bundespatentgericht, 2011, 662.
179 *EuGH*, Rs. 193/95, Slg. 1997, I-4315 Rn. 43.
180 Dazu oben B IV 1 a.
181 Vgl. die Nachweise oben A I 3 b.
182 Vgl. *v.Danwitz*, Produktwerbung in der Europäischen Union zwischen gemeinschaftlichen Kompetenzgrenzen und europäischem Grundrechtsschutz, 1998, 38 f.
183 *Deloitte*, Tobacco Packaging regulation, 2011, 27 f.; *Stein/Rauber*, Rechtliche Grenzen der Bekämpfung des Tabakkonsums im Mehrebenensystem, 2011, 49.
184 *EuGH*, Rs. 92/09 v. 9.11.10, Rn. 77, 79 f., 83, 86.
185 *EuGH*, Rs. 112/00, Slg. 2003, I-5659, Rn. 81; *Kingreen*, in: Calliess/Ruffert (Hg.), EUV/AEUV, 4. Aufl. 2011, Art. 52 Rn. 70.

Eingriff schwerlich noch von einem angemessenen Interessenausgleich die Rede sein.[186]

Das muss umso mehr gelten, als mildere Maßnahmen möglich sind, wie etwa eine Vergrößerung der vorgeschriebenen Aufschriften, ohne dabei das Erkennen der Marke für den Konsumenten weithin unmöglich zu machen. Zudem spricht dafür, dass der Europäische Gerichtshof in seiner Entscheidung zur Tabakprodukt-Richtlinie entscheidend darauf abgehoben hat, dass die Richtlinie noch genügend Raum lässt, auf der Verpackung andere Angaben, insbesondere bezüglich der Zigarettenmarke, anzubringen.[187] Insgesamt sprechen gute Gründe dafür, das ein Verbot von Markenverpackungen in dem dargelegten Sinn zu einem unverhältnismäßigen Eingriff jedenfalls in die Meinungs- und Informationsfreiheit führt.

cc) Dieser Befund muss auch dann gelten, wenn auf Verpackungen derart umfangreiche Warnhinweise verlangt werden, dass dadurch die Marke nicht mehr wirklich zu erkennen ist. Das läuft im Ergebnis auf ein Verbot von Markenverpackungen hinaus. Entscheidend dürfte insoweit sein, ob die Konsumenten bei einem Blick auf die Verpackung noch ihre Marke erkennen. Ist das nicht der Fall, kann man von keiner echten Markenverpackung mehr sprechen.

c) Sondersituation der Hersteller mit vielfältigem Angebot

Schließlich gilt es zu beachten, dass ein Verbot von Markenverpackungen die Hersteller von Tabakprodukten nicht gleichmäßig trifft. Wenn ein Hersteller eine große Zahl unterschiedlicher Zigarettensorten mit jeweils spezifischem Charakter anbietet, dann trifft ihn ein solches Verbot härter als einen Hersteller, der wenige Zigarettensorten mit jeweils hohem Absatz führt. Die Vielfalt der Sorten ist ohne Kennzeichnung durch Markensymbole im Markt nicht zu vermitteln. Das heißt, dass ein Hersteller mit einem vielfältigen Sortiment durch das Verbot von Markenverpackungen schwerer betroffen wird. Die Unverhältnismäßigkeit des Eingriffs wird in solchen Fällen noch ausgeprägter.

2. Verbot der Produktpräsentation in Verkaufseinrichtungen

a) Betroffene Grundrechte und Gewicht des Eingriffs

Das Verbot der Produktpräsentation in Einzelhandelsverkaufseinrichtungen stellt, wie ausgeführt, zunächst einen Eingriff in die Meinungs- und Informationsfreiheit

---

186 Ebenso *Pache*, in: Pache/Schwarz/Sosnitza, Aktuelle Rechtsfragen der Tabakregulierung in Europa, 2012, 105; *Schroeder*, ZLR 2012, 414f. Anders könnte die Situation ausfallen, wenn ein finanzieller Ausgleich erfolgt, der dem wirtschaftlichen Wert der betreffenden Marke entspricht.
187 *EuGH*, Rs. 491/01, Slg. 2002, I-11452 Rn. 132, 152.

des Art. 11 GRCh dar.[188] Weiter liegt darin ein Eingriff in das Eigentumsrecht des Art. 17 GRCh.[189] Schließlich wird auch in die unternehmerische Freiheit des Art. 16 GRCh eingegriffen.[190]

Die belastenden Wirkungen, die von einem solchen Verbot der Produktpräsentation ausgehen, sind beträchtlich, auch wenn sie geringer als beim Verbot der Markenverpackungen ausfallen. Wenn der Konsument sein Tabakprodukt in den Einzelhandelsverkaufseinrichtungen nicht mehr sehen kann, vermag die Marke ihrer Funktion, der Verwechslung mit anderen Produkten vorzubeugen, schwerlich gerecht zu werden.[191] Weiter ergeben sich Probleme bei Neueinführungen oder bei Veränderungen der Rezeptur, weshalb ein Verbot der Produktpräsentation die Fortentwicklung der Produkte behindert. Zusätzlich wird der Konsument in seiner Meinungs- und Informationsfreiheit beeinträchtigt, weil ihm der Zugang zu den Tabakprodukten und den damit verbundenen Informationen verweigert wird.[192]

b) Verhältnismäßigkeit der Maßnahme

aa) Was die *Eignung* des Verbots der Produktpräsentation in Einzelhandelsverkaufseinrichtungen im Hinblick auf den Schutz der Gesundheit angeht, so bestehen Zweifel. So hat das Verbot der Präsentation von Tabakprodukten in Kanada nicht zu einem Rückgang des Konsums geführt.[193] Stattdessen hat der Verkauf illegal gehandelter Produkte zugenommen. Immerhin gibt es auch Befunde zugunsten eines positiven Effekts, auch wenn er nur schwer zu quantifizieren ist.[194] Daher dürfte insoweit der Beurteilungsspielraum des Gesetzgebers zum Tragen kommen.

bb) Im Hinblick auf die *Erforderlichkeit* des Verbots der Produktpräsentation in Einzelhandelsverkaufseinrichtungen und die Notwendigkeit einer ausgewogenen Gewichtung bestehen gravierende Bedenken, insbesondere soweit es um die Meinungs- und Informationsfreiheit geht. Jedenfalls bei diesem Grundrecht ist bedeutsam, dass das Verbot einen sehr gewichtigen Grundrechtseingriff enthält.[195] Daher ist zu erwägen, ob nicht mildere Mittel zur Verfügung stehen, ohne eine Produktpräsentation vollständig auszuschließen. Zumindest sollte der Gesetzgeber stufen-

---

188 Dazu oben B II 1 c.
189 Näher oben B II 2 c.
190 Dazu oben B II 3 c.
191 Vgl. oben A I 3 b.
192 Vgl. oben B II 1 c.
193 So die Untersuchung des Institute of Economic Affairs.
194 Vgl. *Riessen* u.a., Assessing the Impacts of Revising the Tobacco Products Directive, Rand, 2010, 192 ff.
195 Näher oben B III 3 a.

weise vorgehen und sich zunächst mit milderen Maßnahmen begnügen, um dann nach einiger Zeit zu überprüfen, ob sie die gewünschten Effekte erzielen. Insgesamt ist unsicher, ob ein Verbot der Präsentation von Tabakprodukten in Einzelhandelsverkaufseinrichtungen noch einen verhältnismäßigen Grundrechtseingriff darstellt, trotz des Spielraums, der dem Gesetzgeber eingeräumt ist. Noch stärker werden die Zweifel aus den zum Verbot von Markenverpackungen dargelegten Gründen, soweit es um Hersteller geht, die eine große Vielfalt an Tabakproduktsorten anbieten.[196]

3. Verbot von Geruchs- und Geschmacksstoffen

a) Betroffene Grundrechte und Gewicht des Eingriffs

Was das Verbot von Geruchs- und Geschmacksstoffen betrifft, so zeigte sich, dass damit in die unternehmerische Freiheit des Art. 16 GRCh eingegriffen wird.[197] Hinzu tritt ein Eingriff in das Eigentumsrecht des Art. 17 GRCh, soweit die Geruchs- und Geschmacksstoffe eine ein Geschäftsgeheimnis darstellende Produktformel betreffen; denkbar ist zudem, dass die Geruchs- und Geschmacksstoffe für das betreffende Produkt und damit auch für die Markennutzung essentiell sind.[198] Dagegen dürfte die Meinungsäußerungs- und Informationsfreiheit nicht beeinträchtigt sein, obgleich sich das Verbot auch auf die Nutzung der Marke auswirkt. Die Einwirkung auf Art. 11 GRCh ist insoweit zu mittelbar.[199]

Der Eingriff in die unternehmerische Freiheit und gegebenenfalls in das Eigentumsrecht ist für den Hersteller von Tabakprodukten, der bislang seine Produkte mit Geruchs- und Geschmacksstoffen versehen hat, sehr belastend. In diesen Fällen erwartet der Kunde von den Tabakprodukten die durch diese Geruchs- und Geschmacksstoffe bedingten sensorischen Wirkungen. Fehlen sie, dann erhält er nicht mehr das Produkt, auf das es ihm ankommt. Er wird dann überlegen, ob er künftig nicht ein anderes Produkt kaufen soll. Für den Hersteller, der bislang seine Produkte mit bestimmten Geruchs- und Geschmacksstoffen ausgestattet hat, bedeutet das zwangsläufig erhebliche Einbußen. Noch mehr: Genau genommen wird ihm untersagt, ein Produkt in der Weise herzustellen, wie das, orientiert an den Kundenwünschen, sinnvoll ist.

---

[196] Dazu oben B IV 1 c.
[197] Oben B II 3 c.
[198] Dazu oben B II 2 b, c.
[199] Allgemein zu mittelbaren Grundrechtseinwirkungen *Jarass*, Charta der Grundrechte, 2010, Art. 52 Rn. 17.

b) Verhältnismäßigkeit der Maßnahme

aa) Soweit Geruchs- und Geschmacksstoffe mit Gesundheitsrisiken verbunden sind, muss ein Verbot solcher Stoffe angesichts der hohen Bedeutung der Gesundheit als verhältnismäßig eingestuft werden. Das wird bei den Geruchs- und Geschmacksstoffen, die (in Deutschland) durch §2 der Tabakverordnung verboten sind, der Fall sein, da die Vorschrift dem Gesundheitsschutz dient.[200]

bb) Anders stellt sich die Situation bei Geruchs- und Geschmacksstoffen dar, bei denen mit den Stoffen keine Gesundheitsrisiken verbunden sind und die lediglich bestimmten Kundenwünschen gerecht werden. Hier ist zunächst festzuhalten, dass es keinen Beleg für eine Förderung des Gesundheitsschutzes durch einen Verzicht auf solche Stoffe gibt.[201] Vielmehr ist die Verbreitung des Rauchens in Großbritannien und Irland, wo vor allem Zigarettenmarken ohne Zusatzstoffe verkauft werden, nicht geringer als in Ländern, wo überwiegend Zigaretten mit Zusatzstoffen zum Einsatz kommen. Das spricht dafür, dass es an der Eignung der Maßnahme im Hinblick auf das verfolgte Ziel fehlt.

Was die im Rahmen der Verhältnismäßigkeit gebotene Erforderlichkeit und die ausgewogene Gewichtung angeht, so ergeben sich zusätzliche Bedenken. Zwar wird allein in die unternehmerische Freiheit und gegebenenfalls in das Eigentumsrecht eingegriffen, nicht in die Meinungs- und Informationsfreiheit. Der gesetzgeberische Beurteilungsspielraum ist daher, folgt man der Rechtsprechung des Europäischen Gerichtshofs, an sich sehr weit.[202] Doch gilt es zu beachten, dass ein Verbot von Geruchs- und Geschmacksstoffen die Hersteller von Tabakprodukten außerordentlich unterschiedlich trifft. Es gibt Hersteller, die ohnehin keine Geruchs- und Geschmacksstoffe einsetzen. Sie werden durch ein Verbot solcher Stoffe nicht beeinträchtigt. Demgegenüber werden Hersteller von Tabakprodukten mit Geruchs- und Geschmacksstoffen nicht nur für sich empfindlich betroffen. Sie erleiden zudem gegenüber den anderen Herstellern einen Wettbewerbsnachteil. Das Anliegen des Gesundheitsschutzes sollte aber gegenüber allen Herstellern gleichmäßig verfolgt werden.[203] Insgesamt sprechen angesichts der gravierenden Zweifel an der Eignung wie an der ausgewogenen Gewichtung gute Gründe für die Unverhältnismäßigkeit eines Verbots von Geruchs- und Geschmacksstoffen.[204]

---

200 BR-Drs. 479/77, S. 23 f. Zur Tabakverordnung oben A I 1 a.
201 *Riessen* u.a., Assessing the Impacts of Revising the Tobacco Products Directive, Rand, 2010, 177 f.
202 Oben B III 2 b.
203 Dabei wird davon ausgegangen, dass von den eingesetzten Geruchs- und Geschmacksstoffen keine Gesundheitsrisiken ausgehen.
204 Zur Erforderlichkeit von Ausnahme- bzw. Übergangsregelungen oben B III 2 c.

4. Bedeutung additiver Grundrechtseingriffe

a) Grundlagen

Im deutschen Verfassungsrecht ist gerade in jüngerer Zeit zunehmend deutlich geworden, dass bei der Beurteilung der Verhältnismäßigkeit gegebenenfalls zu berücksichtigen ist, wenn sich eine Mehrzahl von Grundrechtseingriffen zu Lasten des gleichen Betroffenen in ihrer belastenden Wirkung verstärken, vorausgesetzt, die Eingriffe kommen im gleichen Zeitraum zum Tragen, verfolgen im Wesentlichen denselben Zweck und berühren dasselbe Grundrecht(sgut). Man spricht dann von „additiven" Grundrechtseingriffen.[205] In solchen Fällen genügt es nicht, jeden Eingriff für sich zu bewerten. Zusätzlich ist erforderlich, auf die Gesamtbelastung für den Betroffenen abzustellen.[206]

Im EU-Recht ist dieser Ansatz bislang, soweit ersichtlich, noch nicht thematisiert werden. In der Sache kann aber nicht zweifelhaft sein, dass im Bereich der EU-Grundrechte nichts anderes gelten kann. Andernfalls könnte ein Grundrechtsverpflichteter die Grundrechtsbindung durch zahlreiche kleine Maßnahmen, also im Wege der Salami-Taktik, unterlaufen.

b) Anwendung im vorliegenden Zusammenhang

Dieser Befund kommt im vorliegenden Zusammenhang vor allem dann zum Tragen, wenn die beschriebenen Maßnahmen der Tabakproduktregulierung kumulativ zur Anwendung kommen. Wird etwa das Verbot der Markenverpackungen mit dem Verbot der Produktpräsentation in Einzelhandelsverkaufseinrichtungen verbunden, dann wird das Markenrecht noch stärker beeinträchtigt. In diesem Falle werden die Gründe für einen unverhältnismäßigen Grundrechtseingriff noch gewichtiger. Ergeht zudem ein Verbot von Geruchs- und Geschmacksstoffen, werden die Hersteller von Tabakprodukten, die solche Stoffe enthalten, noch mehr im Absatz ihrer Produkte behindert, was die Unverhältnismäßigkeit unterstreicht.

Darüber hinaus gilt es zu beachten, dass bereits das geltende Recht, wie dargelegt, die Herstellung und den Vertrieb von Tabakprodukten sehr weit reichenden Beschränkungen unterwirft, sowohl bei der Herstellung wie bei den Verpackungen und der Werbung.[207] Die dadurch bedingten Belastungen der Hersteller von Tabak-

---

205 Näher dazu unten D III 4 a.
206 Unten D III 4 a.
207 Dazu oben A I 1 b; *Schroeder*, ZLR 2012, 407. Vgl. auch die vergleichende Darstellung von Werberegelungen im EU-Recht bei *Marwitz*, K & R 2004, insb. 213 f. Zu den finanziellen Lasten für die Hersteller *Riessen* u.a., Assessing the Impacts of Revising the Tobacco Products Directive, Rand, 2010, 81.

produkten müssen bei der Einführung zusätzlicher Beschränkungen in die Verhältnismäßigkeitsprüfung eingestellt werden. Insgesamt erweist sich daher jedenfalls der kombinierte Einsatz der Verbote als unverhältnismäßig und damit unzulässig.

C. Warenverkehrsfreiheit

I. Allgemeines

1. Verbot der Maßnahmen gleicher Wirkung

Die im primären EU-Recht verankerte Warenverkehrsfreiheit zielt auf eine Beseitigung aller Hemmnisse des die Grenzen innerhalb der Union überschreitenden Handels. Dazu werden in Art. 30 AEUV alle tarifären Handelshemmnisse, wie Zölle, untersagt; für nichttarifäre Handelshemmnisse, also für mengenmäßige Beschränkungen und alle Maßnahmen gleicher Wirkung enthalten die Art. 34–36 AEUV ein entsprechendes Verbot.[208] Im vorliegenden Zusammenhang ist die Regelung des Art. 34 AEUV von Interesse, die neben mengenmäßigen Einfuhrbeschränkungen auch alle Maßnahmen gleicher Wirkung erfasst. Wie sich noch zeigen wird, ist der Anwendungsbereich der Maßnahmen gleicher Wirkung außerordentlich weit und erfasst jede Behinderung des grenzüberschreitenden Handels, jedenfalls wenn inländische Waren nicht den gleichen Behinderungen unterliegen.[209] Sollten daher Regelungen zur Herstellung und zum Verkauf von Tabakprodukten die Aktivitäten eines Tabakherstellers in einem anderen Mitgliedstaat behindern, gilt es die Vorgaben des Art. 34 AEUV zu prüfen.

2. Verpflichtete

aa) Das Verbot des Art. 34 AEUV wendet sich zunächst an die Mitgliedstaaten. Insoweit ist das Verbot in vielen Zusammenhängen zur Anwendung gekommen. Bedeutung hat das im vorliegenden Zusammenhang, wenn Deutschland Regelungen zur Herstellung oder zum Verkauf von Tabakprodukten trifft, ohne dazu durch EU-Recht verpflichtet zu sein.

bb) Daneben verpflichtet Art. 34 AEUV die Union und deren Organe, Einrichtungen und Stellen, obgleich die Union im Regelfall den grenzüberschreitenden Handel nicht behindert, sondern fördert. Der Wortlaut des Art. 34 AEUV ist insoweit durchaus offen.[210] In der Sache wäre schwer nachvollziehbar, wenn die Union „ungehindert" den freien Warenverkehr behindern könnte, handelt es sich doch dabei um einen zentralen Baustein des primären Unionsrechts. Zudem legt Art. 3 Abs. 3 S. 1 EUV die Errichtung des Binnenmarkts als ein Ziel fest, das von der Union

---

208 Vgl. *Kingreen*, in: Calliess/Ruffert (Hg.), EUV/AEUV, 4. Aufl. 2011, Art. 34–36 Rn. 117.
209 Unten C II 1 b.
210 *Schroeder*, in: Streinz (Hg.), EUV/EGV, 2003, Art. 28 Rn. 25.

erreicht werden soll. Dementsprechend hat der Europäische Gerichtshof anerkannt, dass auch die Union an die Vorgaben der Warenverkehrsfreiheit und insbesondere an das Verbot des Art. 34 AEUV gebunden ist. Das gilt etwa für Regelungen der Union über die Etikettierung, Verpackung, Zusammensetzung und Aufmachung von Produkten[211] wie für Herstellungs- und Verkehrsverbote der Union aus Gründen des Gesundheitsschutzes.[212]

II. Anforderungen

1. Anwendungs- bzw. Schutzbereich und Beschränkung

a) Grenzüberschreitender Warenverkehr

Art. 34 AEUV kommt zur Anwendung, wenn Waren in einen anderen Mitgliedstaat exportiert werden, soweit sie aus einem Mitgliedstaat stammen oder sich in den Mitgliedstaaten in freiem Verkehr befinden.[213] Diese Voraussetzung ist im vorliegenden Zusammenhang unschwer erfüllt, wenn die in einem Mitgliedstaat hergestellten Tabakprodukte in einem anderen Mitgliedstaat verkauft werden.

b) Maßnahmen gleicher Wirkung (Grundlagen)

Das Verbot des Art. 34 AEUV wird insbesondere durch Maßnahmen gleicher Wirkung beeinträchtigt. Die klassische Definition der Maßnahmen gleicher Wirkung findet sich in der Dassonville-Formel des Europäischen Gerichtshofs: Danach wird jede Regelung erfasst, „die geeignet ist, den innergemeinschaftlichen Handel unmittelbar oder mittelbar, tatsächlich oder potentiell zu behindern".[214] Der damit umschriebene Anwendungsbereich des Art. 34 AEUV wurde später durch die Keck-Formel eingeschränkt, soweit es um nichtdiskriminierende Regelungen geht. Im vorliegenden Zusammenhang kommt es darauf an, weil die Regelungen zur Herstellung und zum Verkauf von Tabakprodukten einheitlich für Produkte aus allen Mitgliedstaaten gelten sollen. Bei solchen Regelungen sind nur solche als Maßnahmen gleicher Wirkung einzustufen, die rechtlich oder tatsächlich den

---

211 *EuGH*, Rs. 51/93, Slg. 1994 I-3879 Rn. 11 ff.; Rs. 169/99, Slg. 2001, I-5901 Rn. 37 ff.; *Schroeder*, in: Streinz (Hg.), EUV/EGV, 2003, Art. 28 Rn. 29.
212 *EuGH*, Rs. 284/95, Slg. 1998 I-4301 Rn. 62 ff.; *Schroeder*, in: Streinz (Hg.), EUV/EGV, 2003, Art. 28 Rn. 29.
213 *Kingreen*, in: Calliess/Ruffert (Hg.), EUV/AEUV, 4. Aufl. 2011, Art. 34–36 Rn. 120; *Schroeder*, in: Streinz (Hg.), EUV/EGV, 2003, Art. 28 Rn. 20.
214 *EuGH*, Rs. 8/74, Slg. 1974, 837 Rn. 5; ebenso jüngst *EuGH*, Rs. 421/09 v. 9.12.2010, Rn. 26; Rs. 291/09 v. 7.4.2011, Rn. 15; Rs. 456/10 v. 26.4.2012 Rn. 32.

Marktzugang für Erzeugnisse aus einem anderen Mitgliedstaat versperren oder stärker behindern, als sie dies für inländische Erzeugnisse tun.[215]

c) Maßnahme gleicher Wirkung im vorliegenden Zusammenhang

aa) Diese Voraussetzung ist regelmäßig erfüllt, wenn und soweit durch deutsche Regelungen Markenverpackungen, die Produktpräsentation in Einzelhandelsverkaufseinrichtungen oder Geruchs- und Geschmacksstoffe in Tabakprodukten verboten werden, ohne dazu durch EU-Recht verpflichtet zu sein. In diesem Falle bestehen in den anderen Mitgliedstaaten regelmäßig andere Regelungen, was den grenzüberschreitenden Vertrieb von Tabakprodukten zwangsläufig behindert.

bb) Anders stellt sich die Situation dar, wenn die Europäische Union entsprechende Regelungen trifft. Diese gelten dann einheitlich in allen Mitgliedstaaten, was den grenzüberschreitenden Warenverkehr nicht behindert, sondern erleichtert. Allerdings gilt es im vorliegenden Zusammenhang eine Besonderheit zu beachten:

Das Eindringen auf den Markt eines anderen Mitgliedstaat durch einen Hersteller, der bislang dort nicht tätig war, ist regelmäßig sehr viel eher möglich, wenn die Produkte durch eine bestimmte Marke gekennzeichnet sind. In diese Fall kann die Marke zu entsprechenden Werbemaßnahmen eingesetzt werden, die für den ausländischen Hersteller unverzichtbar sind, während sich der inländische Hersteller auf den vorhandenen Kundenstamm stützen kann. Daher befördert der Schutz von Marken den freien Warenverkehr. Dazu passt, dass der Europäische Gerichtshof, wie dargelegt, auch eine Regulierung der Etikettierung, Verpackung, Zusammensetzung und Aufmachung von Produkten durch die Union als Beeinträchtigung des freien Warenverkehr eingestuft hat.[216] Auch hat er festgehalten, dass „Maßnahmen, mit denen die Werbung für Tabakerzeugnisse verboten oder beschränkt wird, den Marktzugang für Erzeugnisse aus anderen Mitgliedstaaten stärker behindern (können) als für inländische Erzeugnisse.[217] Gleiches hat er für ein Vermarktungsverbot für Tabakerzeugnisse zu oralen Gebrauch angenommen,[218] und jüngst für die Großhandelspflicht von Tabakprodukten.[219] Schließlich hat der EFTA-Gerichtshof ein Verbot der Präsentation von Tabakprodukten in Einzelhandelsverkaufseinrichtungen als eine mögliche Maßnahme gleicher Wirkung eingestuft.[220]

---

215 *EuGH*, Rs. 267/91, Slg. 1993, I-6097 Rn. 17; ebenso *EuGH*, Rs. 239/02, Slg. 2004, I-7007 Rn. 51; Rs. 20/03 Slg. 2005, I-4133 Rn. 24.
216 Oben C I 2 bb.
217 *EuGH*, Rs. 380/03, Slg. 2006, I-11573 Rn. 56.
218 *EuGH*, Rs. 434/02, Slg. 2004, I-11825 Rn. 59; *Streinz*, ZUR 2005, 431.
219 *EuGH*, Rs. 456/10 v. 26.4.2012 Rn. 37 ff.
220 EFTA-Gerichtshsof, Rs. E-16/10 v. 12.9.2011, Rn. 42.

Mit dem Verbot von Markenverpackungen wird dem Hersteller ein wichtiges Instrument genommen, auf den Markt eines anderen Mitgliedstaats vorzudringen. Ohne eine solche Kennzeichnung kann der Verbraucher die Besonderheiten des aus einem anderen Mitgliedstaat kommenden Produkts nicht wirklich erkennen. Ähnliches muss für das Verbot der Produktpräsentation in Einzelhandelsverkaufseinrichtungen gelten, da der Verbraucher dann nicht in der Lage ist, das Produkt in den Verkaufsräumen ohne weitere Maßnahmen zu sehen.[221] Schließlich spricht vieles dafür, dass die Regelungen für inländische Hersteller deutlich weniger belastend ausfallen. Dabei gilt es zu beachten, dass es für die Annahme einer Maßnahme gleicher Wirkung bereits ausreicht, wenn die *Möglichkeit* besteht, dass ausländische Hersteller stärker belastet werden; es genügt eine „potentiell" beschränkende Wirkung.[222]

Insgesamt ist festzuhalten, dass ein Verbot von Markenverpackungen, ein Verbot der Produktpräsentation in Einzelhandelsverkaufseinrichtungen wie ein Verbot von Geruchs- und Geschmacksstoffen in Tabakprodukten den grenzüberschreitenden Handel mit solchen Produkten auch dann behindern können, wenn die Verbote einheitlich und unionsweit gelten. Damit liegt eine Beschränkung des Art. 34 AEUV vor. Dem steht nicht entgegen, dass eine unionsweite Regelung den freien Warenverkehr auch fördert. Eine einheitlich unionsweite Regelung kann sehr unterschiedlich ausfallen und durchaus so gestaltet sein, dass sie die Nutzung der Marke beim Eindringen in den Markt eines anderen Mitgliedstaates weiterhin zulässt.

2. Rechtfertigung

a) Zulässige Gründe

Beschränkungen des Art. 34 AEUV sind nicht zwangsläufig unzulässig. Vielmehr können sie unter bestimmten Voraussetzungen gerechtfertigt sein. Rechtliche Grundlage dafür ist zum einen die Ausnahmeregelung des Art. 36 AEUV.[223] Daneben kommt, jedenfalls in bestimmten Fällen, eine Rechtfertigung durch zwingende Erfordernisse des Allgemeininteresses in Betracht.[224] Unter welchen Voraussetzungen die beiden Rechtfertigungsmöglichkeiten zum Tragen kommen, ist mit einigen

---

[221] Auch das Verbot von Geruchs- und Geschmacksstoffen dürfte das Eindringen in den Markt eines anderen Mitgliedstaats behindern, weil gerade bestimmte Zusätze das Produkt von inländischen Produkten abheben können; doch soll die Frage nicht näher untersucht werden.
[222] *EuGH*, Rs. 249/81, Slg. 1982, 4005 Rn. 25; Rs. 125/85, Slg. 1986, 3935 Rn. 7; *Schroeder*, in: Streinz (Hg.), EUV/EGV, 2003, Art. 28 Rn. 37.
[223] Dazu *Becker*, in: Schwarze, EU-Kommentar, 2. Aufl. 2009, Art. 30 Rn. 9 ff.
[224] Dazu *Becker*, in: Schwarze, EU-Kommentar, 2. Aufl. 2009, Art. 30 Rn. 35 ff.

Unsicherheiten behaftet.[225] Doch kommt es darauf im vorliegenden Zusammenhang nicht an. Die Regelung der Herstellung und des Verkaufs von Tabakprodukten soll den Gesundheitsschutz fördern. Darin liegt ein im Rahmen beider Rechtfertigungsmöglichkeiten zulässiger Rechtfertigungsgrund. Insbesondere wird der „Schutz der Gesundheit" in Art. 36 AEUV ausdrücklich aufgeführt. Auch handelt es sich um keinen rein wirtschaftlichen Grund, der Beschränkungen der Warenverkehrsfreiheit nicht zu rechtfertigen vermag. „Rein wirtschaftliche Motive" können eine Beschränkung der Grundfreiheiten nicht rechtfertigen.[226]

b) Verhältnismäßigkeit

Der Schutz der Gesundheit kann allerdings nicht jede Beschränkung des Art. 34 AEUV rechtfertigen. Zwar kommt dem Schutz der Gesundheit des Menschen ein hoher Rang zu. Doch wie alle Beschränkungen des Art. 34 AEUV sind auch Beschränkungen zum Schutze der Gesundheit nur zulässig, wenn sie verhältnismäßig sind.

aa) Das setzt zunächst voraus, dass die fragliche Maßnahme ein *geeignetes Mittel* zur Erreichung des angestrebten Ziels ist, wobei es genügt, wenn das Ziel gefördert wird.[227] Auch kommt dem Gesetzgeber insoweit ein gewisser Beurteilungsspielraum zu.[228] Doch ist insbesondere im Bereich des Gesundheits-, Umwelt- und Verbraucherschutzes eine eingehende und nachvollziehbare Risikoprüfung notwendig, die sich nicht auf hypothetische Erwägungen beschränkt.[229] Dementsprechend hat der EuGH auch im Tabakbereich verlangt, dass die Eignung „nachzuweisen" ist, etwa durch eine entsprechende Untersuchung[230] An der Geeignetheit fehlt es, wenn die relevanten Tatsachen nicht ermittelt werden oder ein widersprüchliches Schutzkonzept zum Einsatz kommt.[231]

bb) Besondere Bedeutung besitzt im Rahmen der Verhältnismäßigkeit das Gebot der *Erforderlichkeit*, das in der Rechtsprechung des Europäischen Gerichtshofs im Mittelpunkt der Verhältnismäßigkeitsprüfung steht.[232] Das Gebot erfordert, dass

---

225 Vgl. *Kingreen*, in: Calliess/Ruffert (Hg.), EUV/AEUV, 4. Aufl. 2011, Art. 34–36 Rn. 82.
226 *EuGH*, Rs. 456/10 v. 26.4.2012 Rn. 53; ebenso EuGH, Rs. 254/98, Slg. 2000, I-151 Rn. 33; *Schroeder*, in: Streinz (Hg.), EUV/EGV, 2003, Art. 30 Rn. 48.
227 *EuGH*, Rs. 152/78, Slg. 1980, I-2299 Rn. 15 ff.
228 *EuGH*, Rs. 293/93, Slg. 1994, I-4249 Rn. 22.
229 *EuGH*, Rs. 41/02, Slg. 2004, I-11375 Rn. 49 ff.; *Kingreen*, in: Calliess/Ruffert (Hg.), EUV/AEUV, 4. Aufl. 2011, Art. 34–36 Rn. 92.
230 *EuGH*, Rs. 456/10 v. 26.4.2012 Rn. 50.
231 Zu Ersterem *EuGH*, Rs. 41/02, Slg. 2004, I-11375 Rn. 59, zu Letzterem *EuGH*, Rs. 67/88, Slg. 1990, I-4285 Rn. 6; *Kingreen*, in: Calliess/Ruffert (Hg.), EUV/AEUV, 4. Aufl. 2011, Art. 34–36 Rn. 92.
232 *Kingreen*, in: Calliess/Ruffert (Hg.), EUV/AEUV, 4. Aufl. 2011, Art. 34–36 Rn. 93.

der angestrebte „Zweck nicht durch Maßnahmen erreicht werden kann, die den innergemeinschaftlichen Handel weniger beschränken".[233] Insoweit stellt der Gerichtshof meist strenge Anforderungen an die Erforderlichkeit, auch im Bereich des Verbraucher- und Gesundheitsschutzes.[234] So sind Verkehrsverbote oder Verbote bestimmter Produktbezeichnungen nicht erforderlich, soweit eine angemessene Information der Verbraucher ausreicht.[235]

Ähnlich wie im Bereich der Grundrechte nimmt der Europäische Gerichtshof häufig keine eigenständige Prüfung der Angemessenheit (als ein drittes Element der Verhältnismäßigkeit) vor. Andererseits findet sich aber bereits in der Erforderlichkeitsprüfung eine gewisse Güterabwägung.[236] In der Sache muss es hier wie allgemein beim Grundsatz der Verhältnismäßigkeit auf eine ausgewogene Gewichtung der betroffenen Interessen ankommen.[237] Insbesondere ist bedeutsam, wie sehr der grenzüberschreitende Handel beeinträchtigt wird.[238]

c) Verhältnis zu den Grundrechten

Mit dem Verhältnis der den Binnenmarkt betreffenden Grundfreiheiten und den Grundrechten hat sich der Europäische Gerichtshof schon mehrfach befasst. Je nach Sachverhalt können sich die Grundrechte und Grundfreiheiten gegenseitig begrenzen oder verstärken.[239] Im vorliegenden Zusammenhang ist Letzteres bedeutsam. So hat der Gerichtshof festgehalten, dass Beschränkungen von Grundfreiheiten auch an den Grundrechten zu messen sind, etwa an der Meinungsäußerungs- und Informationsfreiheit.[240] Und umgekehrt können Einschränkungen der Grundrechte unzulässig sein, weil die Grundfreiheiten entgegen stehen.[241] In solchen Fällen verstärken sich Grundfreiheiten und Grundrechte gegenseitig. Im Rahmen der jeweiligen Verhältnismäßigkeitsprüfung ist das zu beachten.

---

233 *EuGH*, Rs. 25/88, Slg. 1989, 1105 Rn. 13 ff.; Rs. 470/93, Slg. 1995, I-1923 Rn. 15; Rs. 67/97, Slg. 1998, I-8033 Rn. 35.

234 *Schroeder*, in: Streinz (Hg.), EUV/EGV, 2003, Art. 30 Rn. 54. Im Tabakbereich hat der EuGH, wie bei der Geeignetheit, den Nachweis der Erforderlichkeit verlangt; *EuGH*, Rs. 456/10 v. 26.4.2012 Rn. 50.

235 *EuGH*, Rs. 315/92, Slg. 1994, I-317 Rn. 20 ff.; Rs. 470/93, Slg. 1995, I-1923 Rn. 24; Rs. 51/94, Slg. 1995, I-3599 Rn. 34.

236 *Schroeder*, in: Streinz (Hg.), EUV/EGV, 2003, Art. 30 Rn. 55 mit Nachweisen.

237 Vgl. oben B III 2 b.

238 *Kingreen*, in: Calliess/Ruffert (Hg.), EUV/AEUV, 4. Aufl. 2011, Art. 34–36 Rn. 98.

239 Näher *Jarass*, Charta der Grundrechte, 2010, Einl. 24 ff. mit Nachw.

240 *EuGH*, Rs. 260/89, Slg. 1991, I-2925 Rn. 43 f; Rs. 368/95, Slg. 1997, I-3689 Rn. 24 f; *Streinz*, in: Streinz (Hg.), EUV/EGV, 2003, Art. 11 Rn. 6.

241 *Jarass*, Charta der Grundrechte, 2010, Einl. 27.

d) Anwendung im vorliegenden Zusammenhang

Wendet man die Vorgaben zur Verhältnismäßigkeit einer Beschränkung des Art. 34 AEUV im vorliegenden Zusammenhang an, dann werden ganz ähnliche Gesichtspunkte wie bei der Rechtfertigung der Grundrechtseingriffe bedeutsam. Daher kann auf die entsprechenden Ausführungen zur grundrechtlichen Verhältnismäßigkeit des Verbots von Markenverpackungen und des Verbots der Produktpräsentation in Einzelhandelsverkaufseinrichtungen verwiesen werden.[242]

Zusätzlich bzw. abweichend ist aber Folgendes zu beachten: Zunächst beeinträchtigen die untersuchten Regelungen zur Herstellung und zum Verkauf von Tabakprodukten auch den freien Warenverkehr. Im Rahmen der Prüfung der Rechtfertigung ist daher zusätzlich zu berücksichtigen, dass nicht nur die individuellen Interessen der Hersteller (und der Verbraucher) betroffen sind. Vielmehr wird auch das für die Union essentielle Interesse an einem freien Warenverkehr in der Union beeinträchtigt. Das erhöht die Anforderungen an die Rechtfertigung.

Weiter nimmt der Europäische Gerichtshof im Bereich der Grundfreiheiten, anders als im Bereich des Eigentumsrechts und des Rechts der unternehmerischen Freiheit, durchweg eine strenge Verhältnismäßigkeitsprüfung vor. Daher obliegt es dem Gesetzgeber, in jedem Fall den Nachweis der Verhältnismäßigkeit zu führen.[243] Die Notwendigkeit und Erforderlichkeit des Eingreifens ist unter Hinweis auf wissenschaftliche Erkenntnisse oder internationale Standards nachvollziehbar zu belegen.[244]

Im vorliegenden Zusammenhang ist daher bedeutsam, dass der Nutzen der untersuchten Verbote für den Schutz der Gesundheit mit nicht unerheblichen Unsicherheiten behaftet ist oder ein solcher Schutz praktisch nicht auszumachen ist.[245] Andererseits geht es nicht nur, wie dargelegt, um schwere Grundrechtseingriffe,[246] sondern auch um eine bedeutsame Behinderung des freien Warenverkehrs. Das spricht dafür, dass der Gesetzgeber sich auf Maßnahmen beschränken muss, die die Einsatzfähigkeit des Markenrechts nicht völlig entwerten, ist doch der Einsatz dieses Instruments für Aktivitäten der Hersteller von Tabakprodukten in ande-

---

[242] Oben B IV 1 b und B IV 2 b.
[243] *EuGH*, Rs., Slg. 174/82, Slg. 1983, 2445 Rn. 22; Rs. 13/91, Slg. 1992, I-3617 Rn. 18; *Schroeder*, in: Streinz (Hg.), EUV/EGV, 2003, Art. 30 Rn. 57.
[244] *EuGH*, Rs. 17/93, Slg. 1994, I-3537 Rn. 17; Rs. 473/98, Slg. 2000, I-5681 Rn. 40 ff.; Rs. 192/01, Slg. 2003, I-9693 Rn. 46; Rs. 150/00, Slg. 2004, I-3887 Rn. 89.
[245] Vgl. oben B IV 1 b, B IV 2 b und B IV 3 b .
[246] Oben B IV 1 a, B IV 2 a und B IV 3 a.

ren Mitgliedstaaten unverzichtbar.[247] Wenn daher bereits im Rahmen der Grundrechtsprüfung gute Gründe für die Unverhältnismäßigkeit des Verbots der Markenverpackungen sprechen,[248] dann muss das erst recht gelten, wenn zudem die Beschränkung des Art. 34 AEUV berücksichtigt wird. Weiter werden die Bedenken hinsichtlich der Verhältnismäßigkeit eines Verbots der Produktpräsentation in Einzelhandelsverkaufseinrichtungen verstärkt.[249] Die Vorgaben der Warenverkehrsfreiheit erhöhen den Schutz der betroffenen Grundrechte und umgekehrt.

---

247 Auch der EFTA-Gerichtshof hat die Frage als wesentlich eingestuft, ob es nicht ausreichende mildere Maßnahmen als das Verbot der Produktpräsentation gibt; EFTA-Gerichtshsof, Rs.E-16/10 v. 12.9.2011, Rn. 85 ff.
248 Dazu oben B IV 1 b.
249 Zu diesen Bedenken oben B IV 2 b.

D. Grundrechte des Grundgesetzes

I. Grundlagen und beeinträchtigte Grundrechte

1. Grundrechtsverpflichtung und Grundrechtsträger

a) Grundrechtsverpflichtung von EU-Stellen

Im letzten Teil der Untersuchung soll der Frage nachgegangen werden, wieweit ein Verbot von Markenverpackungen, ein Verbot der Produktpräsentation in Einzelhandelsverkaufseinrichtungen und ein Verbot von Geruchs- und Geschmacksstoffen in Tabakprodukten, mit dem Grundgesetz vereinbar wären. Insoweit stellt sich zunächst die Frage, ob und ggf. wieweit Rechtsakte des Unionsrechts an die Grundrechte des Grundgesetzes gebunden sind.[250]

Die Grundrechte des Grundgesetzes binden allein die inländische öffentliche Gewalt. Organe, Einrichtungen und Stellen der Europäischen Union sind daher nicht Verpflichtete der Grundrechte.[251] Auch die Anerkennung, Umsetzung und Anwendung von EU-Akten hängt wegen Art. 23 Abs. 1 GG nicht von ihrer Vereinbarkeit mit den Grundrechten ab, „solange die Europäischen Gemeinschaften, insbesondere die Rechtsprechung des Gerichtshofs der Europäischen Gemeinschaften, einen wirksamen Schutz der Grundrechte gegenüber der Hoheitsgewalt der Gemeinschaften generell gewährleisten, der dem vom Grundgesetz jeweils als unabdingbar gebotenen Grundrechtsschutz im Wesentlichen gleich zu achten ist".[252] Für den Fortfall dieser Voraussetzung genügt es nicht, wenn in Einzelfällen ein solcher Grundrechtsschutz nicht gewahrt wird; vielmehr muss es zu einem flächendeckenden Ausfall kommen.[253] Darin liegt eine hohe, praktisch kaum überwindbare Hürde.[254] Da und solange das Unionsrecht jedenfalls generell einen ausreichenden Grundrechtsschutz bereitstellt, scheidet eine Anwendung deutscher Grundrechte im Hinblick auf Rechtsakte der Union aus.[255]

---

250 Dabei wird die Sicht des deutschen Verfassungsrechts zugrunde gelegt.
251 *Kunig*, in: v.Münch/Kunig, GG-Kommentar, Bd. I, 5. Aufl. 2000, Art. 1 Rn. 52; *Jarass*, in: drs./Pieroth, Grundgesetz, 11. Aufl. 2011, Art. 1 Rn. 46; wohl auch *BVerfGE* 118, 79/95; unklar *BVerfGE* 89, 155/174 f
252 *BVerfGE* 118, 79/95; 73, 339/387; 102, 147/162 ff; 123, 267/335.
253 *BVerfGE* 102, 147/164; BVerfG-K, NVwZ 07, 942.
254 *Streinz*, in: Sachs (Hg.), Grundgesetz, 5. Aufl. 2009, Art. 23 Rn. 41.
255 *BVerfGE* 73, 339/378, 387; 102, 147/164; BVerwGE 85, 24/29 f; *Classen*, in: v.Mangoldt/Klein/Starck, Grundgesetz, 6. Aufl., Bd. II 2010, Art. 23 Rn. 50.

Im vorliegenden Zusammenhang folgt daraus, dass Rechtsakte der Europäischen Union zur Regulierung der Herstellung und des Verkaufs von Tabakprodukten, gleich welcher Art, nicht an den Grundrechten des Grundgesetzes gemessen werden können. Sie unterliegen allein der dargestellten Bindung durch EU-Grundrechte (und sonstigen primärrechtlichen Anforderungen).

b) Grundrechtsverpflichtung deutscher Stellen

Maßnahmen deutscher Stellen sind dagegen an den Grundrechten des Grundgesetzes zu messen, unabhängig davon, ob die Maßnahmen auf das Inland beschränkt sind oder einen Auslandsbezug aufweisen.[256] Das gilt auch für Maßnahmen deutscher Stellen, die zur Umsetzung oder zum Vollzug von EU-Recht ergehen, sofern und soweit das EU-Recht Spielräume belässt.[257] Generell gilt, dass nationale Stellen die Grundrechte des Grundgesetzes voll zu beachten haben, soweit sie EU-rechtlich nicht gebunden sind.[258] Dass im Bereich der Spielräume gleichzeitig EU-Grundrechte zu beachten sind, steht der Anwendung der GG-Grundrechte regelmäßig nicht entgegen, weil die EU-Grundrechte weitergehende nationale Grundrechte nicht ausschließen.[259] Zu beachten ist natürlich der Vorrang sonstigen Unionsrechts.[260] Nur dann, wenn das EU-Recht „keinen Umsetzungsspielraum lässt, sondern zwingende Vorgaben macht", können Umsetzungsakte deutscher Stellen nicht an den deutschen Grundrechten gemessen werden.[261]

Im vorliegenden Zusammenhang ergibt sich daraus, dass der deutsche Gesetzgeber dann, wenn er Regelungen zur Herstellung oder zum Verkauf von Tabakprodukten trifft, ohne dazu durch EU-Recht verpflichtet zu sein, in vollem Umfang an die Grundrechte des Grundgesetzes gebunden ist. Selbst wenn er insoweit zur Umsetzung EU-rechtlicher Vorgaben tätig ist, kommen die deutschen Grundrechte zur Anwendung, soweit das EU-Recht Spielräume belässt.

---

256 *BVerfGE* 6, 290/295; 57, 9/23; *Herdegen*, in: Maunz/Dürig, Grundgesetz, Stand 2010, 71; *Höfling*, in: Sachs (Hg.), Grundgesetz, 5. Aufl. 2009, Art. 1 Rn. 86; *Badura*, in: Merten/Papier (Hg.), Handbuch der Grundrechte, Bd. II, 2006, § 47 Rn. 4.

257 *BVerfGE* 113, 273/300; 118, 79/96

258 *Dreier*, in: Dreier (Hg.), Grundgesetz, Bd. I, 2. Aufl. 2004, Art. 19 III Rn. 13; *Pieroth/Schlink*, Grundrechte, 26. Aufl. 2010, Rn. 191.

259 Zum Verhältnis der beiden Grundrechtsebenen *Jarass*, Charta der Grundrechte, 2010, Art. 53 Rn. 10 ff.

260 Dazu *Jarass*, in: drs./Pieroth, Grundgesetz, 11. Aufl. 2011, Art. 23 Rn. 27.

261 *BVerfGE* 118, 79/95; BVerfG-K, NJW 01, 1267.

c) Grundrechtsträger

Auf die hier relevanten Grundrechte der Berufsfreiheit des Art. 12 GG, der Eigentumsgarantie des Art. 14 GG und der Meinungsfreiheit des Art. 5 GG können sich gem. Art. 19 Abs. 3 GG neben natürlichen Personen auch juristische Personen berufen, soweit sie als inländische juristische Personen einzustufen sind. Diese Voraussetzung ist gegeben, wenn die juristische Person ihren Sitz, d. h. den tatsächlichen Mittelpunkt ihrer Tätigkeit, im Bundesgebiet hat;[262] auf die Staatsangehörigkeit oder den Sitz der Anteilseigner kommt es bei den Jedermann-Grundrechten und damit bei den hier relevanten Grundrechten nicht an.[263] Juristische Personen und Personenvereinigungen aus dem *EU-Bereich* sind kraft Unionsrechts wie inländische Vereinigungen zu behandeln, wie das Bundesverfassungsgericht erst jüngst festgestellt hat.[264]

2. Berufsfreiheit

a) Schutzbereich

Die Berufsfreiheit des Art. 12 GG schützt „jede auf Erwerb gerichtete Beschäftigung, die sich nicht in einem einmaligen Erwerbsakt erschöpft".[265] Bei juristischen Personen ist diese Voraussetzung regelmäßig gegeben, wenn die Führung eines Geschäftsbetriebs zu ihren satzungsmäßigen Zwecken gehört.[266] Geschützt werden neben der Wahl des Berufs dessen Ausübung, d. h. die gesamte berufliche Tätigkeit, insbesondere Form, Mittel und Umfang sowie gegenständliche Ausgestaltung der Betätigung.[267] Das Grundrecht umfasst auch das Recht, Art und Qualität der angebotenen Güter und Dienstleistungen selbst festzulegen.[268] Zudem fällt die berufliche

---

262 BVerfG-K, NJW 09, 2519; *Huber*, in: v.Mangoldt/Klein/Starck, Grundgesetz, Bd. 1, 6. Aufl. 2010, 299; *Tettinger*, in: Merten/Papier (Hg.), Handbuch der Grundrechte, Bd. II, § 51 Rn. 45

263 BVerfG-K, NVwZ 00, 1282; NVwZ 08, 671; *Enders*, in: Epping/Hillgruber (Hg.), Grundgesetz, 2009, 36.

264 BVerfG, 1 BvR 1916/09 v. 19.7.2011; *Dreier*, in: Dreier (Hg.), Grundgesetz, Bd. I, 2. Aufl. 2004, Art. Rn. 83; *Tettinger*, in: Merten/Papier (Hg.), Handbuch der Grundrechte, Bd. HGR II § 51 Rn. 49.

265 *BVerfGE* 97, 228/253.

266 *BVerfGE* 97, 228/253 mit Nachw.

267 *Breuer*, in: Isensee/Kirchhof (Hg.), Handbuch des Staatsrechts, 3. Aufl. 2009, Bd. VIII § 170 Rn. 82; *Manssen*, in: v.Mangoldt/Klein/Starck, Grundgesetz, Bd. 1, 6. Aufl. 2010, Art. 12 Rn. 66; *Gubelt*, in: v.Münch/Kunig, GG-Kommentar, Bd. I, 5. Aufl. 2000, Art. 12 Rn. 38.

268 *BVerfGE* 106, 275/299; 121, 317/345.

Außendarstellung in den Schutzbereich,[269] desgleichen die berufliche Werbung.[270] Geschützt werden schließlich Betriebs- und Geschäftsgeheimnisse.[271]

Vor diesem Hintergrund besteht im vorliegenden Zusammenhang kein Zweifel, dass der Einsatz von Markenverpackungen in den Schutzbereich der Berufsfreiheit fällt. Gleiches gilt für die Präsentation von Tabakprodukten in Einzelhandelsverkaufseinrichtungen.[272] Schließlich wird die Verwendung von Geruchs- und Geschmacksstoffen bei der Herstellung von Tabakprodukten durch die Berufsfreiheit geschützt.

b) Eingriff

Das Verbot von Markenverpackungen, das Verbot der Produktpräsentation in Einzelhandelsverkaufseinrichtungen und das Verbot von Geruchs- und Geschmacksstoffen in Tabakprodukten sind als Eingriffe in die Berufsfreiheit des Art. 12 GG zu qualifizieren.[273] Es handelt sich um verbindliche Vorgaben zu den von Art. 12 GG geschützten Tätigkeiten.[274] Darüber hinaus weisen die Verbote eine berufsregelnde Tendenz auf, da sie typischerweise beruflich ausgeübte Tätigkeiten betreffen.[275]

Schließlich liegt im Verbot der Produktpräsentation in Einzelhandelsverkaufseinrichtungen nicht nur ein Eingriff in die Berufsfreiheit des Einzelhändlers. Da die Maßnahme für den *Hersteller* der Tabakprodukte massive Auswirkungen hat, liegt auch ihm gegenüber ein Eingriff vor, obwohl die Belastung nur mittelbarer Natur ist. Der Hersteller ist sehr viel mehr als der Einzelhändler betroffen, sofern die Tabakprodukte nur einen kleinen Teil des Sortiments bilden, das der Einzelhändler führt. Es handelt sich um eine mittelbare Beeinträchtigung, die nach Zielsetzung und Wirkung einem Eingriff gleichkommt.[276] Zudem handelt es sich um eine bezweckte Wirkung.[277]

---

269 *BVerfGE* 106, 181/192; 112, 255/262.
270 *BVerfGE* 94, 372/389; 105, 252/266; 111, 366/373; BGHZ 147, 71/74; BVerwGE 124, 26/28.
271 *BVerfGE* 115, 205/229.
272 Zur Frage, ob nur der Einzelhändler insoweit in seiner Berufsfreiheit betroffen ist, unten D I 2 b.
273 Ebenso zum Verbot von Markenverpackungen *Stein/Rauber*, Rechtliche Grenzen der Bekämpfung des Tabakkonsums im Mehrebenensystem, 2011, 44; *Schwarz*, in: Pache/ Schwarz/Sosnitza, Aktuelle Rechtsfragen der Tabakregulierung in Europa, 2012, 121.
274 Vgl. *Jarass*, in: drs./Pieroth, Grundgesetz, 11. Aufl. 2011, Art. 12 Rn. 14.
275 *BVerfGE* 97, 228/254; ähnlich *BVerfGE* 111, 191/213.
276 Darauf kommt es für die Annahme einer Grundrechtsbeeinträchtigung an; *BVerfGE* 105, 252/273; 110, 177/191; 116, 202/222.
277 Zur Relevanz dieses Umstands BVerwGE 71, 183/193 f; 90, 112/121 f.

3. Eigentumsgarantie

a) Schutzfähige Positionen

Das Grundrecht des Art. 14 GG schützt nicht nur das Eigentum im Sinne des bürgerlichen Rechts. Geschützt wird vielmehr jedes vom Gesetzgeber gewährte vermögenswerte Recht,[278] jedenfalls wenn es privatrechtlicher Natur ist.[279] Darunter fällt insbesondere das Recht am Warenzeichen bzw. an Marken, wie das Bundesverfassungsgericht und der Bundesgerichtshof festgehalten haben.[280] Das Schrifttum hat sich dem angeschlossen.[281] Zudem werden selbständige vermögenswerte Geschäftsgeheimnisse geschützt.[282]

Unsicher ist die Lage beim Recht am eingerichteten und ausgeübten Gewerbebetrieb, das im vorliegenden Zusammenhang bedeutsam sein könnte. Das Bundesverfassungsgericht hat die Anwendbarkeit von Art. 14 ausdrücklich offen gelassen,[283] während sonst die Anwendbarkeit überwiegend und zu Recht bejaht wird,[284] jedenfalls wenn es um die Substanz dieses Rechts geht.[285] Die Frage kann aber im vorliegenden Zusammenhang auf sich beruhen. Das Verbot der Markenverpackungen betrifft das Markenrecht, das, wie dargelegt, eine schutzfähige Position im Sinne des Art. 14 GG darstellt. Gleiches gilt für das Verbot der Produktpräsentation in Einzelhandelsverkaufseinrichtungen, da bei der Produktpräsentation das Markenrecht in gewichtiger Weise zum Tragen kommt. Schließlich stellt das Verbot von Geruchs- und Geschmacksstoffen dann einen Eingriff in die Eigentumsgarantie dar, wenn die Stoffe ein Geschäftsgeheimnis betreffen.

---

278 *BVerfGE* 24, 367/396; 53, 257/290; 58, 300/336; *Papier*, in: Maunz/Dürig, Grundgesetz, Stand 2010, Art. 14 Rn. 55; *Bryde*, in: v.Münch/Kunig, GG-Kommentar, Bd. I, 5. Aufl. 2000, Art. 14 Rn. 59.

279 Zur Situation bei öffentlich-rechtlichen Positionen *Jarass*, in: drs./Pieroth, Grundgesetz, 11. Aufl. 2011, Art. 14 Rn. 11 ff.

280 *BVerfGE* 51, 193/217; 78, 58/71; 95, 173/188; BGH, GRUR 2009, 678 ff.

281 *Wieland*, in: Dreier (Hg.), Grundgesetz, Bd. I, 2. Aufl. 2004, Art. 14 Rn. 60; *Jarass*, in: drs./Pieroth, Grundgesetz, 11. Aufl. 2011, Art. 14 Rn. 9; *Depenheuer*, in: v.Mangoldt/Klein/Starck, Grundgesetz, Bd. 1, 6. Aufl. 2010, Art. 14 Rn. 15.

282 *Breuer*, in: Isensee/Kirchhof (Hg.), Handbuch des Staatsrecht, 3. Aufl. 2009, Bd. VIII, § 171 Rn. 38; vgl. *BVerfGE* 77, 1/46; BVerwGE 115, 319/325 f; 125, 40 Rn. 7.

283 *BVerfGE* 77, 84/118; 81, 208/227 f; 96, 375/397; 105, 252/278; ebenso BVerwGE 118, 226/241.

284 BGHZ 92, 34/37; BGH, DVBl 2001, 1671; *Papier*, in: Maunz/Dürig, Grundgesetz, Stand 2010, Art. 14 Rn. 95 ff; *Dietlein*, in: Stern, Staatsrecht, Bd. IV/1, 2191; gegen einen Schutz *Wieland*, in: Dreier (Hg.), Grundgesetz, Bd. I, 2. Aufl. 2004, Art. 14 Rn. 52.

285 BGHZ 161, 305/312.

b) Eingriff

Art. 14 GG schützt insbesondere die Nutzung der Eigentumspositionen.[286] Wenn daher die Verwendung der Marke Beschränkungen unterworfen wird, liegt darin ein Eingriff in Art. 14 GG. Das betrifft das Verbot der Markenverpackungen und das Verbot der Produktpräsentation in Einzelhandelsverkaufseinrichtungen. Die Situation unterscheidet sich insoweit maßgeblich von dem Fall, dass Warnhinweise vorgeschrieben werden, ohne dass die auf den jeweiligen Hersteller bezogene Gewährleistungsfunktion beeinträchtigt wird.[287] Weiter stellt ein Verbot, bestimmte vermögenswerte Geschäftsgeheimnisse wie die Rezeptur von Tabakprodukten zu nutzen, einen Eigentumseingriff dar, da es die Nutzung dieses Rechts unmöglich macht.

4. Meinungsfreiheit

Schließlich könnte die Meinungsfreiheit des Art. 5 Abs. 1 GG betroffen sein, soweit es um das Verbot von Markenverpackungen und der Produktpräsentation in Verkaufseinrichtungen geht, da damit die Weitergabe von Informationen an den Verbraucher behindert wird. Das Grundrecht schützt eine Meinungsäußerung auch dann, wenn sie wirtschaftliche Vorteile bringen soll.[288] Die Wirtschaftswerbung wird dementsprechend erfasst, soweit sie „einen wertenden, meinungsbildenden Inhalt hat oder Angaben enthält, die der Meinungsbildung dienen".[289] Allerdings gilt es zu beachten, dass nach Auffassung des Bundesverfassungsgerichts eine Verpflichtung zu Warnhinweisen Produzenten und Händler von Tabakerzeugnissen beim Vertrieb ihrer Waren betrifft, nicht bei der Teilnahme am Prozess der Meinungsäußerung und Meinungsverbreitung, mit der Folge, dass die Kennzeichnungspflicht am Maßstab der Berufsfreiheit, nicht der Meinungsfreiheit zu messen ist.[290] Das spricht dafür, dass auch ein Verbot von Markenverpackungen wie der Produktpräsentation in Einzelhandelsverkaufseinrichtungen Art. 5 Abs. 1 GG nicht berührt.

---

286 *BVerfGE* 88, 366/377; 98, 17/35; 101, 54/75; BGHZ 157, 144/147; *Axer*, in: Epping/Hillgruber (Hg.), Grundgesetz, 2009, 64.
287 Darauf hat *BVerfGE* 95, 173/188 entscheidend abgehoben.
288 *BVerfGE* 30, 336/352.
289 *BVerfGE* 95, 173/182; 102, 347/359; BGHZ 130, 196/203; *Starck*, in: v.Mangoldt/Klein/Starck, Grundgesetz, Bd. 1, 6. Aufl. 2010, Art. 5 Rn. 25; *Wendt*, in: v.Münch/Kunig, GG-Kommentar, Bd. I, 5. Aufl. 2000, Art. 5 Rn. 11.
290 *BVerfGE* 95, 173/181.

Andererseits darf nicht übersehen werden, dass das Bundesverfassungsgericht bei seiner Stellungnahme wesentlich darauf abgehoben hat, dass die Warnweise erkennbar nicht als Meinung des Herstellers ausgestaltet waren.[291] Bei den Einschränkungen der Markenverpackung und der Produktpräsentation fehlt dagegen ein solcher Hinweis. Das könnte dafür sprechen, dass im vorliegenden Zusammenhang die Meinungsfreiheit einschlägig ist.[292] Darüber hinaus wird im Schrifttum nicht zu Unrecht geltend gemacht, dass Art. 5 GG auch die Weitergabe fremder Meinungen schützt.[293]

Auf eine Vertiefung dieser Problematik sei aber verzichtet und im Folgenden die fehlende Einschlägigkeit der Meinungsfreiheit unterstellt. Sowohl das Verbot der Markenverpackungen wie das der Produktpräsentation in Einzelhandelsverkaufseinrichtungen enthalten, wie ausgeführt, einen Eingriff in die Berufsfreiheit des Art. 12 GG und in die Eigentumsgarantie des Art. 14 GG.[294] Gegenüber diesen Grundrechten dürfte die Meinungsfreiheit keinen weitergehenden Schutz vermitteln.[295] Anders als das Eigentumsrecht und die unternehmerische Freiheit auf europäischer Ebene, weisen sowohl die Berufsfreiheit des Art. 12 GG wie die Eigentumsgarantie des Art. 14 GG eine weit reichende Schutzwirkung auf. Insbesondere erfolgt nach der Rechtsprechung des Bundesverfassungsgerichts auch bei diesen Grundrechten eine wirksame Prüfung der Verhältnismäßigkeit.

II. Rechtfertigung der Beeinträchtigungen

1. Berufsfreiheit

a) Gesetzliche Grundlage und Regelungsstufe

aa) Jeder Eingriff in die Berufsfreiheit bedarf einer gesetzlichen Grundlage, nicht notwendig formell-gesetzlicher Natur.[296] Doch muss das Parlament alle für die Grundrechtsausübung *wesentlichen Fragen* selbst regeln, insbesondere beson-

---

291 *BVerfGE* 95, 173/182. Die Hinweise enthielten einen entsprechenden Hinweis.

292 So *Stein/Rauber*, Rechtliche Grenzen der Bekämpfung des Tabakkonsums im Mehrebenensystem, 2011, 41 f.; ebenso zu Warnhinweisen ohne Autorenangabe *Hardach/Ludwigs*, DÖV 2007, 292; *Wachovius*, BayVBl 2005, 618. Interessanter Weise hat der U.S. District Court in Washington am 7.11.2011 eine Anordnung gegen Warnhinweise auf Zigarettenpackungen unter Berufung auf die Meinungsfreiheit erlassen.

293 *Kloepfer*, Produkthinweispflichten bei Tabakwaren als Verfassungsfrage, 1991, 28 ff.; *Kirchhof/Frick*, AfP 1991, 679; *Merten*, DÖV 1990, 768; vgl. auch *Koenig/Kühling*, EWS 2002, 14.

294 Oben D I 2 b, D I 3 b.

295 Vgl. zum Schutz durch die Meinungsfreiheit *Hardach/Ludwigs*, DÖV 2007, 293 f.

296 *Dietlein*, in: Stern, Staatsrecht, Bd. IV/1, 2006, 1884 f.

ders intensive Eingriffe.[297] Weiter muss das einschränkende Gesetz hinreichend bestimmt sein, muss „Umfang und Grenzen des Eingriffs deutlich erkennen" lassen.[298] Die Anforderungen an die Bestimmtheit sind umso größer, je intensiver in die Berufsfreiheit eingegriffen wird.[299]

bb) Die Anforderungen an die Rechtfertigung von Eingriffen in die Berufsfreiheit hängen wesentlich davon ab, auf welcher Stufe die Beeinträchtigung erfolgt. Dabei wird zwischen Berufsausübungsregelungen und subjektiven sowie objektiven Berufswahlregelungen unterschieden.[300] Berufsausübungsregelungen sind dadurch gekennzeichnet, dass sie die Berufswahl nicht beeinflussen. Die Grenze zur Wahlregelung wird überschritten, wenn eine Regelung der beruflichen Betätigung derart gravierend ist, dass eine sinnvolle Ausübung des Berufs unmöglich wird,[301] allerdings nicht nur in Einzelfällen.[302] Trotz der schweren Belastung, die von einem Verbot der Markenverpackungen, von einem Verbot der Produktpräsentation in Einzelhandelsverkaufseinrichtungen oder von einem Verbot von Geruchs- und Geschmacksstoffen ausgehen, dürfte diese Grenze noch nicht überschritten sein.[303] Es gelten daher die Vorgaben für Ausübungsregelungen. Immerhin handelt es sich angesichts des Gewichts der Grundrechtsbeeinträchtigung um einen Grenzfall, was bei der Prüfung der Verhältnismäßigkeit zu berücksichtigen ist.[304]

b) Verhältnismäßigkeit

aa) Eingriffe in die Berufsausübung müssen verhältnismäßig sein.[305] Das setzt voraus, dass die fraglichen Eingriffe zur Erreichung des verfolgten Zwecks *geeignet* sind.[306] Ein Mittel ist „geeignet, wenn mit seiner Hilfe der gewünschte Erfolg gefördert werden kann".[307] Weiter muss die Beeinträchtigung *erforderlich* sein; d. h., der

---

297 BVerfGE 38, 373/381; 94, 372/390; *Manssen*, in: v.Mangoldt/Klein/Starck, Grundgesetz, Bd. 1, 6. Aufl. 2010, Art. 12 Rn. 119; *Wieland*, in: Dreier (Hg.), Grundgesetz, Bd. I, 2. Aufl. 2004, Art. 12 Rn. 98.
298 BVerfGE 86, 28/40.
299 BVerfGE 87, 287/317 f; 98, 49/60; 101, 312/323.
300 Vgl. die Nachweise bei *Jarass*, in: drs./Pieroth, Grundgesetz, 11. Aufl. 2011, Art. 12 Rn. 45 ff.
301 BVerfGE 123, 186/239; *Dietlein*, in: Stern, Staatsrecht, Bd. IV/1, 2006, 1901; *Manssen*, in: v.Mangoldt/Klein/Starck, Grundgesetz, Bd. 1, 6. Aufl. 2010, Art. 12 Rn. 142
302 BVerfGE 30, 292/315 f; 31, 8/29; 68, 155/170 f; BVerwGE 120, 311/334.
303 Ebenso zum Verbot der Markenverpackungen *Stein/Rauber*, Rechtliche Grenzen der Bekämpfung des Tabakkonsums im Mehrebenensystem, 2011, 45.
304 *Jarass*, in: drs./Pieroth, Grundgesetz, 11. Aufl. 2011, Art. 12 Rn. 37.
305 BVerfGE 117, 163/182.
306 BVerfGE 46, 120/145 f; 68, 193/218.
307 BVerfGE 115, 276/308; ebenso BVerfGE 80, 1/24 f; 117, 163/188.

Zweck darf nicht durch ein anderes Mittel erreicht werden können, das den Grundrechtsträger weniger belastet.[308] Dies gilt auch für Berufsausübungsregelungen, wie das Bundesverfassungsgericht immer wieder festgehalten hat.[309] Erforderlich ist die Beeinträchtigung „nur dann, wenn ein anderes, gleich wirksames, aber die Berufsfreiheit weniger fühlbar einschränkendes Mittel fehlt".[310]

Zudem darf der Grundrechtseingriff nicht außer Verhältnis zu dem angestrebten Zweck stehen; er muss „angemessen" sein.[311] Die „Grenze der Zumutbarkeit" muss bei einer Gesamtabwägung zwischen der Schwere des Eingriffs und dem „Gewicht der ihn rechtfertigenden Gründe" gewahrt sein.[312] Insbesondere muss das Gewicht des verfolgten Zwecks umso größer sein, je tiefer in die Berufsfreiheit eingegriffen wird. Bei Berufsausübungsregelungen fällt die Tiefe des Eingriffs typischerweise geringer als bei Berufswahlregelungen aus. Daher kommt hier dem Gesetzgeber ein erheblicher Beurteilungs- und Gestaltungsspielraum zu.[313] Andererseits ist aber zu beachten, dass dann, wenn in die Freiheit der Berufs*ausübung* empfindlich eingegriffen wird, eine Rechtfertigung durch Interessen von entsprechend großem Gewicht erforderlich ist.[314]

bb) Schließlich muss die besondere Belastung von Teilgruppen berücksichtigt werden. Auch wenn eine Regelung für den Großteil der Betroffenen verhältnismäßig ist, kann sie insoweit gegen Art. 12 Abs. 1 iVm Art. 3 Abs. 1 verstoßen, als eine Teilgruppe typischerweise sehr viel härter betroffen ist und daher einer gesonderten Behandlung bedarf.[315] Umgekehrt darf identischen Gefährdungen in einem Gesetz nicht unterschiedliches Gewicht beigemessen werden.[316]

---

308 *BVerfGE* 30, 292/316; 53, 135/145; 69, 209/218 f.
309 *BVerfGE* 101, 331/347; 104, 357/364; 106, 216/219.
310 *BVerfGE* 80, 1/30; 30, 292/316; ebenso *BVerfGE* 75, 246/269; 117, 163/189.
311 *BVerfGE* 117, 163/192 f.
312 *BVerfGE* 102, 197/220; ebenso *BVerfGE* 51, 193/208.
313 *BVerfGE* 116, 202/224 ff; 117, 163/182 f, 189; 121, 317/356.
314 *BVerfGE* 61, 291/311; 77, 84/106; 103, 1/10; 121, 317/355; BSGE 60, 76/78.
315 *BVerfGE* 30, 292/327; 59, 336/355 f; 65, 116/126 f; 68, 155/173; BVerwG, DVBl 01, 743.
316 *BVerfGE* 121, 317/362.

2. Eigentumsgarantie

a) Inhalts- und Schrankenbestimmung, gesetzliche Grundlage, sonstiges Verfassungsrecht

aa) Da Art. 14 GG zwei unterschiedliche Garantiebereiche enthält, fällt die Rechtfertigung von Eigentumsbeeinträchtigungen unterschiedlich aus, je nachdem, ob es um eine Inhalts- und Schrankenbestimmung oder um eine *Enteignung* geht. Während sich die Rechtfertigung einer Enteignung nach den strengen Vorgaben des Art. 14 Abs. 3 GG bestimmt, ist die Rechtfertigung einer Inhalts- und Schrankenbestimmung an Art. 14 Abs. 1 S. 2 GG und an Art. 14 Abs. 2 GG zu messen. Daher stellt sich zunächst die Frage, ob die hier zu untersuchenden Maßnahmen eventuell als Enteignung einzustufen sind. Immerhin führt das Verbot der Markenverpackungen und das Verbot der Produktpräsentation in Einzelhandelsverkaufseinrichtungen zu einem weitgehenden Bedeutungsverlust des Markenrechts und damit einer durch Art. 14 GG geschützten Rechtsposition.[317]

Der Begriff der Enteignung im Sinne des Art. 14 Abs. 3 GG wird in der neueren Rechtsprechung des Bundesverfassungsgerichts sehr eng gezogen. Die Enteignung „ist auf die vollständige oder teilweise Entziehung konkreter subjektiver Eigentumspositionen im Sinne des Art. 14 Abs. 1 Satz 1 GG zur Erfüllung bestimmter öffentlicher Aufgaben gerichtet".[318] Im vorliegenden Zusammenhang könnte man eventuell von einer teilweisen Entziehung des Markenrechts sprechen. Es fehlt aber an der Voraussetzung, dass es zur Erfüllung einer öffentlichen Aufgabe eingesetzt werden soll. Damit sind die hier interessierenden Verbote als Inhalts- und Schrankenbestimmung einzustufen, jedenfalls wenn man der Rechtsprechung des Bundesverfassungsgerichts folgt.

bb) Eine Inhalts- und Schrankenbestimmung kann durch jede Rechtsnorm erfolgen. Voraussetzung ist eine formell-gesetzliche Ermächtigung.[319] Das Gesetz muss dabei die Kompetenzordnung des Grundgesetzes wahren.[320] Aber auch allen anderen Verfassungsnormen muss eine Inhalts- und Schrankenbestimmung gerecht

---

317 Im Schrifttum wird denn auch von einer Enteignung ausgegangen; *Kunz-Hallstein*, in: Bender/Schülke/Winterfeldt (Hg.), 50 Jahre Bundespatentgericht, 2011, 668.

318 *BVerfGE* 70, 191/199 f; 72, 66/76; 102, 1/15; ähnlich *BVerfGE* 104, 1/9; BGHZ 99, 24/28; *BVerwGE* 77, 295/297; *Papier*, in: Maunz/Dürig, Grundgesetz, Stand 2010, Art. 14 Rn. 527.

319 *Depenheuer*, in: v.Mangoldt/Klein/Starck, Grundgesetz, Bd. 1, 6. Aufl. 2010, Art. 14 Rn. 220; a. A. *Papier*, in: Maunz/Dürig, Grundgesetz, Stand 2010, Art. 14 Rn. 339

320 *BVerfGE* 34, 139/146; 58, 137/145.

werden.[321] Insbesondere sind die Vorgaben des Gleichheitssatzes in Art. 3 Abs. 1 GG zu beachten.[322]

b) Verhältnismäßigkeit

Jede Inhalts- und Schrankenbestimmung hat den Grundsatz der Verhältnismäßigkeit zu wahren.[323] Dazu muss die betreffende Regelung im Hinblick auf das entsprechende Ziel geeignet sein,[324] muss es fördern. Weiter darf die Inhalts- und Schrankenbestimmung den Eigentümer nicht mehr beeinträchtigen, als es der gesetzgeberische Zweck erfordert;[325] es darf keine mildere Alternative zur Verfügung stehen.[326] Schließlich muss die Belastung des Eigentümers in einem angemessenen Verhältnis zu den mit der Regelung verfolgten Interessen stehen und damit angemessen bzw. zumutbar sein.[327] Die „schutzwürdigen Interessen des Eigentümers sowie die Belange des Gemeinwohls" müssen in ein ausgewogenes Verhältnis gebracht werden.[328] Schließlich sind die grundgesetzliche Anerkennung des Privateigentums durch Art. 14 Abs. 1 S. 1 GG als auch das Sozialgebot des Art. 14 Abs. 2 GG zu beachten.[329]

Im Rahmen der Verhältnismäßigkeitsprüfung ist bedeutsam, dass dem Gesetzgeber ein nicht unerheblicher Beurteilungs- und Prognosespielraum zustehen kann.[330] Ob und wieweit das der Fall ist, hängt von verschiedenen Faktoren ab. Relevant ist insbesondere die Intensität, Schwere und Tragweite der Eigentumsbeeinträchtigung, kommt es doch gerade darauf im Rahmen der Angemessenheit wesentlich an.[331]

---

321 *BVerfGE* 62, 169/183; 102, 1/17; 110, 1/28; *Wieland*, in: Dreier (Hg.), Grundgesetz, Bd. I, 2. Aufl. 2004, Art. 14 Rn. 129; *Papier*, in: Maunz/Dürig, Grundgesetz, Stand 2010, Art. 14 Rn. 326.
322 *BVerfGE* 79, 174/198; 87, 114/139; 102, 1/17; 126, 331/360.
323 *BVerfGE* 75, 78/97 f; 76, 220/238; 92, 262/273; 110, 1/28; *Dietlein*, in: Stern, Staatsrecht, Bd. IV/1, 2247; *Bryde*, in: v.Münch/Kunig, GG-Kommentar, Bd. I, 5. Aufl. 2000, Art. 14 Rn. 63.
324 *BVerfGE* 70, 278/286; 76, 220/238.
325 *BVerfGE* 75, 78/97 f; 79, 179/198; 100, 226/241; 110, 1/28.
326 *Jarass*, in: drs./Pieroth, Grundgesetz, 11. Aufl. 2011, Art. 14 Rn. 38b.
327 *BVerfGE* 74, 203/214 f; BGHZ 81, 152/175.
328 *BVerfGE* 110, 1/28; 98, 17/37; 100, 226/240; *BVerwGE* 88, 191/194 f; *Papier*, in: Maunz/Dürig, Grundgesetz, Stand 2010, Art. 14 Rn. 310
329 *BVerfGE* 52, 1/29; 71, 230/246 f; 81, 208/220.
330 *BVerfGE* 53, 257/293; *Papier*, in: Maunz/Dürig, Grundgesetz, Stand 2010, Art. 14 Rn. 321 ff.
331 *BVerfGE* 31, 229/243; ; 79, 29/41; 126, 331/363; *Jarass*, in: drs./Pieroth, Grundgesetz, 11. Aufl. 2011, Art. 14 Rn. 40.

c) Sachlicher sowie finanzieller Ausgleich

Um eine unverhältnismäßige Inhalts- und Schrankenbestimmung zu vermeiden, kann es geboten sein, den Interessen der betroffenen Eigentümer durch geeignete Ausgleichsmaßnahmen Rechnung zu tragen. Das können Übergangsregelungen, Ausnahme- und Befreiungsvorschriften oder andere Ausgleichsregelungen sein.[332] Übergangsregelungen können insbesondere aus Gründen des Vertrauensschutzes geboten sein, der im Bereich der Eigentumsbeeinträchtigungen unmittelbar durch Art. 14 GG gewährleistet wird.[333] An Ausnahmeregelungen ist zu denken, wenn Teilgruppen sehr viel stärker als die Mehrheit der von der Regelung Betroffenen in ihrem Eigentum beeinträchtigt werden.[334]

Ist ein sachlicher Ausgleich nicht möglich oder mit dem verfolgten Ziel nicht vereinbar, kann ein *finanzieller Ausgleich* oder gar eine Übernahme des Eigentums durch die öffentliche Hand (zum Verkehrswert) notwendig sein.[335] Wenn eine Inhaltsbestimmung in ihren Wirkungen einer Enteignung gleichkommt, ist das häufig der Fall.[336] Aber auch bei weniger weit reichenden Maßnahmen kann ein finanzieller Ausgleich geboten sein. In Betracht kommt das vor allem bei individuellen, gravierenden Härten einer generell unbedenklichen gesetzlichen Regelung.[337]

III. Verhältnismäßigkeit im vorliegenden Zusammenhang

1. Verbot der Markenverpackung

a) Betroffene Grundrechte und Gewicht des Eingriffs

Das Verbot von Markenverpackungen im Bereich der Tabakprodukte enthält, wie dargelegt, zum einen einen Eingriff in die Berufsfreiheit des Art. 12 GG,[338] der (nur) als Regelung der Berufsausübung zu qualifizieren ist.[339] Andererseits handelt

---

332 BVerfGE 100, 226/245 f; BVerwG, DVBl 03, 1075; DVBl 09, 1454; *Becker*, in: Stern/Becker, Grundrechte-Kommentar, 2010, Art. 14 Rn. 191.
333 BVerfGE 75, 78/104 f; 76, 220/244 f; 95, 64/82; 101, 239/257.
334 Vgl. BVerfGE 30, 292/327; 59, 336/355 f; 65, 116/126 f; 68, 155/173; BVerwG, DVBl 01, 743 jeweils zur Berufsfreiheit.
335 BVerfGE 100, 226/245 f; BVerwGE 87, 332/383; 94, 1/12; *Becker*, in: Stern/ Becker, Grundrechte-Kommentar, 2010, Art. 14 Rn. 186.
336 Vgl. BVerfGE 83, 201/212 f; 100, 226/245 f; 126, 331/363 f.; BVerwGE 88, 191/197.
337 *Wieland*, in: Dreier (Hg.), Grundgesetz, Bd. I, 2. Aufl. 2004, Art. 14 Rn. 133; *Jarass*, in: drs./Pieroth, Grundgesetz, 11. Aufl. 2011, Art. 14 Rn. 46.
338 Dazu oben D I 2 b.
339 Oben D II 1 a.

es sich um einen schweren Eingriff in die Berufsausübung, da der Einsatz von Markenverpackungen für den Verkauf von Tabakprodukten essentiell, ja unverzichtbar ist. Markenfreie Tabakprodukte spielen keine nennenswerte Rolle. Ohne Markenverpackungen lassen sich Tabakprodukte nur schwer absetzen.

Weiter enthält ein Verbot von Markenverpackungen einen Eingriff in die Nutzung des Markenrechts und damit in eine durch die Eigentumsgarantie des Art. 14 GG geschützte Position.[340] Das Markenrecht wird dabei empfindlich betroffen. Speziell bei Tabakprodukten stellt der Einsatz von Markenverpackungen die wichtigste Nutzung des Markenrechts dar. Sind hier Markenverpackungen nicht mehr möglich, wird das Markenrecht eines Tabakprodukts weitgehend entwertet.

b) Verhältnismäßigkeit der Maßnahme

aa) Was die *Eignung* eines Verbots von Markenverpackungen angeht, den Schutz der Gesundheit zu fördern, kann auf die entsprechenden Ausführungen zu den EU-Grundrechten verwiesen werden.[341] Von der Eignung der Maßnahme wird dementsprechend auch im Zusammenhang mit der Berufsfreiheit des Art. 12 GG und der Eigentumsgarantie des Art. 14 GG ausgegangen.[342]

bb) Hinsichtlich der *Erforderlichkeit* des Verbots von Markenverpackungen bestehen nicht unerhebliche Zweifel. Eine Beeinträchtigung der Berufsausübung ist, wie dargelegt, nur zulässig, wenn ein anderes, gleich wirksames, aber die Berufsfreiheit weniger fühlbar einschränkendes Mittel fehlt.[343] Als alternatives Mittel ist an eine Vergrößerung der Warnhinweise auf den Verpackungen zu denken, ohne dabei die Funktion der Verpackung, die Marke ausreichend deutlich werden zu lassen, (nennenswert) zu beeinträchtigen.[344] Ein solcher Weg könnte für den Gesundheitsschutz ebenso wirksam, wenn nicht wirksamer sein.

cc) Aber auch wenn man aus diesem Grunde dem Beurteilungsspielraum des Gesetzgebers hohes Gewicht einräumt und damit die Erforderlichkeit noch bejaht, fehlt es an dem dritten Element der Verhältnismäßigkeit, an der *Angemessenheit*. Gegenüber der beschriebenen Alternative kann ein Verbot von Markenverpackungen für den Gesundheitsschutz allenfalls geringfügige Vorteile haben. Dieser geringe Nutzen kann aber die schweren Eingriffe in die Berufsausübung und in das durch

---

340 Dazu oben D I 3 b.
341 Oben B IV 1 b aa.
342 Ablehnend *Schwarz*, in: Pache/Schwarz/Sosnitza, Aktuelle Rechtsfragen der Tabakregulierung in Europa, 2012, 124 f.
343 Oben D II 1 b.
344 Vgl. oben B IV 1 b bb.

Art. 14 GG geschützte Markenrecht nicht legitimieren. Das Gewicht des Eingriffs steht in keinem angemessenen Verhältnis zu dem eventuell erzielbaren Nutzen.[345]

Was speziell die Berufsfreiheit angeht, so belastet das Verbot von Markenverpackungen den Verkauf von Tabakprodukten an einer sehr empfindlichen Stelle und bildet für die Berufsausübung insbesondere des Herstellers von Tabakprodukten eine hohe Hürde. Zudem dürfte ein solches Verbot dazu führen, dass sich die Marktverhältnisse zwischen den verschiedenen Sorten von Tabakprodukten nur noch schwer verändern lassen. Das Verbot von Markenprodukten führt zu einer deutlichen Verfestigung der Marktsituation.[346] Die Maßnahme beeinträchtigt damit auch die Funktion der Berufsfreiheit, den Wettbewerb zu fördern.[347]

Des Weiteren führt das Verbot von Markenverpackungen, wie dargelegt, zu einer weitgehenden Entwertung des Markenrechts.[348] Ein solcher Eingriff in Art. 14 GG kann nur angemessen sein, wenn er ein hochrangiges Ziel verfolgt und der Nutzen belegbar und von hohem Gewicht ist. Ersteres ist im vorliegenden Zusammenhang zu bejahen, da es um den Schutz der Gesundheit geht. Dagegen steht der Nutzen im Vergleich zu der beschriebenen Alternativmaßnahme in einem Missverhältnis zu einem so schweren Grundrechtseingriff.[349] Wie zu den EU-Grundrechten dargelegt, gibt es mildere Maßnahmen, die den Gesundheitsschutz kaum weniger gut fördern, gleichwohl aber dem Markenrecht sehr viel besser Rechnung tragen.[350]

Insgesamt muss man ein Verbot von Markenverpackungen als unverhältnismäßig einstufen. Wegen der Schwere des Eingriffs vermag daran der Beurteilungsspielraum, der dem Gesetzgeber bei Berufsausübungsregelungen und bei Inhalts- und Schrankenbestimmungen zusteht, nichts zu ändern. Das gilt jedenfalls für die Hersteller von Tabakprodukten, die eine große Zahl von Sorten anbieten und daher aus den dargelegten Gründen in besonderer Weise auf den Einsatz von Markenverpackungen angewiesen sind.[351]

---

345 *Schwarz*, in: Pache/Schwarz/Sosnitza, Aktuelle Rechtsfragen der Tabakregulierung in Europa, 2012, 126 f.

346 *Stein/Rauber*, Rechtliche Grenzen der Bekämpfung des Tabakkonsums im Mehrebenensystem, 2011, 46.

347 Zu dieser Funktion *Jarass*, in: drs./Pieroth, Grundgesetz, 11. Aufl. 2011, Art. 12 Rn. 2; *Ruffert*, in: Epping/Hillgruber (Hg.), Grundgesetz, 2009 Art. 12 Rn. 159; *Manssen*, in: v. Mangoldt/Klein/Starck, Grundgesetz, Bd. 1, 6. Aufl. 2010, Art. 12 Rn. 70.

348 Oben D III 1 a.

349 Ebenso *Stein/Rauber*, Rechtliche Grenzen der Bekämpfung des Tabakkonsums im Mehrebenensystem, 2011, 49.

350 Oben B IV 1 b bb.

351 Dazu oben B IV 1 c.

2. Verbot der Produktpräsentation in Verkaufseinrichtungen

a) Betroffene Grundrechte und Gewicht des Eingriffs

Das Verbot der Präsentation von Tabakprodukten in Einzelhandelsverkaufseinrichtungen enthält zunächst einen Eingriff in die Berufsfreiheit des Art. 12 GG.[352] Dabei geht es um eine Berufsausübungsregelung. Was das Gewicht des Eingriffs angeht, so fällt es geringer als beim Verbot der Markenverpackungen aus. Gleichwohl ist das Gewicht aus den zu den EU-Grundrechten dargelegten Gründen durchaus erheblich.[353]

b) Verhältnismäßigkeit der Maßnahme

Was die Verhältnismäßigkeit dieser Maßnahme betrifft, so dürfte hier dem Beurteilungs- und Prognosespielraum des Gesetzgebers ein deutlich höheres Gewicht zukommen. Gleichwohl bedarf noch näherer Prüfung, ob ein ausreichender Gesundheitsschutz nicht auch dadurch erzielt werden kann, dass lediglich die Werbung für Tabakprodukte in Einzelhandelsverkaufseinrichtungen eingeschränkt wird. Jedenfalls sprechen insoweit, wie zu den EU-Grundrechten dargelegt, gute Gründe dafür, dass der Gesetzgeber stufenweise vorgeht, und sich zunächst mit der milderen Maßnahme begnügt und erst dann zu schärferen Mitteln greift, wenn sich die milderen Maßnahmen als unzureichend erwiesen haben.[354] Daher muss man gegenwärtig ein vollständiges Verbot der Produktpräsentation in Einzelhandelsverkaufseinrichtungen als unverhältnismäßig einstufen, trotz des Spielraums, der dem Gesetzgeber eingeräumt ist. Jedenfalls im Hinblick auf Hersteller von Tabakprodukten, die wegen ihrer Produktvielfalt besonders auf die Produktpräsentation angewiesen sind, ist der Befund deutlich.[355]

3. Verbot von Geruchs- und Geschmacksstoffen

a) Betroffene Grundrechte und Gewicht des Eingriffs

Das Verbot von Geruchs- und Geschmacksstoffen bei Tabakprodukten greift in die Berufsfreiheit des Art. 12 GG ein.[356] Unter bestimmten Voraussetzungen kann

---

352 Oben D I 2 b.
353 Dazu oben B IV 2 b.
354 Oben B IV 2 b.
355 Vgl. dazu oben B IV 1 c.
356 Dazu oben D 1 2 b.

auch ein Eingriff in die Eigentumsgarantie des Art. 14 GG vorliegen.[357] Für die Hersteller von Tabakprodukten, die Geruchs- und Geschmacksstoffe enthalten, ist eine solche Maßnahme zwangsläufig sehr belastend, Insoweit kann auf die entsprechenden Ausführungen zu den EU-Grundrechten verwiesen werden.[358]

b) Verhältnismäßigkeit der Maßnahme

aa) Bei der Beurteilung der Verhältnismäßigkeit eines Verbots von Geruchs- und Geschmacksstoffen ist zwischen Stoffen zu unterscheiden, die (als solche) Gesundheitsrisiken aufwerfen, und solchen, bei denen das nicht der Fall ist. Im ersten Fall ist die Verhältnismäßigkeit jedenfalls dann zu bejahen, wenn die Risiken nicht völlig fern liegend sind. Das ist nach der Amtlichen Begründung bei den in § 2 der Tabakverordnung aufgeführten Geruchs- und Geschmacksstoffen der Fall.[359]

bb) Ist das dagegen nicht der Fall, dann ist die Verhältnismäßigkeit gravierenden Bedenken ausgesetzt, obgleich hier der Beurteilungsspielraum des Gesetzgebers eine nicht unerhebliche Bedeutung entfaltet. Im Einzelnen stellt sich die Situation ganz ähnlich wie auf der EU-rechtlichen Ebene dar. Vieles spricht dafür, dass es bereits an der Eignung der Maßnahme fehlt, den Gesundheitsschutz zu fördern.[360] Jedenfalls wird der Eingriff dem Gebot der Angemessenheit nicht gerecht. Insoweit ist der Vergleich mit den Herstellern von Tabakprodukten, die Tabakprodukte ohne Geruchs- und Geschmacksstoffe produzieren, bedeutsam: Im Bereich der Berufsfreiheit spielt eine Rolle, ob Teilgruppen besonders schwer belastet werden.[361] Im Bereich der Eigentumsgarantie ist zu prüfen, ob der Eingriff mit dem allgemeinen Gleichheitssatz vereinbar ist.[362] Dem wird es schwerlich gerecht, wenn eine Maßnahme allein zu Lasten eines Teils der Hersteller von Tabakprodukten geht und andere unbehelligt bleiben. Für eine solche Ungleichbehandlung gibt es keinen ausreichenden Grund, soweit die Geruchs- und Geschmacksstoffe mit keinen zusätzlichen Gesundheitsrisiken behaftet sind.

---

357 Oben D I 3 b.
358 Dazu oben B IV 3 b.
359 BR-Drs. 479/77, S. 23 f. Zur Tabakverordnung oben A I 1 a.
360 Vgl. oben B IV 3 b.
361 Dazu oben D II 1 b bb.
362 Oben D II 2.

4. Bedeutung additiver Grundrechtseingriffe

a) Grundlagen

Für die Verhältnismäßigkeit von Grundrechtseingriffen spielt, wie dargelegt, eine wichtige Rolle, wie belastend die Maßnahme für den Grundrechtsträger ist. Wird nun der Grundrechtsträger durch ein Gesetz mehrfach belastet, dann wird es häufig nicht genügen, jede Beeinträchtigung für sich auf ihre Verhältnismäßigkeit zu überprüfen; vielmehr kann es geboten sein, eine Gesamtbeurteilung der Belastungen vorzunehmen. Dieser Befund wird in jüngerer Zeit durch das Stichwort des „additiven" Grundrechtseingriffs gekennzeichnet: So ist es nach Auffassung des Bundesverfassungsgerichts „möglich, dass verschiedene, für sich betrachtet geringfügige Eingriffe in grundrechtlich geschützte Bereiche in ihrer Gesamtwirkung zu einer schwerwiegenden Beeinträchtigung führen, die das Maß der rechtsstaatlich hinnehmbaren Eingriffsintensität überschreitet".[363] Der Bundesgerichtshof und das Bundessozialgericht sind dem gefolgt.[364] Auch im Schrifttum wird die Auffassung geteilt.[365] Voraussetzung für eine additive Belastung ist dabei, dass die Beeinträchtigungen den gleichen Adressaten treffen, im gleichen Zeitraum auftreten und im Wesentlichen demselben Zweck dienen sowie dasselbe Grundrecht(sgut) berühren.[366] Ist das der Fall, dann sind die Belastungen im Rahmen der Verhältnismäßigkeitsprüfung zusammen zu rechnen.[367]

b) Anwendung im vorliegenden Zusammenhang

Im vorliegenden Zusammenhang ergibt sich daraus, dass dann, wenn mehrere der untersuchten Verbote eingeführt werden sollen, deren Belastungswirkung für die Hersteller von Tabakprodukten zusammenzurechnen sind.[368] Das Verbot von Markenverpackungen belastet ebenso wie das Verbot der Produktpräsentati-

---

363 *BVerfGE* 123, 186/265, ebenso *BVerfGE* 112, 304/319 f.; 114, 196/247; dabei greift das Gericht den Begriff des „additiven" Einriffs auf.

364 *BGH*, NJW 2009, 3448/3458 Rn. 99; *BSG*, GesR 2010 554/558 Rn. 26

365 Etwa *Peine*, in: Merten/Papier (Hg.), Handbuch der Grundrechte, Bd. III, 2009, § 57 Rn. 53; *Lücke*, DVBl 2001, 1469 ff.; *Kirchhof*, NJW 2006, 732; *Jarass*, in: drs./Pieroth, Grundgesetz, 11. Aufl. 2011, Vorb. 47 vor Art. 1.

366 *Peine*, in: Merten/Papier (Hg.), Handbuch der Grundrechte, Bd. III, 2009, § 57 Rn. 53; *Hillgruber*, in: Isensee/Kirchhof (Hg.), Handbuch des Staatsrechts, Bd. IX, 2011, § 200 Rn. 97; *Lücke*, DVBl 2001, 1470; etwas großzügiger *Kirchhof*, NJW 2006, 734.

367 *Hofmann*, AöR 133 (2008), 540 ff.; *Lücke*, DVBl 2001, 1477 f.; *Peine*, in: Merten/Papier (Hg.), Handbuch der Grundrechte, Bd. III, 2009, § 57 Rn. 54.

368 Ebenso im vorliegenden Zusammenhang *Schwarz*, in: Pache/Schwarz/Sosnitza, Aktuelle Rechtsfragen der Tabakregulierung in Europa, 2012, 109 f.

on in Einzelhandelsverkaufseinrichtungen und das Verbot von Geruchs- und Geschmacksstoffen den Hersteller der jeweiligen Tabakprodukte. Weiter kommen die Belastungen im gleichen Zeitraum zum Tragen. Endlich verfolgen die Verbote den gleichen Zweck und betreffen die gleichen Rechtsgüter, die Berufsausübung einerseits und das Eigentum andererseits. Soweit sich daher bereits bei der Einzelanalyse zeigte, dass die Grenze der Unverhältnismäßigkeit überschritten wird oder jedenfalls gewichtige Zweifel an der Verhältnismäßigkeit bestehen, wird dieser Befund durch die kumulative Anwendung der Instrumente noch erheblich verstärkt. Insoweit kann auf die entsprechenden Ausführungen im Bereich der EU-Grundrechte verwiesen werden.[369]

Des Weiteren ist auch auf der Ebene der nationalen Grundrechte zu beachten, dass bereits das geltende Recht zu Lasten der Hersteller von Tabakprodukten weit reichende Einschränkungen aufweist.[370] Dies muss bei der Beurteilung neuer und zusätzlicher Belastungen berücksichtigt werden.[371]

---

369 Dazu oben B IV 4 b.
370 Oben A I 1 a.
371 Auch insoweit kann auf die entsprechenden Ausführungen zu den EU-Grundrechten verwiesen werden; oben B IV 4 b.

E. Zusammenfassung

I. Ausgangslage

1. *Gegenstand der Untersuchung* sind drei weit reichende Regelungsvorschläge, die zu einer gravierenden Verschärfung der Anforderungen an die Herstellung und den Verkauf von Tabakprodukten führen: die Verpflichtung zu einer Einheitsverpackung ohne markenspezifische Gestaltung (Verbot von Markenverpackungen), das Verbot der Präsentation von Tabakprodukten in Einzelhandelsverkaufseinrichtungen (unter Einschluss der Werbung für solche Produkte) und das Verbot von Geruchs- und Geschmacksstoffen in Tabakprodukten (oben S. 17–19).
2. Im vorliegenden Zusammenhang spielt die Nutzung von *Markenrechten* eine gewichtige Rolle. Daher ist bedeutsam, dass den Marken aufgrund ihrer gesetzlichen und tatsächlichen Funktionen in einer Marktwirtschaft überragende Bedeutung zukommt und sie einen wesentlichen, ja unverzichtbaren Bestandteil eines Systems unverfälschten Wettbewerbs bilden (oben S. 19–21).

II. Grundrechte der Europäischen Union

3. Die Grundrechte der Union haben ihre primärrechtliche *Grundlage* in der (rechtsverbindlichen) Charta der Grundrechte und in den vom EuGH als allgemeine Rechtsgrundsätze entwickelten Grundrechten. Als Rechtserkenntnisquellen sind die EMRK und die Erläuterungen des Präsidiums zur Grundrechte-Charta bedeutsam (oben S. 24–25).
4. Die Grundrechte *verpflichten* umfassend alle Stellen der Union. Die Mitgliedstaaten werden gebunden, soweit sie EU-Recht durchführen, insb. wenn sie Unionsrecht umsetzen oder vollziehen (oben S. 25–26).
5. Die *Meinungsäußerungs- und Informationsfreiheit* des Art. 11 GRCh schützt auch alle Äußerungen und Informationsweitergaben im wirtschaftlichen Bereich. Darunter fällt die Verwendung von Produktmarken. Daher greifen das Verbot der Markenverpackungen wie das der Produktpräsentation in Einzelhandelsverkaufseinrichtungen in das Grundrecht ein (oben S. 27–29).
6. Das *Eigentumsrecht* des Art. 17 GRCh schützt das Recht an einer Marke sowie Geschäftsgeheimnisse. Folglich enthalten das Verbot der Markenverpackungen wie das der Produktpräsentation in Einzelhandelsverkaufseinrichtungen Beeinträchtigungen des Eigentumsrechts. Beim Verbot der Geruchs- und Geschmacksstoffe gilt das vor allem, wenn ein Geschäftsgeheimnis nicht mehr genutzt werden kann (oben S. 29–31).

7. Die *unternehmerische Freiheit* des Art. 16 GRCh enthält eine Spezialregelung für die unternehmerische Berufsfreiheit. Das Verbot von Markenverpackungen greift ebenso wie das Verbot der Produktpräsentation in Einzelhandelsverkaufseinrichtungen und das von Geruchs- und Geschmacksstoffen in das Grundrecht ein (oben S. 31–33).
8. *Einschränkungen* der Meinungsäußerungs- und Informationsfreiheit sind nur unter den Voraussetzungen des Art. 10 Abs. 2 EMRK möglich. Insb. ist der Grundsatz der Verhältnismäßigkeit zu wahren. Einschränkungen des Eigentumsrechts müssen die Vorgaben des Art. 17 Abs. 1 S. 3 GRCh und zudem die des Art. 1 EMRK-ZP beachten. Insoweit kommt der Grundsatz der Verhältnismäßigkeit ebenfalls zum Einsatz. Auch bei Einschränkungen der unternehmerischen Freiheit ist dieser Grundsatz zu beachten, trotz des Hinweises auf das Unionsrecht und die einzelstaatlichen Rechtsvorschriften in Art. 16 GRCh (oben S. 34–37).
9. Im primären EU-Recht spielt der Grundsatz der Verhältnismäßigkeit nicht nur bei Einschränkungen von Grundrechten eine Rolle. Vielmehr kennt der EuGH in ständiger Rechtsprechung ein eigenständiges *allgemeines Gebot der Verhältnismäßigkeit*, das in seinen Anforderungen mit denen der grundrechtlichen Verhältnismäßigkeit übereinstimmt und dessen Konkretisierung (auch) im Bereich der Grundrechte genutzt werden kann (oben S. 38–39).
10. Die Verhältnismäßigkeit setzt die *Eignung* der Maßnahme im Hinblick auf das verfolgte Ziel voraus. Die weiter notwendige *Erforderlichkeit* verlangt zunächst, dass das am wenigsten belastende, aber gleich wirksame Mittel zum Einsatz kommt. Darüber hinaus müssen die betroffenen Interessen *ausgewogen gewichtet* werden, eine Vorgabe, die in Deutschland als eigenständiges drittes Element der Verhältnismäßigkeit eingestuft wird. Unter Umständen kann die Verhältnismäßigkeit Übergangs- und Ausnahmeregelungen oder eine Entschädigung notwendig machen, auch im Bereich der unternehmerischen Freiheit und der Meinungsäußerungs- und Informationsfreiheit (oben S. 39–40).
11. Die *gerichtliche Kontrolldichte* fällt nach der Rechtsprechung des EuGH im Bereich der Meinungsäußerungs- und Informationsfreiheit grundsätzlich höher als im Bereich des Eigentumsrechts und der unternehmerischen Freiheit aus, auch und gerade bei schweren Grundrechtseingriffen (oben S. 41–42).
12. Das *Verbot von Markenverpackungen* dürfte noch als geeignet einzustufen sein. Dagegen bestehen im Hinblick auf die Erforderlichkeit bzw. die Verpflichtung zu ausgewogener Gewichtung bei dieser Maßnahme schwere Bedenken, zumal mildere Mittel zur Verfügung stehen, die den Schutz der Gesundheit fast ebenso gut fördern, dem Markenrecht aber sehr viel besser Rechnung tragen. In besonderer Weise gilt das für Hersteller mit einem vielfältigen Angebot. Der Befund dürfte auch für eine übermäßige Verpflichtung zu Warnhinweisen auf

Zusammenfassung

den Verpackungen gelten, die dazu führt, dass der Konsument seine Marke nicht mehr mit einem Blick erkennt (oben S. 42–45).

13. Das *Verbot der Produktpräsentation* in Einzelhandelsverkaufseinrichtungen unterliegt geringeren Bedenken. Im Hinblick auf das Gebot der Erforderlichkeit spricht aber vieles dafür, dass es geboten ist, zunächst mildere Maßnahmen zu nutzen und dann deren Wirkungen zu überprüfen (oben S. 45–47).

14. Das *Verbot von Geruchs- und Geschmacksstoffen* dürfte verhältnismäßig sein, soweit mit den Stoffen selbst Gesundheitsrisiken verbunden sind. Ist das nicht der Fall, bestehen bereits an der Eignung des Verbots, die Gesundheit (durch eine Reduzierung des Tabakkonsums) zu fördern, gewichtige Zweifel. Jedenfalls wird ein Verbot solcher Stoffe, trotz des gesetzgeberischen Spielraums, nicht der Verpflichtung zu ausgewogener Gewichtung gerecht, zumal es unter Beeinträchtigung der Wettbewerbsgleichheit nur einen Teil der Hersteller trifft (oben S. 47–48).

15. Schließlich sind Grundrechtseingriffe zu Lasten des gleichen Betroffenen, die im gleichen Zeitraum zum Tragen kommen, im Wesentlichen den gleichen Zweck verfolgen und dasselbe Grundrechtsgut betreffen, im Rahmen der Verhältnismäßigkeit zusammenzurechnen (*additive Eingriffe*). Das verstärkt im vorliegenden Zusammenhang die Bedenken gegen die Verhältnismäßigkeit (oben S. 49–50).

III. Warenverkehrsfreiheit

16. Das Verbot der Maßnahmen gleicher Wirkung in Art. 34 AEUV *verpflichtet* die Mitgliedstaaten, aber auch die Union (oben S. 51–52).

17. Eine *Maßnahme gleicher Wirkung* ist bei nichtdiskriminierenden Regelungen gegeben, wenn sie rechtlich oder tatsächlich den Marktzugang für Erzeugnisse aus einem anderen Mitgliedstaat versperren oder stärker behindern, als sie dies für inländische Erzeugnisse tun. Diese Voraussetzung ist im Hinblick auf das Verbot von Markenverpackungen und das Verbot der Produktpräsentation in Einzelhandelsverkaufseinrichtungen erfüllt, auch wenn die Union solche Regelungen trifft. Die genannten Verbote führen zu einer weitgehenden Entwertung des Markenrechts und erschweren damit den Marktzugang eines Herstellers von Tabakprodukten in anderen Mitgliedstaaten stärker als für inländische Hersteller (oben S. 52–54).

18. Beschränkungen des Verbots der Maßnahmen gleicher Wirkung können *gerechtfertigt* sein. Voraussetzung ist die Verhältnismäßigkeit der Beschränkung. Insoweit stellt der EuGH strenge Anforderungen, auch im Bereich des Gesundheits- und Verbraucherschutzes. Im Rahmen der Verhältnismäßigkeit ist zu be-

rücksichtigen, wenn die Beschränkung der Warenverkehrsfreiheit gleichzeitig in Grundrechte eingreift (oben S. 54–56).

19. Angesichts des Umstands, dass einerseits das Markenrecht ein wichtiges Element des grenzüberschreitenden Warenverkehrs ist, andererseits aber dieses Recht durch ein Verbot von Markenverpackungen wie durch ein Verbot der Produktpräsentation in Einzelhandelsverkaufseinrichtungen weithin entleert wird, sprechen *im vorliegenden Zusammenhang* gute Gründe gegen die Verhältnismäßigkeit der Beschränkung des Art. 34 AEUV (oben S. 57–58).

IV. Grundrechte des Grundgesetzes

20. Die Grundrechte des Grundgesetzes *verpflichten* nicht die Union, insb. nicht beim Erlass von Rechtsakten. Dagegen wird der deutsche Normgeber gebunden, soweit das EU-Recht keine Regelungen trifft oder den Mitgliedstaaten Spielräume belässt. Dies betrifft insb. die Umsetzung und den Vollzug von EU-Recht. Bedeutung hat das im vorliegenden Zusammenhang bei der Umsetzung von Richtlinien zur Tabakherstellung und zum Tabakverkauf (oben S. 59–61).

21. Ein Verbot von Markenverpackungen, ein Verbot der Produktpräsentation in Einzelhandelsverkaufseinrichtungen wie ein Verbot von Geruchs- und Geschmacksstoffen in Tabakprodukten greifen in die *Berufsfreiheit* des Art. 12 GG ein; insb. handelt es sich um berufsspezifische Regelungen. Weiter liegt im Verbot der Markenverpackungen wie der Präsentation von Tabakprodukten ein Eingriff in die *Eigentumsgarantie* des Art. 14 GG, da die Nutzung des Markenrechts gravierend eingeschränkt wird; beim Verbot der Geruchs- und Geschmacksstoffe gilt das jedenfalls insoweit, als die Nutzung eines Geschäftsgeheimnisses ausgeschlossen wird. Unsicher ist, ob die beiden Verbote auch an der *Meinungsfreiheit* des Art. 5 Abs. 1 GG zu messen sind. Anders als auf der europäischen Ebene dürfte aber dieses Grundrecht keinen weitergehenden Schutz als Art. 12 GG und Art. 14 GG vermitteln, weshalb die Anwendbarkeit offen bleiben kann (oben S. 61–65).

22. Was die Voraussetzungen der *Rechtfertigung* angeht, so sind die Eingriffe in die Berufsfreiheit eher als Berufsausübungsregelungen einzustufen, allerdings sehr gewichtiger Art. Ähnlich spricht vieles dafür, dass die Verbote Inhalts- und Schrankenbestimmungen (und keine Enteignungen) bilden. Als solche müssen sie verhältnismäßig sein und dem Gleichheitsgrundsatz gerecht werden. Ggf. kann auch eine Entschädigung geboten sein (oben S. 65–70).

23. Das *Verbot von Markenverpackungen* enthält einen schweren Eingriff sowohl in die Berufsfreiheit wie in die Eigentumsgarantie. Diese Eingriffe können nicht mehr als angemessen eingestuft werden, da mildere Mittel zur Verfügung ste-

Zusammenfassung

hen, die den Schutz der Gesundheit kaum geringer fördern, aber dem Markenrecht sehr viel besser Rechnung tragen (oben S. 70–72).

24. Beim *Verbot der Produktpräsentation* in Einzelhandelsverkaufseinrichtungen spielt der Beurteilungsspielraum des Gesetzgebers eine größere Rolle. Doch sprechen gute Gründe dafür, dass die Verhältnismäßigkeit den Einsatz milderer Mittel und die Überprüfung ihrer Wirksamkeit verlangt (oben S. 73).

25. Beim *Verbot von Geruchs- und Geschmacksstoffen* kommt es darauf an, ob mit den Stoffen selbst Gesundheitsrisiken verbunden sind. Ist das der Fall, wird man die Verhältnismäßigkeit zu bejahen haben. Im Übrigen dürfte die Verhältnismäßigkeit bereits an der fehlenden Erforderlichkeit scheitern. Jedenfalls wird das Gebot der Angemessenheit nicht gewahrt, trotz des nicht unerheblichen Spielraums des Gesetzgebers (oben S. 73–74).

26. Der Rechtsprechung des BVerfG entsprechend ist in den Fällen des *additiven Grundrechtseingriffs* eine Gesamtbetrachtung der Belastungen notwendig. Zum Tragen kommt das, wenn die Belastungen den gleichen Grundrechtsträger zum gleichen Zeitpunkt treffen und im Wesentlichen den gleichen Zweck verfolgen sowie das gleiche Rechtsgut betreffen. Im vorliegenden Zusammenhang führt das zu einer Verstärkung der Bedenken gegen die Verhältnismäßigkeit der untersuchten Verbote (oben S. 75–76).

A. Initial situation and Problem Definition

I. Regulation of tobacco production and the sale of tobacco

1. Tobacco product regulation on national, European and international levels

a) German law provisions

In Germany the regulation of tobacco products is stipulated in the Provisional Tobacco Act (*Vorläufiges Tabakgesetz*, VTG), which was originally issued as the Foodstuffs and Commodities Act (*Lebensmittel- und Bedarfsgegenständegesetz*).[372] The Act stipulates numerous requirements for the tobacco products defined in Sec. 3 VTG. In particular, Sec. 21a VTG contains far-reaching prohibitions on tobacco advertising and sponsorship to transpose Directive 2003/33/EC relating to advertising and sponsorship of tobacco products[373].

Of greater importance in this context are the provisions in the statutory ordinances issued on the basis of the Provisional Tobacco Act. One example is the Tobacco Product Ordinance (*Tabakprodukt-Verordnung*) of 20.11.2002.[374] This ordinance serves to transpose Directive 2001/37/EC of 5.6.2001.[375] Under sections 2–4 it regulates the permissible levels of tar, nicotine and carbon monoxide in cigarettes. Sec. 5 concerns the obligation to provide information on additives. Sections 6–9 stipulate the requirements for information and notifications on the packages.

Also of significance is the regulation on tobacco products (*Tabakverordnung*) of 20.12.1977.[376] It regulates in a detailed manner the permissibility of additives in the production of tobacco products. Sec. 1 contains a positive list of allowed substances or substance groups. Sec. 2 provides for a general exclusion of certain odorous

---

[372] Of 15.8.1974, republished on 9.9.1997 (Federal Gazette I 2296), last amended on 9.12.2010 (Federal Gazette I 1934). Through the act of 1.9.2005 (Federal Gazette I 2618) the original Foodstuffs and Commodities Act was to a large extent replaced by the Food, Commodities and Feed Code (*Lebensmittel-, Bedarfsgegenstände- und Futtermittelgesetzbuch*). Only the tobacco-related provisions were retained; at the same time the act was renamed Provisional Tobacco Act.

[373] On this directive, A I 1 b below.

[374] Federal Gazette I 4434; last amended by Art. 360 of the Regulation of 31.10.2006 (Federal Gazette I 2407). As to the interpretation of the regulation, see the explanatory memorandum to the draft of 9.10.2002 (BR-Drs. 758/02).

[375] More on this directive, A I 1 b below.

[376] Federal Gazette I 2831; last amended by Art. 1 of the Regulation of 28.6.2010 (Federal Gazette I 851). As to the interpretation of the regulation, see the explanatory memorandum to the draft of 13.10.1977 (BR-Drs. 479/77).

substances and flavouring agents.[377] Maximum amounts of other substances are stipulated under Sec. 3a. There are also further provisions that in part also cover related issues other than the use of additives. For instance Sec. 5a stipulates rules on the use of tobacco products.

b) Provisions under European law

At the European level tobacco products are regulated through Directive 2001/37/EC on the manufacture, presentation and sale of tobacco products (Tobacco Products Directive) of 5.6.2001.[378] The Directive was based on the EC Treaty, in particular Art. 95 TEC (today Art. 114 Treaty on the Functioning of the European Union – TFEU) and Art. 133 TEC (today Art. 207 TFEU). The purpose of the Directive is, according to Art. 1, the approximation of laws in the area concerned, taking as a basis "a high level of health protection". Art. 3 and 4 stipulate regulations on the maximum tar, nicotine and carbon monoxide content of cigarettes. Art. 5 regulates the labelling of tobacco product packaging. Art. 6 concerns product information provided by manufacturers and importers of tobacco products. Requirements pertaining to product descriptions are included in Art. 7. Additional requirements are set in Art. 8–12. On the other hand, Art. 13 protects the free movement of goods concerning tobacco products, under the condition that those products are in accordance with the requirements of the Directive.

The distribution of tobacco products is regulated in Directive 2003/33/EC on advertising and sponsorship of tobacco products of 26.5.2003.[379] The Directive stipulates far-reaching restrictions on advertising and sponsoring in printed material, radio and the Internet and at events.[380] There are also special regulations for excise duties on tobacco products.[381]

c) International provisions

At the international level there is the WHO Framework Convention on Tobacco Control that was adopted at the 56th World Health Assembly on 21.5.2003.[382] The

---

[377] As indicated in the explanatory memorandum of the draft, the tobacco ordinance serves to protect health (BR-Drs. 479/77, p. 23 f.).

[378] OJ L 194/26; amended by Regulation (EC) No. 596/2009 (OJ L 188/14). On the Directive *Hardach/Ludwigs*, DÖV 2007, 288; *Marwitz*, K & R 2004, 214; *Riessen inter alia*, Assessing the Impacts of Revising the Tobacco Products Directive, Rand, 2010, 3 f.

[379] OJ L 152/16, corrected on 5.3.2004 (OJ L 67/34).

[380] See *Marwitz*, K & R 2004, 214.

[381] Compare the latest amendment to this Directive through Directive 2010/12/EC (OJ L 50/1).

[382] WHO Framework Convention on Tobacco Control.

treaty was signed by almost every country, including Germany. However, it only applies in Germany if mandated by a domestic act.[383] The Convention contains far-reaching obligations on production, sale, distribution, advertising and taxation of tobacco products.[384]

2. New dimensions of tobacco product regulation as the subject of this study

There is currently a major discussion, in particular at the European Union level, on whether and – if so – to what extent, the provisions on tobacco production and tobacco sales should be tightened to reduce the negative effects of smoking and thereby promote good health.[385] The Health and Consumers Directorate-General of the European Commission has carried out a public consultation in the English language on the possible revision of the Tobacco Products Directive 2001/37/EC. The questions concerned six areas:

1. Scope of the Directive
2. Smokeless tobacco products
3. Consumer information
4. Reporting and registration of ingredients
5. Regulation of ingredients
6. Access to tobacco products

The response to the consultation was surprisingly high. The findings of the consultation were summarised by the Directorate General in its "Report on the public consultation on the possible revision of the Tobacco Products Directive (2001/37/EC)" of 27.7.2011.

Numerous political options were presented in the consultation on which the public could express an opinion.[386] These also included very extensive amendments to existing law. These options are the subject of this study and can be described as "new dimensions" in tobacco product regulation. This refers to the following proposals (hereinafter referred to as regulatory proposals to be examined):

---

383 *BVerfGE* (Decisions of the Federal Constitutional Court) 73, 339/375; *Jarass*, in: drs./Pieroth, Grundgesetz, 11th ed. 2011, Art. 25 para. 1a; Art. 59 para. 17.

384 See *Pauling*, VuR 2010, 444 f.

385 To the extent that the legal act is based on Art. 114 TFEU, the approximation of laws must be the primary aim. However, in addition, health issues may also be pursued.

386 See *Pauling*, VuR 2010, 443 f.

(1) Prohibition of brand packaging

The first proposal addresses plain packaging and also speaks of standardized packaging.[387] In German, this could be referred to as *"schlichte Verpackung"*, *"standardisierte Verpackung"* or as *"Einheitsverpackung"*. This involves prohibition of the use of brand emblems, brand colours and similar design features of the packaging of tobacco products, apart from the name of the company and the product.[388] The packages should also have a uniform shape and colour, such as black and white.[389] Since the consumer does not only recognise a brand through a word, but also to a large extent through figures and colours, which will be explained in further detail,[390] this is essentially a prohibition of brand packaging. The concepts of plain or standardized packaging are euphemistic and do not sufficiently describe the weight and the meaning of the measure. Therefore, in this study, it is called a "prohibition of brand packaging".

(2) Prohibition of product display in retail facilities

Another proposal is designated as a "retail display ban".[391] This involves prohibiting the presentation and visibility of tobacco products at points of retail sale. This is a prohibition of product display in retail facilities. The purchaser should only see the products if he so requests; the products are kept "under the counter". This includes a prohibition of advertising for tobacco products in retail sales facilities.

(3) Prohibition of odorous substances and flavouring agents

The third proposal that will be assessed in this study is the complete prohibition of odorous substances and flavouring agents as a means of reducing the attractiveness of the products.[392] A prohibition of odorous substances and flavouring agents

---

[387] Inter alia "Report on the public consultation on the possible revision of the Tobacco Products Directive (2001/37/EC)" of 27.7.2011, p. 14.

[388] *Kunz-Hallstein*, in: Bender/Schülke/Winterfeldt (ed.), 50 Jahre Bundespatentgericht, 2011, 661.

[389] KOM (2007) 754 final, p. 12; *Pauling*, VuR 2010, 443; *Ziegenaus*, GRUR Prax 2010, 475.

[390] Below A I 3 a.

[391] Inter alia "Report on the public consultation on the possible revision of the Tobacco Products Directive (2001/37/EC)" of 27.7.2011, p. 20.

[392] Cf. "Report on the public consultation on the possible revision of the Tobacco Products Directive (2001/37/EC)" of 27.7.2011, p. 18. A more circumspect solution would be a positive and a negative list.

Initial situation and Problem Definition

has far-reaching consequences for the manufacturer since the product expected by the consumer is characterised by these substances.[393]

3. The brand as a basic element of competition

a) Trademark law and the concept of a brand

The examined proposals for a regulation of tobacco production and the sale of tobacco – which are the subject of this study – have particularly grave consequences for the individual tobacco brands and their use. The prohibition of brand packaging has obvious consequences since it affects a central instrument, or possibly *the* central instrument, of the manufacturer, to exploit the opportunities associated with a brand. As will be demonstrated, the type and manner of packaging can be registered as a trademark.[394] The prohibition of product display in retail sales facilities also essentially diminishes the potential exploitation of a trademark or brand.[395]

Given the significance of trademark law in this connection, it is only appropriate to first take a brief look at the meaning and function of brands and their legal protection. On the one hand, the relevant requirements of EU trademark law are taken as a basis, namely Directive 2008/95/EC on trademarks (Trademark Directive)[396] and Council Regulation EC 207/2009 on the Community trademark (CTMR).[397] Additionally, this study will address German trademark law by means of the German Act on the protection of trademarks and other symbols (Trademark Act).[398]

According to Art. 2 of the Trademark Directive and Sec. 3 (1) and Sec. 8 (1) of the Trademark Act, all symbols which can be graphically illustrated and which are suitable to distinguish goods[399] of one company from those of another company – such as words (in particular names), pictures, letters, numbers and the shape and design of the goods – can function as trademarks. As the Court of Justice of the European

---

393 Accordingly, the *ECJ*, case 273/00, ECR 2002, I-11737 para. 44 ff., 69 ff. considered an odour to be capable of constituting a trademark which identifies a product, and odour only failed to pass this test since it was not possible to visualise it.

394 More under A I 3 a.

395 Below B II 2 b bb.

396 Of 22.10.2008 (ABl L 299/25).

397 Of 22.10.2009 (ABl L 78/1).

398 *"Gesetz über den Schutz von Marken und sonstigen Kennzeichen"* of 25.10.1994 (BGBl I, 3082), last amended through Art. 17 of the Act of 22.12.2010 (GBGl I, 2253).

399 This also applies for services which is, however, not relevant to the following.

Union has emphasised, this also includes colours and colour combinations and the packaging of goods, in particular their graphic and colour design.[400]

b) The meaning and function of trademarks

Trademarks play an extremely significant role in modern economic systems. The following statement was made in a recently published textbook on German and European trademark law: "In highly developed economic systems trade marks are of paramount importance. They are central instruments in commercial marketing. They enable communication with the consumer and frequently shape the appearance of the company in the public eye. Trade marks can be very valuable and are in many cases the most valuable economic asset of a company".[401]

The reasons for this statement can be found in the function of trademarks, which have especially been elaborated by the Court of Justice of the European Union. In a competitive economy a company must be able to attract customers by the quality of its goods. This requires distinguishing elements to facilitate the identification of the goods.[402] The trademark should serve as a guarantee of the origin of the goods to the end user by enabling him to distinguish the goods without the likelihood of confusion with goods of another origin.[403] The trademark should ensure that all goods marked with the trademark are manufactured under the control of a single company responsible for the quality of the goods.[404] This also takes into account the interests of the owner of the trademark to protect the particular reputation of its products.[405]

In addition to the function of the trademark to provide proof of origin, which according to the case law of the Court of Justice of the European Union is its main purpose, there are other functions such as the effect of advertising, denoting trust and quality, an indicative function and a communicative function.[406] The German

---

[400] *ECJ*, case 218/01, ECR 2004, I-1725 para. 37, 44; case 49/02, ECR 2004, I-6129 para. 22; *Lange*, Marken- und Kennzeichenrecht, 2006, §1 para. 8.

[401] *Sosnitza*, Deutsches und europäisches Markenrecht, 2010, §3 para. 13.

[402] ECJ, case 517/99, ECR 2001, I-6959 para. 21 f.; case 206/01, ECR 2002, I-10273 para. 47 f.; case 228/03, ECR 2005, I-2337 para. 25 f.; *Lange*, Marken- und Kennzeichenrecht, 2006, §1 para. 11.

[403] *ECJ*, case 143/00, ECR 2002, I-3759 para. 12; case 329/02, ECR 2004, I-8317 para. 23; case 304/06, ECR 2009, I-3297 para. 66; case 265/09 of 9.10.2010, para. 31.

[404] *ECJ*, case 299/99, ECR 2002, I-5475 para. 30; case 273/00, ECR 2002, I-11737 para. 35; case 371/02, ECR 2004, I-5791 para. 20; *Lange*, Marken- und Kennzeichenrecht, 2006, §1 para. 11; *Fezer*, Handbuch der Markenpraxis, Vol. 1, 2007, Intro. 66.

[405] *ECJ*, case 349/95, ECR 1997, I-6227 para. 22; case 63/97, ECR 1999, I-905 para. 52.

[406] *Lange*, Marken- und Kennzeichenrecht, 2006, §1 para. 12; *Ingere/Rohnke*, Markengesetz, 3rd ed. 2010, Intro. 72; *Fezer*, Handbuch der Markenpraxis, Vol. 1, 2007, Intro. 69 ff.

Federal Constitutional Court has also emphasised the function as a guarantee that a product has certain characteristics, as well as the advertising purpose, in addition to the function as an indicator of origin.[407] Taking all of this into account, the significance of trademarks mentioned above is not surprising. It also confirms the thesis of the Court of Justice of the European Union that trademarks are a significant, even indispensable part of the system of undistorted competition, which is established through EU primary legislation.[408]

II. The problem definition and method of examination

1. Problem definition

a) Levels of regulation

The regulation of tobacco products can take place on various levels. At the European level, there are two possibilities: the European Union can enact directly applicable regulations which are valid in the Member States pursuant to Art. 288 (2) (2) TFEU without requiring special transposition or it can also enact directives pursuant to Art. 288 (3) TFEU which must be transposed by the Member States through national law to become binding under the law of the Member States.[409] On the other hand, regulations can also be enacted at the national level, for example through German laws, even if they are not required by EU law, provided that such national regulations do not contradict EU law.

As to the presented proposals to drastically increase tobacco product regulation, it is yet uncertain whether they will be transposed and – if so – on which level this would happen. For this reason, the law both at the European level and at the national German level will be examined.

b) Problems concerning fundamental rights and freedoms as well as other issues

The proposals presented above to drastically tighten tobacco product regulation could only become applicable law if they are compatible with the fundamental rights. In the case of EU regulations, compatibility with the fundamental rights of

---

407 *BVerfGE* 51, 193 (216).

408 *ECJ*, case 39/97, ECR 1998, I-5507 para. 28; case 299/99, ECR 2002, I-5475 para. 78; case 104/01, ECR 2003, I-3797 para. 48; *Fezer*, Handbuch der Markenpraxis, Vol. 1, 2007, Intro. 65 f.

409 In so far as directives are directly applicable, they are to by applied in the Member States without any transposition.

the European Union is of chief significance. Provisions of secondary EU law can only be recognised as legal if they are in accordance with the fundamental rights' requirements that are established in primary legislation.[410] A legal act that infringes on fundamental rights is not valid.[411] German provisions must respect the fundamental rights of the German Constitution (basic rights of the German Basic Law). Again, laws are only valid if all fundamental rights are respected.[412] Provisions at both levels must also satisfy the requirements of the basic freedoms of the TFEU. With respect to the proposals' far-reaching consequences, it is effectively uncertain whether they are compatible with fundamental rights and freedoms. This will, therefore, be addressed in greater detail below.

Moreover, if they are carried out at the European level, the above-mentioned proposals raise serious issues pertaining to competencies.[413] It is not possible to address these competence issues here. However, the limited competencies must be respected in addition to the limits of substantive law.

2. Method of examination

In its first part, the following study will address the compatibility of the proposals to regulate tobacco products with the fundamental rights of the EU. First, the legal basis of the fundamental rights of the EU and those bearing these obligations will be addressed in B I below. Next, it will be clarified which fundamental rights are infringed in B II. Subsequently, the conditions under which such infringement can be justified will be discussed in B III. Finally, the key requirement of proportionality will be examined in further detail in B IV.

The study will also address the proposals' compatibility to regulate tobacco products with the free movement of goods. The prohibition of measures having equivalent effect to a quantitative restriction of the free movement of goods will be outlined. Further, it will examine who is under the obligation to respect the free movement of goods in C I. The requirements that arise from the prohibition of equivalent measures will be assessed as well in C II.

---

410 *ECJ*, case 112/00, ECR 2003, I-5659 para. 73; case 402/05, ECR 2008, I-6513 para. 284; case 45/08, ECR 2009, I-12073 para. 41.

411 ECJ, case 92/09 of 9.11.2010, para. 45 f.

412 *BVerfGE* 84, 9/20; Schulze-Fielitz, in: Dreier (ed.), Grundgesetz, Vol.II, 2nd ed. 2006, Art. 20 para. 84; *Jarass*, in: drs./Pieroth, Grundgesetz, 11th ed. 2011, Art. 20 para. 33; *Sommermann*, in: v.Mangoldt/Klein/Starck, Grundgesetz, 6th ed., Vol.II 2010, Art. 20 para. 256.

413 In general, on the competency issues of tobacco regulation *Pache*, in: Pache/Schwarz/Sosnitza, Aktuelle Rechtsfragen der Tabakregulierung in Europa, 2012, 21 ff.; *Pauling*, VuR 2010, 444; *Stein/Rauber*, Rechtliche Grenzen der Bekämpfung des Tabakkonsums im Mehrebenensystem, 2011, 15 ff.; *Koenig/Kühling*, EWS 2002, 17 ff.

The study's last section will address the proposals' compatibility to regulate tobacco products with the basic rights of German Basic Constitutional Law. This will first involve reviewing who is bound by these fundamental rights and which fundamental rights are being interfered with, looked at in D I. In order for infringements of basic rights to be justified, certain conditions must be fulfilled, examined in D II. Finally the key requirement, proportionality, which is also significant in the context of the German basic rights, will be examined in further detail in D III.

B. Fundamental Rights of the European Union

I. General

1. Principles of the fundamental rights of the European Union

aa) The examination of the compatibility of the regulatory proposals with the fundamental rights of the European Union inevitably has to involve the individual fundamental rights concerned. However, first a few issues must be addressed which are of overriding significance and therefore relevant to all fundamental rights concerned. This applies initially to the question of what the fundamental rights of the European Union are based on.

Since 1.12.2009 the "Charter of Fundamental Rights of the European Union" (CFR) is binding law, pursuant to Art. 6 (1) of the EU Treaty. It has the same legal value as the treaties, thus the rank of primary EU law. In addition, under Art. 6 (3) of the EU Treaty, the fundamental rights, as established by the European Court of Justice, are general legal principles and remain valid EU law. The Charter, as stated in paragraph 4 of its Preamble, aims to make the protection of the fundamental rights, as established by the European Court of Justice, more "visible". It thus seems sensible to interpret the fundamental rights of both sources as coordinated and harmonised with one another.[414] Perhaps these are just two different sources of the fundamental rights.[415] In the following guidelines to the Charter and the case law of the European Court of Justice, they will be handled together accordingly.

bb) An important source for fundamental rights of the European Union can be found in the "European Convention for the Protection of Human Rights and Fundamental Freedoms" (ECHR). Some of the fundamental rights contained in the Charter are regulated similar to the rights of the Convention.[416] For this purpose, Art. 52 (3) (1) CFR stipulates that these Charter Rights have the same meaning and scope as the respective rights of the Convention. However, pursuant to Art. 52 (3) (2) CFR, the Charter can grant further protection, exceeding the scope of the ECHR. This means that the fundamental rights of the Charter can never be interpreted as less protective than the requirements of the Convention.[417] This also applies to

---

414 *Jarass*, Charta der Grundrechte, 2010, Intro. 33.

415 *Skouris*, in: Merten/Papier (ed.), Handbuch der Grundrechte, Vol.VI/1, 2010, § 157 para. 45.

416 In this connection this concerns the freedom of expression and information and the right to property.

417 Explanations relating to the charter of fundamental rights, OJ 2007 C 303/33; *Heringa/Verhey*, MJ 2001, 17; *Jarass*, Charta der Grundrechte, 2010, Art. 52 para. 63; *Hilf*, in: Merten/Papier (ed.), Handbuch der Grundrechte, Vol.VI/1, § 164 para. 46.

the interpretation of the Convention through the case law of the European Court of Human Rights.[418]

Finally, the "Explanations relating to the Charter of Fundamental Rights" prepared by the Praesidium of the Convention provide important considerations for the interpretation of the Charter. Pursuant to Art. 6 (1) sub-section 3 of the EU Treaty and Art. 52 (7) CFR, the explanations must be duly taken into account when interpreting the Charter. This does not make them binding, but they are an important source of knowledge.[419]

2. The parties bound and those entitled to fundamental rights

a) The parties bound by the EU fundamental rights (scope of application)

aa) The issue of whom is bound by the fundamental rights of the European Union is also an overriding question. It is addressed in Art. 51 CFR under the heading "Scope". Under this provision the fundamental rights of the European Union are initially addressed to the bodies, institutions and other agencies *of the Union*. This applies to all activities of the Union and its institutions.[420] In particular, it covers enacting secondary legislation, which is of importance in the present case.

bb) *The Member States* are also subject to obligations arising out of the fundamental rights of the European Union. However, pursuant to Art. 51 (1) (1) CFR, this only applies when they are implementing EU law.[421] The term "implementing" is to be interpreted in a very broad sense and includes both the transposition of EU law by the Member States, in particular transposition of directives[422], and the execution of EU law through administrative activities.[423] The fundamental rights of the European Union must also be observed when national regulations are issued, if they result in a restriction of basic freedoms.[424] This includes the application of national

---

[418] *ECJ*, case 400/10 of 5.10.2010, para. 53; case 279/09 of 22.10.2010, para. 35; *Jarass*, Charta der Grundrechte, 2010, Art. 52 para. 65.

[419] *Jarass*, Charta der Grundrechte, 2010, Art. 52 para. 87; *Scheuing*, EuR 2005, 185.

[420] *Borowski*, in: Meyer (ed.), Charta der Grundrechte, 3rd ed. 2011, Art. 51 para. 21; *Jarass*, Charta der Grundrechte, 2010, Art. 51 para. 4.

[421] Similarly, in the past, the ECJ only applied the fundamental rights within the scope of application of EU law.

[422] *ECJ*, case 74/95 ECR 1996, I-6609 para. 25; case 275/06, ECR 2008, I-271 para. 68; Borowski, in: Meyer (ed.), Charta der Grundrechte, 3rd ed. 2011, Art. 51 para. 27.

[423] *Jarass*, Charta der Grundrechte, 2010, Art. 51 para. 17.

[424] *ECJ*, case 260/89, ECR 1991, I-2925 para. 43 f; case 368/95, ECR 1997, I-3689 para. 24 f case 60/00, ECR 2002, I-6279 para. 40.

law enacted to implement EU law, in particular directives (indirect execution).[425] If fundamental rights of the EU are binding for the Member States, not only the states themselves are bound, but, as a result of the direct applicability of the fundamental rights, also all of their institutions and bodies are bound. [426]

In the present case, this means that the EU fundamental rights bind the German legislator if it transposes EU directives regulating tobacco into German law. Both German administration and German courts have to respect the EU fundamental rights if they interpret or apply EU provisions or the German provisions enacted to implement them.

b) Parties entitled to the fundamental rights of the European Union

To begin with, all natural persons are entitled to the fundamental rights of the European Union unless the fundamental right is expressly limited to citizens of the European Union. Legal entities are also entitled to the fundamental rights, even though only a few of the fundamental rights explicitly mention this.[427] This can be seen from the case law of the European Court of Justice on fundamental rights (as general legal principles).[428] However, this does not apply to all fundamental rights; in character some are only applicable to natural persons. However, there is no doubt with regard to the fundamental rights concerned here: Legal entities can rely on the freedom of expression and information.[429] The same applies to the right to property[430] and the freedom to conduct a business.[431] Thus, in this regard, tobacco producing companies or retailers can, as legal entities, assert the relevant fundamental rights.

---

[425] *ECJ*, case 74/95, ECR 1996, I-6609 para. 25; case 275/06, ECR 2008, I-271 para. 68; Borowski, in: Meyer (ed.), Charta der Grundrechte, 3rd ed. 2011, Art. 51 para. 28; *Jarass*, Charta der Grundrechte, 2010, Art. 51 para. 17.

[426] *Rengeling/Szczekalla*, Grundrechte in der EU, 2004, § 4 para. 330; *Jarass*, Charta der Grundrechte, 2010, Art. 51 para. 12.

[427] Thus, the converse argument cannot be used; *Tettinger*, in: Merten/Papier (ed.), Handbuch der Grundrechte, Vol. II, 2006, § 51 para. 76; *Ladenburger*, in: Tettinger/Stern (ed.), Europ. Grundrechte-Charta, 2006, Art. 51 para. 3.

[428] *ECJ*, case 11/70, ECR 1970, 1125 para. 4 ff.; case 265/87, ECR 1989, I-2237 para. 15.

[429] *Calliess*, in: Calliess/Ruffert (ed.), EUV/AEUV, 4th ed. 2011, Art. 11 para. 9; *Jarass*, Charta der Grundrechte, 2010, Art. 11 para. 13.

[430] *Duschanek*, in: Duschanek/Griller (ed.), Grundrechte für Europa, 2002, 64; cf. *ECJ, case 200/96*, ECR 1998, I-1953 para. 21 ff; case 368/96, ECR 1998, I-7967 para. 61 ff, 79 ff; case 20/00, ECR 2003, I-7411 para. 2, 66 ff.

[431] *Ruffert*, in: Calliess/Ruffert (ed.), EUV/AEUV, 4.ed. 2011, Art. 16 para. 3; *Schwarze*, EuZW 2001, 518; *Streinz*, in: Streinz (ed.), EUV/EGV, 2003, Art. 16 para. 7.

II. Infringement of fundamental rights

1. Freedom of expression and information

a) Principles

Art. 11 (1) CFR guarantees the right to freedom of expression in the broadest sense. As the provision expressly states, in addition to the freedom of expression, the freedom to receive and impart information and ideas without interference by public authority is ensured. Even before the Charter came into force, the European Court of Justice acknowledged the freedom of expression as a general legal principle of Community or EU law.[432] This includes the freedom of information.[433] As stated, this case law must also be considered when interpreting Art. 11 CFR.[434]

Moreover, as stated in the Charter Explanations, the fundamental right of Art. 11 CFR corresponds to the fundamental right in Art. 10 ECHR.[435] Pursuant to Art. 52 (3) CFR, Art. 11 CFR may not take a back seat to the provisions of this law, including its substantiation through the European Court of Human Rights.

b) Scope of protection

aa) Art. 11 (1) CFR refers to opinions, information and ideas. This makes it clear that all content of communication is to be included regardless of its nature. In particular, the content and the quality of the content are irrelevant.[436] The fundamental right does "not only apply to information and ideas which are approved or those considered insignificant or harmless".[437] The form and presentation of the content are also protected.[438]

The freedom of expression and freedom of information as guaranteed at the European level are of particular importance in the economic sector. In particular, every type of advertising falls under the scope of protection, especially that of an

---

432 *ECJ, case* 112/00, ECR 2003, I-5659 para. 79; case 380/03, ECR 2006, I-11573 para. 154; case 421/07, ECR 2009, I-2629 para. 26.
433 *ECJ,* case 479/04, ECR 2006, I-8089 para. 64.
434 B I 1 above.
435 Charter Explanations
436 *Calliess*, in: Calliess/Ruffert (ed.), EUV/AEUV, 4th ed. 2011, Art. 11 para. 6.
437 *ECJ, case* 274/99, ECR 2001, I-1611 para. 39; *Kugelmann*, EuGRZ 2003, 20.
438 *Jarass*, Charta der Grundrechte, 2010, Art. 11 para. 10.

economic nature.[439] This must also apply to the utilisation of a trademark. As stated, the trademark is the central instrument of commercial marketing and, thus, the means of communication between manufacturer and consumer.[440] This concerns information from and the opinions of the manufacturer, and, thus, it also involves activities protected by Art. 11 CFR.

The situation differs somewhat from German fundamental rights in this respect since the German Federal Constitutional Court assumes precedence of the freedom of profession in some cases, as will be demonstrated.[441] At the European level, the fundamental right, in contrast to the German level, also protects all statements of facts from the outset. Thus, the corresponding official heading of Art. 11 CFR is, "Freedom of expression and information".[442] In the light of this, the type and design of brand packaging and use thereof are to be understood as imparting opinions, or information and ideas, within the meaning of Art. 11 CFR.

c) Infringement

The prohibition of brand packaging or the significant restriction of its impact constitutes an encroachment of the fundamental rights of the manufacturer as creator of the respective information and opinion.[443] This also applies to the prohibition of product display in retail sales facilities since it blocks an important means to spread information and symbols on the packaging. The prohibition of product display also impairs the consumer in its fundamental right, pursuant to Art. 11 CFR, since the consumer is hindered from receiving information associated with the presentation of the products.[444] It is recognised that Art. 11 CFR also protects the reception of

---

439 *AG Fenelly,* case 376/98, ECR 2000, I-8419 para. 153; *AG Trstenjak,* case 316/09 v. 24.11.2010, no. 77; *Stern,* in: Tettinger/Stern (ed.), Europ. Grundrechte-Charta, 2006, Art. 11 para. 25; implicitly *ECJ,* case 245/01, ECR 2003, I-12489 para. 72 f.; case 71/02, ECR 2004, I-3025 para. 72 f.

440 A I 3 b above.

441 D I 4 below.

442 Further, the European Court of Human Rights applies this fundamental right in particular in an economic context. This is very likely also due to the lack of fundamental rights protecting the freedom of profession or entrepreneurial freedom in the ECHR.

443 *Pache,* in: Pache/Schwarz/Sosnitza, Aktuelle Rechtsfragen der Tabakregulierung in Europa, 2012, 112; *Schroeder,* ZLR 2012, 416 f. If an infringement is rejected with regard to warnings since negative freedom of expression is not protected (*Wachovius,* BayVBl 2005, 620 f.), this is of no significance in the present case since this is about positive freedom of expression and information. Art. 11 CFR also protects the negative freedom of expression and information (*Jarass,* Charta der Grundrechte, 2010, Art. 11 margin no 10; *Koenig/Kühling,* EWS 2002, 13 f.; *Kühling,* in: Heselhaus/Nowak, Handbuch der europ. Grundrechte, 2006, § 23 para. 23).

444 *Schroeder,* ZLR 2012, 417 f.

information by the consumer.⁴⁴⁵ Overall, it can be said that both the prohibition of tobacco brand packaging and the prohibition of presentation of tobacco products in retail facilities constitute an infringement of the fundamental right of Art. 11 CFR. Even more so, the prohibition on advertising even "primarily" affects the freedom of expression and information.⁴⁴⁶ There can be no other interpretation for restrictions on trademark utilisation.

2. Right to property

a) Basic principles

Art. 17 CFR grants the right to own, use, dispose of and bequeath property. The heading is "Right to property". The European Court of Justice has since long ranked this fundamental right as a general legal principle and thus as binding primary law.⁴⁴⁷ Furthermore, according to the Charter Explanations (which are significant pursuant to Art. 52 (7) CFR), the right to property corresponds with the fundamental right of Art. 1 ECHR Additional Protocol.⁴⁴⁸ Therefore, pursuant to Art. 52 (3) CFR, it conveys at least the same protection as Art. 1 ECHR Additional Protocol, taking into account the interpretation and application of this fundamental right by the European Court of Human Rights.⁴⁴⁹

b) Scope of protection

aa) The term property under Art. 17 CFR is to be understood in a broad sense and is by no means limited to legal positions described as "property" under the law of the Member States, as emphasised in the French and English versions ("ses biens"/"his possessions"). This includes *every asset (vermögenswertes Recht)*⁴⁵⁰ that is of significance and attributed to an individual for use in his own responsibility.⁴⁵¹ Also, "*intellectual property*" is protected, as Art. 17 (2) CFR expressly states, because

---

445 *AG Trstenjak*, case 316/09 of 24.11.2010, para. 85.
446 *AG Trstenjak*, case 316/09 of 24.11.2010, para. 76.
447 *ECJ, case* 293/97, ECR 1999, I-2603 para. 54; case 491/01, ECR 2002, I-11453 para. 149; case 154/04, ECR 2005, I-6451 para. 126.
448 *Charter Explanations,* OJ 2007 C 303/23.
449 *ECJ*, case 402/05, ECR 2008, I-6513, para. 356; *Charter Explanations,* OJ 2007 C 303/23.
450 Cf. *European Court of Human Rights,* no. 15375/89 of 23.2.1995, para. 53; *Meyer-Ladewig*, ECHR, 3rd ed. 2011, Art. 1 ZP para. 8.
451 Cf. *European Court of Human Rights,* no. 73049/01 of 11.1.2007, para. 63, 76.

of its increasing importance⁴⁵². That was assumed even before the Charter came into force.⁴⁵³

This includes, in particular, trademark rights and associated property rights.⁴⁵⁴ In the Charter Explanations, protection of trademark law is expressly covered by the protection of intellectual property under Art. 17 (2) CFR.⁴⁵⁵ If one considers the value of trademark rights and the investments made to establish a trademark, no other interpretation is possible. Within the meaning of Art. 17 CFR a company's right of disposal over assets, such as *trade secrets*, is also considered property, in particular if the secrets concern its products.⁴⁵⁶ The European Court of Justice shares this opinion.⁴⁵⁷ Such trade secrets with asset value fall under the scope of protection of the right to property, at least when they are protected as a legal position through EU law or the right of the Member State concerned.

bb) With regard to the protected aspects, the right to use property is comprised, as expressly stated under Art. 17 CFR. This applies to all types of use.⁴⁵⁸ Accordingly, the use of trademark rights, in particular the use of the trademark on packaging or in retail facilities, is covered under the protection of Art. 17 CFR. Therefore, the prohibition of brand packaging and the prohibition of product display in retail facilities involves protected aspects of Art. 17 CFR.⁴⁵⁹

The situation regarding the use of odorous substances and flavouring agents is more complicated. According to the case law of the European Court of Justice, a prohibition to market certain products, such as orally used tobacco products, only concerns the market share of a company that is not protected by the right to property.⁴⁶⁰ This is also likely to apply to a prohibition of odorous substances and flavouring agents. However, the situation differs if the formula for the odorous substances and flavouring agents constitutes a trade secret that is carefully protected vis-à-vis

---

452 *Charter Explanations,* OJ 2007 C 303/23.

453 *ECJ,* case 479/04, ECR 2006, I-8089 para. 65; case 275/06, ECR 2008, I-271 para. 62.

454 *Charter Explanations,* OJ 2007 C 303/23; *Depenheuer,* in: Tettinger/Stern (ed.), Europ. Grundrechte-Charta, 2006, Art. 17 para. 30; *Calliess,* in: Ehlers (ed.), Europ. Grundrechte und Grundfreiheiten, 3rd ed. 2009, § 16.4 para. 17; also *European Court of Human Rights,* no. 19247/03 of 29.1.2008, para. 34 ff; cf. *ECJ,* case 368/96, ECR 1998, I-7967 para. 78.

455 *Charter Explanations,* OJ 2007 C 303/23.

456 *Heselhaus,* in: Heselhaus/Nowak (ed.), Handbuch der europäischen Grundrechte, 2006, § 32 para. 50; *Jarass,* Charta der Grundrechte, 2010, Art. 17 para. 9.

457 *ECJ, case* 368/96, ECR 1998, I-7967 para. 81 ff; case 453/03, ECR 2005, I-10423 para. 82, 87.

458 *Jarass,* Charta der Grundrechte, 2010, Art. 17 para. 13.

459 *Pache,* in: Pache/Schwarz/Sosnitza, Aktuelle Rechtsfragen der Tabakregulierung in Europa, 2012, 99 f.

460 *ECJ,* case 210/03, ECR 2004, I-11893 para. 73; also *ECJ,* case 295/03, ECR 2005, I-5673 para. 88; case 120/06, ECR 2008, I-6513 para. 185.

third parties and is clearly an asset. In this case, the trade secret is protected pursuant to Art. 17 CFR.[461] After all, Art. 6 (2) (2) Directive 2001/37 expressly mentions the protection of trade secrets. The disputed issue, whether Art. 17 CFR also protects the right to establish and exercise business operations,[462] is not relevant in this sense.

c) Infringement

An infringement of the right to property exists, in particular, when a provision hinders the use of a protected position. The prohibition of brand packaging significantly restricts the possibilities of using a trademark. Since the trademark is protected under Art. 17 CFR, the prohibition constitutes an infringement of the right to property, to which the owner of the trademark is entitled.[463] The prohibition of product display in retail sales facilities also hinders the use of the trademark, which also constitutes an infringement of the right to property. The prohibition of odorous substances and flavouring agents in tobacco products constitutes an infringement of the right to property if, and to the extent that, the substances concern the formula of the product and the formula is a trade secret. Additionally, such a prohibition may interfere with the use of a trademark if the odorous substances and flavouring agents form an essential element of the trademark.

3. Freedom to conduct a business

a) Principles

The Charter of Fundamental Rights of the European Union guarantees in Art. 15 (1) CFR the freedom to choose an occupation and the right to engage in work and, in Art. 16 CFR, the freedom to conduct a business. The Charter does not contain any further details with regard to differentiating between these two fundamental rights. It is correctly assumed that the protection of entrepreneurial activity is only regulated in Art. 16 CFR, and the freedom of profession, pursuant to Art. 15 CFR, is not applicable in this respect,[464] whereby it is unclear where to draw the line between both rights. This depends to a large extent on what is deemed an activity of conducting a business, i.e., an entrepreneurial activity. Some consider that activi-

---

461 The fact that development of the formula for the respective odorous substances and flavouring agents and their impartation on consumers require quite significant investments also suggests this.
462 Cf. *Jarass*, Charta der Grundrechte, 2010, Art. 17 para. 12.
463 *Schroeder*, ZLR 2012, 412 f.
464 *AG Trstenjak*, case 316/09 of 24.11.2010, para. 83 *Nowak*, in: Heselhaus/Nowak (ed.), Handbuch der europäischen Grundrechte, 2006, § 30 para. 58; Jarass, EuZW 2011, 360 f.

ties are not entrepreneurial if the overriding interests are personal.[465] This does, however, make it difficult to differentiate. The exact definition of entrepreneurial activity will not have to be addressed here. In this context, there is no doubt that the tobacco producers exercise such activity within the meaning of Art. 16 CFR. One would also have to affirm this with regard to retailers.

The European Court of Justice has considered the freedom of profession or entrepreneurial freedom as a general principle of EU law in numerous decisions. The court often mentioned the freedom to pursue a trade or profession.[466] In most cases, this involved entrepreneurial activities. Therefore, the case law of the European Court of Justice on the freedom to pursue a profession is of great significance in the context of Art. 16 CFR. Protection under Art. 16 CFR can hardly be deemed as more restrictive than under the jurisprudence, since otherwise it would be necessary to revert to the fundamental right developed by the courts, as general legal principle.[467]

b) Scope of protection

Art. 16 CFR protects *entrepreneurial activity*, i.e., economic or business activities.[468] This includes any activity that serves an economic purpose and is established for a certain period.[469] It must also be an *independent* activity[470]. Only then can one speak of entrepreneurial activity.

The commencement and termination of the entrepreneurial activities, and all aspects of their implementation, are among the activities that are protected.[471] The manner and way in which one operates a company is protected.[472] In particular, advertising and sponsoring fall within the scope of protection.[473] This also includes

---

465 *Bernsdorff*, in: Meyer (ed.), Charta der Grundrechte, 3rd ed. 2011, Art. 16 para. 10; *Nowak*, in: Heselhaus/Nowak (ed.), Handbuch der europäischen Grundrechte, 2006, § 30 para. 32.

466 *ECJ*, case 210/03, ECR 2004, I-11883 para. 72; case 295/03, ECR 2005, I-5673 para. 86; case 120/06, ECR 2008, I-6513 para. 183.

467 Cf. the comments on Art. 6 (3) EU-Treaty, B I 1 above.

468 *Bernsdorff*, in: Meyer (ed.), Charta der Grundrechte, 3rd ed. 2011, Art. 16 para. 11; *Frenz*, Handbuch Europarecht, Vol. 4, 2009, para. 2679.

469 *Nowak*, in: Heselhaus/Nowak (ed.), Handbuch der europäischen Grundrechte, 2006, § 30 para. 38; *Frenz*, Handbuch Europarecht, Vol. 4, 2009, para. 2684.

470 *Ruffert*, in: Calliess/Ruffert (ed.), EUV/AEUV, 4th ed. 2011, Art. 16 para. 3; *Frenz*, Handbuch Europarecht, Vol. 4, 2009, para. 2686.

471 *Frenz*, Handbuch Europarecht, Vol. 4, 2009, para. 2693 f.

472 *ECJ, case* 116/82, ECR 1986, 2519 para. 27; *Ruffert*, in: Ehlers (ed.), Europ. Grundrechte und Grundfreiheiten, 3rd ed. 2009, § 16.3 para. 13; *Jarass*, Charta der Grundrechte, 2010, Art. 16 para. 10.

473 *AG Trstenjak*, case 316/09 of 24.11.2010, no. 83.

the role of economic operators as competitors as indicated through the reference to free competition in the Charter Explanations.[474]

In this context, there is no doubt that the use of brand packaging is protected under Art. 16 CFR. The same applies to product presentation in retail facilities. Finally, the composition of tobacco products and, therefore, the use of odorous substances and flavouring agents fall under the scope of the freedom to conduct a business.

c) Infringement

An infringement of the fundamental rights of Art. 16 CFR occurs when a party bound by the fundamental rights establishes a regulation that aims at, or *directly results in*, a disadvantage for the entrepreneurial activities of a party entitled to those fundamental rights.[475] The decisive factor is whether the measure "has [a] sufficiently direct and significant effect on freedom to exercise a trade or profession".[476] This is the case, particularly if certain entrepreneurial activities are prohibited. It can thus be said that the prohibition of brand packaging infringes the fundamental right of Art. 16 CFR.[477] The same applies to the prohibition of product display in retail facilities and the prohibition of odorous substances and flavouring agents. The prohibition of product display is aimed primarily at retailers. However, since the prohibition very significantly burdens manufacturers of tobacco products, their indirect negative effect must be sufficient to assume an infringement.[478]

III. Justification of the infringements

1. Basic principles

a) Freedom of expression and information

Restrictions on the freedoms of expression and information may be justified. The general limitations provided for under Art. 52 (1) CFR are not relevant in this respect, at least not primarily. As also indicated in the Charter Explanations, Art. 52 (3) CFR

---

[474] *ECJ*, case 280/93, ECR 1994, I-4973 para. 81; *Charter Explanations,* OJ 2007 C 303/23.
[475] *ECJ*, case 200/96, ECR 1998, I-1953 para. 28; *Jarass*, Charta der Grundrechte, 2010, Art. 17 para. 12; *Frenz*, Handbuch Europarecht, Vol. 4, 2009, para. 2734.
[476] *ECJ*, case 435/02, ECR 2004, I-8663 para. 49.
[477] As here *Schroeder*, ZLR 2012, 417; *Pache*, in: Pache/Schwarz/Sosnitza, Aktuelle Rechtsfragen der Tabakregulierung in Europa, 2012, 107.
[478] Cf. *Jarass*, Charta der Grundrechte, 2010, Art. 16 para. 13 with evidence and D I 2 b below.

incorporates the restrictions of Art. 10 (2) ECHR.[479] First, a sufficiently specific legal basis is required in EU law or in domestic law.[480] The restriction also has to serve the purposes indicated in Art. 10 (2) ECHR. In the present context, it is significant that the "protection of health" is among these aims.[481]

Finally, pursuant to Art. 10 (2) ECHR, each restriction must be necessary in a democratic society, meaning it is justified by a pressing social need and is proportionate to the legitimate aim pursued.[482] Here, the principle of proportionality plays a role. In particular, the restriction must be suitable with regard to the aim pursued.[483] Furthermore, no less severe means may be available;[484] Art. 10 (2) ECHR requires the limitation to be "necessary". Finally, the restriction of the fundamental right must be "reasonable in proportion to the justified aim being pursued".[485] The measure may not result in a "disproportionate and unacceptable interference".[486] If it involves a particularly far-reaching infringement, such as a ban on advertising, the requirements concerning legality are particularly high.[487] What this means in the present case will be examined more closely.[488]

b) Right to property

aa) The legality of infringements on the right to property under Art. 17 CFR depends on whether it concerns the deprivation of property or a regulation of property use. The justification for the deprivation of property is provided by Art. 17 (1) (2) CFR; the justification for the regulation of property use is found in Art. 17 (1) (3) CFR.[489] There are significant uncertainties associated with the distinction between these two forms of restricting property. Any formal expropriation is to be con-

---

[479] *ECJ*, case 479/04, ECR 2006, I-8089 para. 64; *Charter Explanations,* OJ 2007 C 303/21.
[480] *ECJ*, case 274/99, ECR 2001, I-1611 para. 42; case 380/03, ECR 2006, I-11573 para. 154.
[481] *ECJ*, case 491/01, ECR 2002, I-11453 para. 150.
[482] *ECJ,* case 112/00, ECR 2003, I-5659 para. 79; case 71/02, ECR 2004, I-3025 para. 50; case 421/07, ECR 2009, I-2629 para. 26.
[483] *ECJ, case* 112/00, ECR 2003, I-5659 para. 80; *Kühling*, in: Heselhaus/Nowak (ed.), Handbuch der europäischen Grundrechte, 2006, 23 para. 49.
[484] *Kühling*, in: Heselhaus/Nowak (ed.), Handbuch der europäischen Grundrechte, 2006, § 23 para. 50.
[485] *ECJ*, case 380/03, ECR 2006, I-11573 para. 154 f; also *ECJ,* case 71/02, ECR 2004, I-3025 para. 50; *Kühling*, in: Heselhaus/Nowak (ed.), Handbuch der europäischen Grundrechte, 2006, § 23 para. 51 ff.
[486] *ECJ, case* 112/00, ECR 2003, I-5659 para. 80.
[487] *AG Trstenjak*, case 316/09 of 24.11.2010, para. 80.
[488] B IV below.
[489] The main difference in the legal consequences is that divestment always requires compensation, whereby this is only the case with particularly serious cases of utilisation regulations; see below B III 2 c.

sidered a deprivation of property. However, there is also *de facto expropriation*,[490] which does not formally affect the position as owner, but takes all of the rights associated therewith from the owner and imposes on the owner the effects of expropriation.[491] This requires that the owner be excluded from *any* "reasonable" use or disposal.[492] The European Court of Justice rejected the deprivation of property accordingly in a case involving a far-reaching restriction on use that still allowed the owner to sell, even though the price was significantly lower.[493] It is yet unclear where the lines are to be drawn.[494]

In the case at hand, the prohibition of brand packaging results in a severe infringement of trademark law and renounces a significant part of the meaning of trademark law. The effect on trademark law is all the more intense when viewed together with the prohibition of product display in retail facilities. On the other hand, the owner of the trademark continues to have some possibilities to use the trademark, even if they are few. It is thus a borderline case. Although the Court of Justice's case law is ambiguous, Article 17 CFR is assumed to be a use regulation. However, even a utilisation regulation may infringe the right to property to a degree that amounts to deprivation of property. A similar principle applies to trade secrets regarding the formula for odorous substances and flavouring agents.

bb) Regulations of property use are permissible if they meet the requirements of Art. 17 (1) (3) CFR, which are in accordance with the requirements of Art. 1 (2) ECHR Additional Protocol, applicable via Art. 52 (3) (1) CFR. The initial requirement has a sufficiently specific legal basis in EU law or domestic law.[495] Furthermore, the utilisation regulation pursuant to Art. 17 (1) (3) CFR must serve the "objectives of general interest". This also includes the protection of health.

Finally, the utilisation regulation must observe the principle of proportionality.[496] Based on Art. 52 (1) (2) CFR, it must "genuinely" meet or serve the objectives

---

490 *Bernsdorff*, in: Meyer (ed.), Charta der Grundrechte, 3rd ed. 2011, Art. 17 para. 20.

491 *European Court of Human Rights, no.* 7151/75 of 23. 9. 1982, para. 63; *Cremer*, in: Grote/Marauhn (ed.), EMRK/GG, 2006, Ch. 22 para. 92.

492 *ECJ*, case 347/03, ECR 2005, I-3785 para. 122; also *European Court of Human Rights*, no. 14556/89 of 24.6.1993, para. 43 f; *Cremer*, in: Grote/Marauhn (ed.), EMRK/GG, 2006, Ch. 22 para. 95.

493 *ECJ, case* 44/79, ECR 1979, 3727 para. 19. Thus, it is confirmed that the *ECJ* takes a formal view; *Grabenwarter*, EuR 2001, 15 f; *Calliess*, in: Ehlers (ed.), Europ. Grundrechte und Grundfreiheiten, 3rd ed. 2009, § 16.4 para. 20.

494 *Calliess*, in: Ehlers (ed.), Europ. Grundrechte und Grundfreiheiten, 3rd ed. 2009, § 16.4 para. 29.

495 *EuGH*, case 347/03, ECR 2005, I-3785 para. 125; *Heselhaus*, in: Heselhaus/Nowak (ed.), Handbuch der europäischen Grundrechte, 2006, § 32 para. 78.

496 *ECJ*, case 491/01, ECR 2002, I-11453 para. 149; case 347/03, ECR 2005, I-3785 para. 125; case 402/05, ECR 2008, I-6351 para. 55; *Heselhaus*, in: Heselhaus/Nowak (ed.), Handbuch der europäischen Grundrechte, 2006, § 32 para. 82.

pursued, and thus be suitable.[497] It must support the objective of the regulation. Also, there may be no alternative measure available that is milder but has the same effect.[498] Ultimately, "there must exist a reasonable relationship between the means employed and the aim sought to be realised".[499] They "cannot constitute in relation to the aim pursued a disproportionate and intolerable interference, impairing the very substance of the rights guaranteed".[500] A "fair balance" is necessary between the requirements of the general interest and the safeguarding of the fundamental rights of the individual.[501]

c) Freedom to conduct a business

It is expressly stated that the freedom to conduct a business is (only) "recognised in accordance with Union law and national laws and practices". This can hardly constitute a limitation of the scope of protection since Art. 16 CFR would then take a back seat to the freedom to conduct a business as was established by the European Court of Justice, where the scope of protection regularly included all entrepreneurial activity. Instead, this should be understood as a reservation leaving room for regulations to develop and regulate the protected right, which enables the legislator to make far-reaching provisions (*Ausgestaltungs- und Regelungsvorbehalt*).[502]

Thus, limitations of the freedom to conduct a business are possible with a sufficiently specific legal basis in EU or domestic law. With a reservation regarding structure and regulation, the permissible objectives that allow limitations are particularly broad and, in any event, include the protection of health. On the other hand, the limitation has to observe the principle of proportionality despite the

---

497 *ECJ*, case 379/08, ECR 2010, I-0000, para. 86; *v.Danwitz*, in: v.Danwitz/Depenheuer/Engel (ed.), Bericht zur Lage des Eigentums, 2002, 253.

498 *ECJ*, case 379/08, ECR 2010, I-2007, para. 86; *Depenheuer*, in: Tettinger/Stern (Ed.) Europ. Grundrechte-Charta, 2006, Art. 17 para. 53.

499 *ECJ*, case 402/05, ECR 2008, I-6351 para. 360; *Heselhaus*, in: Heselhaus/Nowak (ed.), Handbuch der europäischen Grundrechte, 2006, §32 para. 84; *Frenz*, Handbuch Europarecht, Vol. 4, 2009, para. 2981 f.

500 *ECJ, case* 44/94, ECR 1995, I-3115 para. 55; case 368/96, ECR 1998, I-7967 para. 79; case 20/00, ECR 2003, I-7411 para. 68; case 154/04, ECR 2005, I-6451 para. 126.

501 *European Court of Human Rights*, No. 7151/75 of 23. 9.1982, para. 69; no. 21151/04 of 8.4.08 para. 79; *v.Danwitz*, in: v.Danwitz/Depenheuer/Engel (ed.), Bericht zur Lage des Eigentums, 2002, 253 f; *Cremer*, in: Grote/Marauhn (ed.), EMRK/GG, 2006, Ch. 22 para. 116.

502 Cf. *Bernsdorff*, in: Meyer (ed.), Charta der Grundrechte, 3rd ed. 2011, Art. 16 para. 15; *Durner*, in: Merten/Papier(ed.), Handbuch der Grundrechte, §162 para. 38.

reservation regarding structure and regulation.[503] Otherwise, it would result in a contradiction to the case law of the European Court of Justice on entrepreneurial freedom. In its decisions on the freedom of profession, the Court of Justice generally measured limitations with regard to proportionality, even if they concerned companies, which was usually the case. If one were to interpret differently Art. 16 CFR, then pursuant to Art. 6 (3) EC Treaty, the freedom to conduct a business as established by the European Court of Justice (as a general principle) would apply. Finally, in this regard it must be taken into account that in the Charter Explanations Art. 16 CFR is based on the provision of Art. 119 (1) and (3) TFEU (ex Art. 4 (1), (3) EC Treaty) whereby the Union (and the Member States) are committed to free competition.[504] Infringements of trademark rights are, however, particularly problematic in a competition system.[505]

2. Proportionality

a) Proportionality in general and with regard to fundamental rights

The previous deliberations have shown that the justification of limitations of all fundamental rights concerned essentially depends on whether the limitation of the fundamental right demonstrates proportionality. As a result, the way in which the European Court of Justice understands and specifies the principle of proportionality is of material importance. For this issue not only is the case law of the Court of Justice on limitations of fundamental rights significant, it cannot be overlooked that according to settled case law the Court of Justice has extracted from Community or EU law an independent principle of proportionality as a general legal principle,[506] which is also reflected in Art. 5 (4) subpara. 1 EU Treaty.[507] The Court of Justice then examines, without any connection to a certain fundamental right,

---

503 *AG Tizzano*, case 453/03, ECR 2005, I-10423 para. 75; *AG Trstenjak*, case 316/09 of 24.11.2010, para. 84; *Durner*, in: Merten/Papier(ed.), Handbuch der Grundrechte, Vol.VI/1, 2010, § 162 para. 38; *Frenz*, Handbuch Europarecht, Vol. 4, 2009, para. 2758.
504 Charter Explanations, OJ 2007 C 303/23: Jarass, EuGRZ 2011, 360.
505 On the function of trade marks in a competitive system A I 3 b above.
506 *ECJ*, case 133/93, ECR 1994, I-4863 para. 41; case 296/93, ECR 1996, I-795 para. 30; case 210/00, ECR 2002, I-6453 para. 59; case 380/03, ECR 2006, I-11573 para. 144. This applies when the measure in question encroaches upon protected interest; *ECJ*, case 329/01, ECR 2004, I-1899, para. 59.
507 Art. 5 (4) EU Treaty concerns primarily the relationship to the Member States; cf. *ECJ*, case 165/09 of 26.5.2011, para. 89.

whether the burdens are disproportionate when measured against the objectives that the measure pursues.[508]

This approach differs greatly from the German approach that usually applies proportionality as a restrictive control within the assessment of a fundamental right, which can also be found in the case law of the European Court of Justice.[509] In some cases, both assessments fall within *one* decision, possibly even with references.[510] The requirements do not differ, as is evident from the references. Therefore, the decision of the Court of Justice on the general principle of proportionality can also be used in the context of a review of fundamental rights. This is important because there are some statements of the Court of Justice that are more specific in this respect. The principle of proportionality based on fundamental rights can hardly be less strict than proportionality, in general.

b) *Elements of proportionality*

In its approach to substantiate the principle of proportionality, the European Court of Justice usually takes a two-step approach:[511] First, it requires that the "means used are suitable to achieve the objectives pursued". [512] In particular, the reasons therefore must be "correct".[513]

Furthermore, the means used must not "exceed what is necessary to attain the objective pursued". [514] This means that measures may only go as far as actually required for attaining the objective. This applies with regard to material aspects, time and with regard to the personal scope of application.[515] Furthermore, no other measure may be available which can attain the objective just as easily but with less

---

508 *ECJ*, case 157/96, ECR 1998, I-2211 para. 47 ff; case 180/96, ECR 1998, I-2265 para. 96–11; case 60/00, ECR 2002, I-6279 para. 43 ff; cf. *Penski/Elsner,* DÖV 2001, 273.

509 E.g. *ECJ*, case 296/93, ECR 1996, I-795 para. 25–45, 63–65; case 418/97, ECR 1997, I-4475 para. 66–75; case 368/96, ECR 1998, I-7967 para. 66–86; *ECJ*, case 65/98, ECR 2003, II-4653 para. 170–173, 201–205.

510 Cf. *ECJ*, case 368/96, ECR 1998, I-7967 para. 83; case 293/97, ECR 1999, I-2603 para. 57; case 453/03, ECR 2005, I-10423 para. 88; *Koch,* Der Grundsatz der Verhältnismäßigkeit in der Rechtsprechung des EuGH, 2003, 255 ff.

511 E.g. *ECJ,* case 58/08 of 8.6.2010, para. 51; case 92/09 of 9.11.10, para. 74.

512 On proportionality in general *ECJ*, case 28/05, ECR 2006, I-5431 para. 72; case 368/96, ECR 1998, I-7967 para. 66; case 171/03, ECR 2004, I-10945 para. 51.

513 *ECJ, case* 274/99, ECR 2001, I-1611 para. 41.

514 On proportionality in general *ECJ*, case.28/05, ECR 2006, I-5431 para. 72; case 171/03, ECR 2004, I-10945 para. 51; case 37/06 of 17.1.2008 para. 35.

515 Cf. *ECJ,* case 265/08 of 20.4.10, para. 35–38.

infringement of the fundamental right[516]: "When there is a choice between several appropriate measures recourse must be had to the least onerous".[517]

According to the case law of the European Court of Justice, the necessity of the measure also requires that the interests affected are properly balanced.[518] It is possible to view the appropriateness as an independent element of proportionality and not as a second part of the requirement of necessity, as under German constitutional law. Regardless of this dogmatic issue, a proper balance between the interests of the Union or the Member State, on the one hand, and the party entitled to the fundamental rights, on the other, is necessary.[519] In those circumstances, the "interests" involved "must be weighed having regard to all the circumstances of the case in order to determine whether a fair balance was struck between those interests".[520] The adverse effects must be "proportionate in light of the legitimate objective pursued".[521] Similarly, the European Court on Human Rights requires a "fair balance" between the general public interest and the necessity to protect the fundamental rights of the individual.[522]

c) Transitional regulations, exceptions and compensation

In some cases, the principle of proportionality may only be observed if the legislator foresees *transitional provisions*.[523] In hardship cases, *exceptions* may also be necessary; due to the possibility for exceptions, the European Court of Justice affirmed proportionality accordingly.[524] If certain groups are typically affected more severely, special provisions may be necessary. To name just one example, there are special packaging forms for certain tobacco products that necessitate special provisions.

---

516 Cf. *ECJ*, case 265/87, ECR 1989, 2237 para. 21; case 254/94, ECR 1996, I-4235 para. 55.

517 On proportionality in general *ECJ*, case 375/96, ECR 1998, I-6629 para. 63; similarly *ECJ*, case 296/93, ECR 1996, I-795 para. 30; case 171/03, ECR 2004, I-10945 para. 51.

518 Particularly clear *ECJ*, case 92/09 of 9.11.10, para. 76 f.

519 *ECJ*, case 402/05, ECR 2008, I-6351 para. 360; case 92/09 of 9.11.10, para. 77, 80.

520 *ECJ*, case 112/00, ECR 2003, I-5659, para. 81; *Kingreen*, in: Calliess/Ruffert (ed.), EUV/AEUV, 4th ed. 2011, Art. 52 para. 70.

521 *ECJ*, case112/00, ECR 2003, I-5659 para. 79; similarly *ECJ*, case 60/00, ECR 2002, I-6279 para. 42; case 482/01, ECR 2004, I-5257 para. 99; also, on proportionality in general *ECJ*, case 37/06 of 17.1.08 para. 35; case 171/03, ECR 2004, I-10945 para. 51.

522 *European Court of Human Rights, no.* 12033/86 of 18.2.91, para. 51; no. 15375/89 of 23.2.1995, para. 62; no. 25404/94 of 21.10.1997, para. 43; *Grabenwarter*, ECHR, 4th ed. 2009, § 18 margi no. 16.

523 *ECJ*, case 68/95, ECR 1996, I-6085 para. 40; cf. *ECJ, case* 306/93, ECR 1994, I-5555 para. 28; case 347/03, ECR 2005, I-3785 para. 133.

524 *ECJ*, case 68/95, ECR 1996, I-6085 para. 40, 42 f.

Similarly, the proportionality of a limitation of a fundamental right can depend on whether *compensation* is granted. With initial regard for infringements of property, the European Court of Justice stated (also in the form of regulations of property use), "in the absence of compensation[,] restrictions on ownership constitute an intolerable interference with respect to the aims pursued".[525] However, such a requirement is also mentioned in the event of a restriction of entrepreneurial freedom of profession and, thereby, of entrepreneurial freedom.[526] This also applyies with regard to a restriction on the freedom of expression and information even if the Court of Justice has not yet made such statements.

3. Intensity (standard) of control

a) Freedom of expression and information

The effects of the requirement of proportionality differ depending on the intensity or standard of judicial control required. The statements made by the European Court of Justice differ in this respect on the various fundamental rights:

There is a clear emphasis placed on judicial controls in the area of the freedom of expression and information pursuant to Art. 11 CFR. The parties bound by the fundamental rights are, however, allowed a certain assessment leeway with regard to appropriateness or proper balancing.[527] In particular, the intensity of control for statements in business transactions or in the pursuit of commercial interests, particularly advertising, is lower.[528] Then again, the greater the infringement of the freedom of expression is, the more accurate the control.[529] This is also significant with commercial issues. Just recently, in a case of far-reaching interference, such as a ban on advertising, the requirements for the justification as stated by the Advocate General were high.[530]

b) Right to property and freedom to conduct a business

The intensity of judicial control is much more restrained in the case law of the European Court of Justice on the right to property. The intensity of control vis-à-vis

---

[525] *ECJ*, case 20/00, ECR 2003, I-7411 para. 79; case 120/06, ECR 2008, I-6513 para. 184; *Frenz*, Handbuch Europarecht, Vol. 4, 2009, para. 2985 f.

[526] *ECJ*, case 120/06, ECR 2008, I-6513 para. 184.

[527] *ECJ*, case 274/99, ECR 2001, I-1611 para. 49; case 112/00, ECR 2003, I-5659 para. 81 f.

[528] *ECJ*, case 71/02, ECR 2004, I-3025 para. 51; case 380/03, ECR 2006, I-11573 para. 155; case 421/07, ECR 2009, I-2629 para. 27.

[529] *ECJ, case* 340/00, ECR 2001, I-10269 para. 18.

[530] *AG Trstenjak*, case 316/09 of 24.11.2010, para. 80.

the legislator is reduced overall.⁵³¹ The measure to be assessed is only impermissible if it is "obviously unsuitable".⁵³² And the assessment of the necessity only must be corrected if it is "obviously" incorrect.⁵³³ The appropriateness is often not examined in great detail.⁵³⁴

The same applies with regard to entrepreneurial freedom. In this case, the party bound by the fundamental right is granted a certain amount of leeway in its assessment.⁵³⁵ A measure must be obviously unsuitable or obviously unnecessary.⁵³⁶ If the party bound must assess the effect of a measure, the assessment can only be contested if it appears to be obviously erroneous with respect to the party's knowledge at the time of assessment.⁵³⁷

In legal commentary, this general reduction of the intensity of judicial control in the area of property and entrepreneurial freedom is correctly criticised as being deficient,⁵³⁸ in particular, because the European Court of Justice accepted the proportionality without any detailed review. It is at any rate questionable whether it seriously interferes with the freedom of the party entitled to the fundamental rights. On the other hand, it should not be overlooked that case law to date primarily referred to areas such as agricultural policy and similar fields that are characterised by intensive market regulations and, in some cases, are highly subsidised;⁵³⁹ in such cases, the leeway with regard to fundamental rights must be greater.

---

531 *ECJ, case* 402/05, ECR 2008, I-6351 para. 360.
532 *ECJ, case* 306/93, ECR 1994, I-5555 para. 21; case 296/93, ECR 1996, I-795 para. 31; *CFI, case* 13/99, ECR 2002, II-3305 para. 166.
533 *ECJ, case* 280/93, ECR 1994, I-4973 para. 94.
534 *Calliess,* in: Ehlers (ed.), Europ. Grundrechte und Grundfreiheiten, 3rd ed. 2009, § 16.4 para. 47.
535 *ECJ, case* 44/94, ECR 1995, I-3115 para. 57; case 296/93, ECR 1996, I-795 para. 31; *Penski/Elsner,* DÖV 2001, 273.
536 *ECJ, case* 280/93, ECR 1994, I-4973 para. 90; case 306/93, ECR 1994, I-5555 para. 21, 27; case 44/94, ECR 1995, I-3115 para. 58.
537 *ECJ, case* 280/93, ECR 1994, I-4973 para. 90.
538 *Streinz,* in: Streinz (ed.), EUV/EGV, 2003. Art. 16 para. 4; *Bernsdorff,* in: Meyer (ed.), Charta der Grundrechte, 3rd ed. 2011, Art. 15 para. 18; *Ruffert,* in: Ehlers (ed.), Europ. Grundrechte und Grundfreiheiten, 3rd ed. 2009, § 16.3 para. 39; *Koch,* Der Grundsatz der Verhältnismäßigkeit in der Rechtsprechung des Gerichtshofs, 2003, 399 ff; a.A. *Kischel,* EuR 2000, 395 ff.
539 *Streinz,* in: Streinz (ed.), EUV/EGV, 2003, Art. 15 para. 6, Art. 16 GC Rn. 4; *Ruffert,* in: Ehlers (ed.), Europ. Grundrechte und Grundfreiheiten, 3rd ed. 2009, § 16.3 para. 3.

IV. Proportionality in the present context

1. Prohibition of brand packaging

a) Infringement of fundamental rights and severity of the infringement

aa) The findings can now be applied to the prohibitions at issue. First, it must be clarified whether the prohibition of brand packaging is in line with the principle of proportionality. This prohibition infringes the freedom of expression and information of Art. 11 (1) CFR.[540] The right to property pursuant to Art. 17 CFR is also infringed.[541] The prohibition on brand packaging ultimately results in an infringement of the freedom to conduct a business pursuant to Art. 16 CFR.[542]

bb) With regard to the severity of these infringements, a prohibition of brand packaging leads to a far-reaching devaluation of trademark rights.[543] Without effective packaging, the consumer can hardly recognize "his" brand. The name of the brand alone is hardly sufficient. The brand should, as stated, enable the end user to recognise the goods without the risk of confusion with goods of other origin; it should ensure that all goods that it distinguishes are manufactured or performed under the control of a single company responsible for the quality of the goods.[544] All of this is impossible in practice if brand packaging, which differs in colour and graphics, is no longer permitted. Therefore, a prohibition of brand packaging must be seen as a serious infringement of the legal position and thereby of the fundamental rights of the trademark owner.

This is all the more true since brands are the central instruments of commercial marketing and are of great importance, especially in highly developed economic systems.[545] The prohibition of brand packaging would destroy market values that have been established at a considerable cost over decades.

---

540 B II 1 c above.

541 B II 2 c above.

542 B II 3 c above.

543 In detail *Sosnitza*, in: Pache/Schwarz/Sosnitza, Aktuelle Rechtsfragen der Tabakregulierung in Europa, 2012, 133 f.

544 A I 3 b above, with evidence from the case law of the ECJ.

545 A I 3 b above.

b) The proportionality of the measure

aa) The extent to which a prohibition of brand packaging contributes to protecting health is difficult to assess,[546] since such radical measures have never been implemented previously. However, for the requirement of suitability, it is sufficient if the attainment of the objectives is promoted.[547] Therefore, the suitability of the measure cannot be excluded, at least not if one grants the legislator leeway in its assessment, in light of the uncertainties.[548]

bb) There are serious concerns with regard to the necessity of a prohibition of brand packaging and the need for proper balance with regard to this issue, in spite of the fact that the legislator does have significant leeway, not only with respect to the right to property and the freedom of profession, but also in the areas of the freedom of expression and information since this concerns commercial freedom of expression. Additionally, the protection of health is also a very significant objective.[549]

However, as stated, it cannot be overlooked that a prohibition of brand packaging constitutes a very significant encroachment of fundamental rights.[550] It must also be taken into consideration, as the European Court of Justice has stated, that brands are a significant indispensable element of a system of fair competition that should be safeguarded through EU Primary Law.[551] The market would be cemented if there were a prohibition on brand packaging; it would make any future changes in the market difficult, and, in particular, access to the market would become problematic.[552] Finally, uniform packaging would also lead to an increase in product imitations.[553]

In the light of these findings the requirements to justify a prohibition on brand packaging must be very strict, at any rate, in the areas of the freedom of expression and information. A "proper balance" between the interests of the Union or the Member State, on the one hand, and the party entitled to fundamental rights, on

---

546 Cf. *Riessen* e.g., Assessing the Impacts of Revising the Tobacco Products Directive, Rand, 2010, 131, 134; *Deloitte*, Tobacco Packaging regulation, 2011, 24 ff.

547 B II 2 b above.

548 Expressing doubts *Schroeder*, ZLR 2012, 414; In addition, in 2009, the responsible minister in Great Britain was of the view that there was no sufficient evidence; cf. *Kunz-Hallstein*, in: Bender/ Schülke/ Winterfeldt (ed.), 50 Jahre Bundespatentgericht, 2011, 662.

549 *ECJ*, case 193/95, ECR 1997, I-4315 para. 43.

550 B IV 1 a above.

551 Cf. the evidence under A I 3 b above.

552 Cf. *v.Danwitz*, Produktwerbung in der Europäischen Union zwischen gemeinschaftlichen Kompetenzgrenzen und europäischem Grundrechtsschutz, 1998, 38 f.

553 *Deloitte*, Tobacco Packaging regulation, 2011, 27 f.; *Stein/Rauber*, Rechtliche Grenzen der Bekämpfung des Tabakkonsums im Mehrebenensystem, 2011, 49.

the other, is necessary.⁵⁵⁴ In those circumstances, "the interests involved must be weighed having regard to all the circumstances of the case in order to determine whether a fair balance was struck between those interests".⁵⁵⁵ In view of the uncertainties with respect to the health benefits of a prohibition on brand packaging, this can hardly be considered a reasonable balance of interests for such a serious infringement.⁵⁵⁶

This is particularly true since less severe measures are possible such as enlarging the required labelling on the packages without making it impossible for the consumer to recognise the brand. Thus, in its decision on the tobacco product directive the European Court of Justice emphasised that the directive leaves enough space for other information on the package, in particular with regard to the brand of cigarettes.⁵⁵⁷ Overall, there are good reasons to suggest that a prohibition of brand packaging in the scope described leads to a disproportionate infringement, at any rate, of the freedom of expression and information.

cc) This finding must also apply if labelling requirements on packaging are imposed to such an extent that the brand becomes impossible to recognise. This would effectively result in a prohibition of brand packaging. The decisive question will be whether consumers can recognize the brand at first sight based on the packaging. If this is not the case, one can no longer truly qualify this as brand packaging.

c) *Special situation of manufacturers with a wide assortment*

It must also be taken into consideration that a prohibition on brand packaging does not affect all manufacturers of tobacco products equally. If a manufacturer offers many different types of cigarettes, each with a specific character, then such a prohibition would be more severe compared to a manufacturer who has fewer brands, but distributes greater amounts of those few brands. The variety of products cannot be communicated on the market without brand symbols. Therefore, a prohibition of brand packaging hits harder a manufacturer with a wide assortment. The disproportionate effects of the infringement are more pronounced in such cases.

---

554 *ECJ*, case 92/09 of 9.11.10, para. 77, 79 f., 83, 86.

555 *ECJ*, case 112/00, ECR 2003, I-5659, para. 81; *Kingreen*, in: Calliess/Ruffert (ed.), EUV/AEUV, 4th ed. 2011, Art. 52 para. 70.

556 Also *Pache*, in: Pache/Schwarz/Sosnitza, Aktuelle Rechtsfragen der Tabakregulierung in Europa, 2012, 105; *Schroeder*, ZLR 2012, 414 f. The situation would be different if there were financial compensation that amounted to the economic value of the brand concerned.

557 *ECJ*, case 491/01, ECR 2002, I-11452 para. 132, 152.

2. Prohibition of product display in retail facilities

a) Fundamental rights affected and the severity of the encroachment

The prohibition of product display in retail facilities infringes, as stated, the freedom of expression and information pursuant to Art. 11 CFR.[558] Furthermore, it interferes with the right to property pursuant to Art. 17 CFR.[559] Finally, it also encroaches upon the freedom to conduct a business pursuant to Art. 16 CFR.[560]

The implications that result from such a prohibition of product display are considerable, even if they are less severe than the implications of a prohibition of brand packaging. If the consumer can no longer see his tobacco product in the retail sales facilities then the brand can hardly fulfil its function of preventing confusion between other brands.[561] Problems also arise with regard to introducing new products or changing formulas, which is why a prohibition on product display hinders the further development of products. In addition, the consumer is impaired in his freedom of information since he is not provided access to the tobacco products and the associated information.[562]

b) Proportionality of the measure

aa) There are doubts about the *suitability* of the prohibition of product display in retail sales facilities with respect to the protection of health. In Canada, the prohibition against displaying tobacco products has not resulted in a decrease in consumption.[563] Instead, the sale of illegally traded products has increased. There are also studies that reveal a positive effect, although it is difficult to quantify.[564] In this respect, the legislator's leeway for assessment is relevant.

bb) With regard to the *necessity* of the prohibition of product display in retail facilities and the need for proper balance, there are serious doubts, particularly with regard to the freedom of expression and information. With regard to this fundamental right, the prohibition constitutes a severe encroachment of the fundamental rights.[565] It must therefore be taken into consideration whether there are less severe

---

558 B II 1 c above.
559 B II 2 c above.
560 B II 3 c above.
561 See A I 3 b above.
562 See B II 1 c above.
563 According to the examination by the Institute of Economic Affairs.
564 See *Riessen*, e.g., Assessing the Impacts of Revising the Tobacco Products Directive, Rand, 2010, 192, 134; Deloitte, Tobacco Packaging regulation, 2011, 24 ff.
565 B III 3 a above.

measures available that do not fully exclude product display. The legislator should at least take an incremental approach and initially try milder measures, afterwhich it may assess whether the measures have produced the desired effect. Overall, it is uncertain whether a prohibition against the display of tobacco products in retail facilities constitutes an infringement of fundamental rights that still observes the principle of proportionality, despite the leeway that the legislator has been granted. As stated above, the doubts are even greater when the manufacturer offers a great variety of tobacco products.[566]

3. Prohibition of odorous substances and flavouring agents

a) Fundamental rights affected and severity of the infringement

With regard to the prohibition of odorous substances and flavouring agents, it is apparent that the freedom to conduct a business pursuant to Art. 16 CFR is infringed.[567] The right to property pursuant to Art. 17 CFR is also infringed, insofar as the odorous substances and flavouring agents concern a product formula which is a business secret. It is also plausible that the odorous substances and flavouring agents are essential for the product concerned and thus their use is essential to the brand.[568] However, it is unlikely that the freedom of expression and information are encroached upon, although the prohibition does have implications for the use of the trademark. The impact on Art. 11 CFR is too indirect in this respect.[569]

The encroachment of entrepreneurial freedom, and possibly of the right to property, presents a significant burden for the manufacturer of tobacco products who has used odorous substances and flavouring agents in its products in the past. In these cases the consumer expects the sensory effects from the tobacco products caused by these odorous substances and flavouring agents. If they are missing, the consumer does not receive the product that he seeks. The consumer will then consider whether he should purchase a different product in the future. For manufacturers who have used certain odorous substances and flavouring agents in their products in the past, this is inevitably a considerable loss. What is more, to be precise, is that the manufacturer is forbidden from producing the goods in a manner which is expedient with regard to the wishes of the customers.

---

566 B IV 1 c above.

567 B II 3 c above.

568 B II 2 b, c above.

569 In general, on indirect impacts on fundamental rights *Jarass*, Charta der Grundrechte, 2010, Art. 51 para. 17.

b) Proportionality of the measure

aa) Considering the importance of health, a prohibition of odorous substances and flavouring agents must be considered proportional to the extent to which such substances are associated with health risks. This is the case for the odorous substances and flavouring agents prohibited (in Germany) under Sec. 2 of the regulation on tobacco products, since the provision serves to protect health.[570]

bb) The situation differs for odorous substances and flavouring agents which are not associated with health risks and only serve to satisfy the wishes of the customers. Here it must be stated that there is no evidence that forgoing such substances promotes the protection of health.[571] Smoking is no less popular in Great Britain and Ireland, where cigarette brands without additives are predominantly sold, than in countries where most of the cigarettes have additives. This suggests that the measure is not suitable to achieve the aim pursued.

Doubts also arise with regard to the necessity and proper balancing required under the principle of proportionality. The freedom to conduct a business, and possibly the right to property, are encroached upon, but not the right to expression and information. The legislative leeway is thus in principle very broad if one follows the case law of the European Court of Justice.[572] With regard to a prohibition on odorous substances and flavouring agents, it must be taken into consideration that the effects on the manufacturers of tobacco products vary greatly. There are manufacturers that do not use any odorous substances and flavouring agents anyway, so such a prohibition would not affect them. By contrast, the prohibition would induce serious consequences for manufacturers of tobacco products with odorous substances and flavouring agents. They would suffer a competitive disadvantage vis-à-vis the other manufacturers. The protection of health should be pursued equally vis-à-vis all manufacturers.[573] Overall, considering the serious doubts regarding the suitability and proper balancing, the evidence suggests that a prohibition of odorous substances and flavouring agents is disproportionate.[574]

---

570 Gazette of the Bundesrat 479/77, p. 23 f. On the tobacco regulation A I 1 a above.

571 *Riessen* inter alia, Assessing the Impacts of Revising the Tobacco Products Directive, Rand, 2010, 177 f.

572 B III 2 b above.

573 Here it is assumed that no health risks result from the odorous substances and flavouring agents used.

574 On the necessity of exceptions and transitional provisions B III 2 c above.

4. Consequences of cumulative infringements of fundamental rights

a) Principles

Recently in German constitutional law it has become increasingly clear that, with the assessment of proportionality, the legislator must take into account that multiple and simultaneous interferences with fundamental rights may intensify one another, pursue essentially similar purposes, and affect the same legal interest. These are called "cumulative" infringements of fundamental rights.[575] In such circumstances it is not enough to assess each infringement separately. In addition, the overall burden on the party concerned must be assessed.[576]

As far as can be seen, this issue has not yet been dealt with in EU law. There is, however, no doubt that nothing else can apply with regard to the fundamental rights of the European Union. Otherwise, the party bound by the fundamental right could circumvent the binding nature of the fundamental rights through numerous small measures, or a piecemeal approach.

b) Applicability in the present context

In the present context these findings apply when the measures described to regulate tobacco products are implemented cumulatively. If, for example, the prohibition on brand packaging is combined with the prohibition of product display in retail facilities then the trademark rights are infringed to an even greater degree. In this case, the grounds for an unreasonable infringement of fundamental rights are even more important. Underscoring this unreasonableness, a prohibition against odorous substances and flavouring agents hinders the sales of manufacturers of tobacco products that contain such substances to a greater extent.

Moreover, it must also be taken into consideration that applicable law already stipulates far-reaching restrictions on the distribution and production of tobacco products with regard to both production and packaging.[577] The existing burden on the manufacturers of tobacco products must also be considered when examining the principle of proportionality regarding the introduction of additional restrictions. Thus, the combination of the prohibitions proves, at any rate, to be disproportionate and thus impermissible.

---

575 D III 4 a below.

576 D III 4 a below.

577 A I 1 b above; *Schroeder*, ZLR 2012, 414f. Also see the comparative description of advertising regulations in EU law by *Marwitz*, K & R 2004, esp. 213f. On the financial burdens on manufacturers *Riessen* inter alia, Assessing the Impacts of Revising the Tobacco Products Directive, Rand, 2010, 81.

C. Free movement of goods

I. General

1. Prohibition of measures having equivalent effect

The free movement of goods, which is firmly established in EU primary law, aims to eliminate all restraints on cross-border trade within the Union. To this end all means of restricting trade through tariffs, such as customs duties, are prohibited under Art. 30 TFEU; restrictions that are non-tariff based, such as quantitative restrictions, and all measures having equivalent effect are prohibited under Art. 34–36 TFEU.[578] Art. 34 TFEU that, in addition to quantitative restrictions, also includes all measures having equivalent effect is of interest in the present context. It will become apparent that the scope of application of measures having equivalent effect is extremely broad and includes every hindrance of cross-border trade, at least if domestic goods are not subject to the same hindrances.[579] Therefore, if the regulations on the production and sale of tobacco products hinder the activities of a tobacco manufacturer in another Member State, the requirements of Art. 34 TFEU must be examined.

2. Parties bound

aa) The prohibition under Art. 34 TFEU initially addresses the Member States. In this respect the prohibition has been applied in many cases. This is of significance in the present case if Germany issues regulations on the production or sale of tobacco products without being obliged to do so under EU law.

bb) In addition, Art. 34 TFEU binds the Union and its bodies, institutions and offices. According to principle, the Union promotes cross-border trade rather than hinders it. The wording of Art. 34 TFEU is in this respect open to interpretation.[580] It is difficult to understand why the Union would be "unrestricted" in infringing the free movement of goods since this is a central component of primary EU law. In addition, Art. 3 (3) (1) EU Treaty stipulates the establishment of an internal market as a goal to be achieved by the Union. The European Court of Justice has acknowledged accordingly that the Union is also bound by the requirements pertaining to the free movement of goods and, in particular, the prohibition set out under Art. 34

---

[578] Cf. *Kingreen*, in: Calliess/Ruffert (ed.), EUV/AEUV, 4the ed. 2011, Art. 34–36 para. 117.
[579] C II 1 b below.
[580] *Schroeder*, in: Streinz (ed.), EUV/EGV, 2003, Art. 30 para. 25.

TFEU. This applies to regulations of the Union on labelling and packaging and the composition and presentation of products[581] as well as for the Union's prohibitions of production and movement based on health protection grounds.[582]

II. Requirements

1. Scope of protection and restrictions

a) Cross-border movement of goods

Art. 34 TFEU applies when goods are exported to another Member State if they originate from a Member State or if they move freely in a Member State.[583] This requirement is easily fulfilled in the present case when the tobacco products manufactured in one Member State are sold in another Member State.

b) Measures with equivalent effect (principles)

The prohibition under Art. 34 TFEU is particularly impaired through measures having equivalent effect. The classic definition of measures having equivalent effect can be found in the Dassonville formula of the European Court of Justice: all legislation "which is capable of hindering, directly or indirectly, actually or potentially, intra-Community trade".[584] The scope of the application of Art. 34 TFEU thereby described was subsequently limited by the Keck decision in the case of non-discriminatory regulations. This is important in the present case since the regulations on tobacco production and the sale of tobacco products would apply uniformly to products from all Member States. Only regulations that, in law or in fact, obstruct the market access of products from another Member State, hinder them more than they obstruct, or hinder domestic products are to be considered measures having equivalent effect.[585]

---

[581] *ECJ*, case 51/93, ECR 1994 I-3879 para. 11 ff.; case 169/99, ECR 2001, I-5901 para. 37 ff.; *Schroeder*, in: Streinz (ed.), EUV/EGV, 2003, Art. 28 para. 29.

[582] *ECJ*, case 284/95, ECR 1998 I-4301 para. 62 ff.; *Schroeder*, in: Streinz (ed.), EUV/EGV, 2003, Art. 28 para. 29.

[583] *Kingreen*, in: Calliess/Ruffert (ed.), EUV/AEUV, 4th ed. 2011, Art. 34–36 para. 120; *Schroeder*, in: Streinz (ed.), EUV/EGV, 2003, Art. 28 para. 20.

[584] *ECJ*, case 8/74, ECR 1974, 837 para. 5; also recently *ECJ*, case 421/09 of 9.12.2010, para. 26; case 291/09 of 7.4.2011, para. 15; case 456/10 of 26.4.2012, para. 32.

[585] *ECJ*, case 267/91, ECR 1993, I-6097 para. 17; also *ECJ*, case 239/02, ECR 2004, I-7007 para. 51; case 20/03 ECR 2005, I-4133 para. 24.

c) Measures having equivalent effect in the present context

aa) This requirement is generally fulfilled if and to the extent that brand packaging, product display in retail sales facilities or odorous substances and flavouring agents are prohibited by German regulations if there is no such obligation under EU law. In such cases, there are differing provisions in the other Member States that inevitably hinder the cross-border distribution of tobacco products.

bb) The situation differs when the European Union has issued regulations accordingly. These then apply uniformly in all Member States, which does not interfere with cross-border trade, but rather facilitates it. However, there is a peculiarity that must be noted in the present case:

It is much more probable that a manufacturer who has not yet been active in a national market will be able to penetrate the market of another Member State if the products are branded with a specific trademark. In this case, the trademark can be used for advertising, which is indispensable for the foreign manufacturer, whereby domestic manufacturers can rely on the existing customer base. The protection of trademarks thus promotes the free movement of goods. Thus, the European Court of Justice has deemed that the Union's regulation of labelling, packaging, content and presentation of products does impair the free movement of goods.[586] The ECJ has also stated that, "measures prohibiting or restricting the advertising of tobacco products are liable to impede access to the market for products from other Member States more than they impede access for domestic products."[587] The same applies for a prohibition of advertising for tobacco products for oral use,[588] as well as in a recent decision on wholesale obligations for tobacco products.[589] Finally, the EFTA Court considered a prohibition against the display of tobacco products in retail sales facilities as a measure potentially having equivalent effect.[590]

Through the prohibition of brand packaging, the manufacturer loses an important instrument for penetrating the market of another Member State. Without such branding the consumer is not really able to recognize the special features of products from another Member State. A similar analysis applies for the prohibition of product display in retail facilities since the consumer is not able to see the product in

---

586 C I 2 bb above.
587 *ECJ*, case 380/03, ECR 2006, I-11573 para. 56.
588 *ECJ*, case 434/02, ECR 2004, I-11825 para. 59; *Streinz*, ZUR 2005, 431.
589 ECJ, case 456/10 of 26.4.2012 para. 37 ff.
590 EFTA Court, case E-16/10 of 12.9.2011, para. 42.

the stores without taking any further actions.⁵⁹¹ Ultimately, there is a strong indication that the regulations burden domestic manufacturers far less. Here it has to be noted that to assume a measure having equivalent effect, it is sufficient if there is the *possibility* that the burden on foreign manufacturers is greater; a "potentially" restricting effect is sufficient.⁵⁹²

In summary, prohibitions of brand packaging, of product display in retail sales facilities and of odorous substances and flavouring agents in tobacco products can also hinder cross-border trade of such products, if the prohibitions apply uniformly and throughout the European Union. That constitutes a restriction of Art. 34 TFEU. This does not mean that a regulation that applies throughout the European Union cannot promote the free movement of goods. A uniform regulation that applies throughout the European Union can vary greatly and can be structured so that it still allows the use of the trademark to penetrate the market of another Member State.

2. Justification

a) Permissible grounds

Restrictions of Art. 34 AEUV are not necessarily impermissible, and can indeed be justified under certain conditions. Art. 36 TFEU provides the legal basis for such exceptions.⁵⁹³ In addition, at least in certain cases, it may be possible to justify them with overriding requirements related to the public interest.⁵⁹⁴ There are uncertainties with regard to the circumstances under which both of these possible justifications apply.⁵⁹⁵ However, that is not relevant in the present case. Regulation of the manufacturing and sale of tobacco products should promote the protection of health. In the context of both possible justifications this is an admissible reason. In particular, Art. 36 TFEU expressly states the "protection of health". It is also not a purely economic reason. "Purely economic grounds" cannot justify restrictions of fundamental freedoms.⁵⁹⁶

---

591 The prohibition of odorous substances and flavouring agents could also hinder penetration into the market of another Member State since certain additives can distinguish the product from domestic products; however, this issue will not be examined in further detail.

592 *ECJ*, case 249/81, ECR 1982, 4005 para. 25; case 125/85, ECR 1986, 3935 para. 7; *Schroeder*, in: Streinz (ed.), EUV/EGV, 2003, Art. 28 para. 37.

593 *Becker*, in: Schwarze, EU Commentary, 2nd ed., 2009, art. 30 para. 9 ff.

594 *Becker*, in: Schwarze, EU Commentary, 2nd ed., 2009, art. 30 para. 35 ff.

595 Cf. *Kingreen*, in: Calliess/Ruffert (ed.), EUV/AEUV, 4th ed. 2011, Art. 34–36 para. 82.

596 *ECJ*, case 456/10 of 26.4.2012, also case 254/98, ECR 2000, I-151 para. 33; *Schroeder*, in: Streinz (ed.), EUV/EGV, 2003, Art. 30 para. 48.

Free movement of goods

b) Proportionality

The protection of health cannot, however, justify every restriction of Art. 34 TFEU. Human health is indeed very important. However, just as with all restrictions of Art. 34 TFEU, restrictions to protect health are only permissible if they observe the principle of proportionality.

aa) This first requires that the questionable measure is a *suitable means* of achieving the aim whereby it is sufficient if it supports the aim.[597] The legislator has a certain assessment leeway in this respect.[598] Particularly in the area of the protection of health, protection of the environment and consumer protection, it is necessary to conduct an extensive and comprehensible risk assessment that is not limited to hypothetical considerations.[599] Thus, also with regard to tobacco products, the ECJ requires the suitability to be "shown", e.g. by way of a relevant study.[600] If the relevant facts have not been ascertained, or if a contradictory protection concept is implemented, one cannot speak of suitability.[601]

bb) The next element of proportionality, the requirement of *necessity*, is of particular importance since it plays a central role in the case law of the European Court of Justice.[602] It requires that the "objective pursued cannot be achieved by measures which are less restrictive on intra-Community trade".[603] In this respect, the Court of Justice usually applies strict standards on necessity, especially in the areas of consumer protection and health protection.[604] Thus, prohibitions on trade and prohibitions of certain product designations are not necessary if appropriate information of the consumers is sufficient.[605]

Similarly to the area of fundamental rights, the European Court of Justice often does not conduct an independent review of the appropriateness (as a third element

---

[597] *ECJ*, case 152/78, ECR1980, I-2299 para. 15 ff.

[598] *ECJ*, case 293/93, ECR 1994, I-4249 para. 22.

[599] *ECJ*, case 41/02, ECR 2004, I-11375 para. 49 ff.; *Kingreen*, in: Calliess/Ruffert (ed.), EUV/AEUV, 4th ed. 2011, Art. 34–36 para. 92.

[600] ECJ, case 456/10 of 26.4.2012, para. 50.

[601] In the first case *ECJ*, case 41/02, ECR 2004, I-11375 para. 59, in the latter case *ECJ*, case 67/88, ECR 1990, I-4285 para. 6; *Kingreen*, in: Calliess/Ruffert (ed.), EUV/AEUV, 4th ed. 2011, Art. 34–36 para. 92.

[602] *Kingreen*, in: Calliess/Ruffert (ed.), EUV/AEUV, 4th ed. 2011, Art. 34–36 para. 93.

[603] *ECJ*, case 25/88, ECR 1989, 1105 para. 13 ff.; case 70/93, ECR 1995, I-1923 para. 15; case 67/97, ECR 1998, I-8033 para. 35.

[604] *Schroeder*, in: Streinz (ed.), EUV/EGV, 2003, Art. 30 para. 55. Concerning tobacco products, the ECJ has required, as for the question of suitability, the necessity of a measure to be shown, ECJ case 456/10 of 26.4.2012, para. 50.

[605] *ECJ*, case 315/92, ECR 1994, I-317 para. 20 ff.; case 470/93, ECR 1995, I-1923 para. 24; case 51/94, ECR 1995, I-3599 para. 34.

of proportionality). On the other hand, a certain balancing of the benefits and restrictions does take place during the assessment of necessity.[606] In this matter, and in general, the principle of proportionality depends on a balanced weighting of the interests concerned.[607] The extent to which cross-border trade is impaired is of particular importance.[608]

c) In relation to fundamental rights

The European Court of Justice has often addressed the relationship between the fundamental freedoms concerning the internal market and the fundamental rights. Depending on the circumstances, the fundamental rights and the fundamental freedoms can limit or strengthen one another.[609] The latter is of importance in the present context. The Court of Justice stated that restrictions of fundamental freedoms must also be measured against the fundamental rights such as the freedom of expression and information.[610] Conversely, restrictions of fundamental rights can be impermissible if they contradict the fundamental freedoms.[611] In such cases, the fundamental freedoms and the fundamental rights reinforce one another. This must be noted in the context of the respective assessments of proportionality.

d) Applicability in the present context

If one applies the requirements with regard to the proportionality of an Art. 34 TFEU restriction in the present context, then the key issues are similar to those where the justification of infringements of fundamental rights is concerned. It is thus possible to refer to the relevant comments on the proportionality of the prohibition of brand packaging and the prohibition of product display in retail sales facilities.[612]

In addition, or in derogation, the following must be noted: first, the regulations of the production and sale of tobacco products also impair the free movement of goods. In the context of assessing the justification, it must therefore be taken into account that not only the individual interests of the manufacturer (and the consumer)

---

606 *Schroeder*, in: Streinz (ed.), EUV/EGV, 2003, Art. 30 para. 54. with evidence.
607 B III 2 b above.
608 *Kingreen*, in: Calliess/Ruffert (ed.), EUV/AEUV, 4th ed. 2011, Art. 34–36 para. 98.
609 For details *Jarass*, Charta der Grundrechte, 2010, Intro. 24 ff. with evidence.
610 *ECJ, case* 260/89, ECR 1991, I-2925 para. 43 f; case 368/95, ECR 1997, I-3689 para. 24 f; *Streinz*, in: Streinz (ed.), EUV/EGV, 2003, Art. 11 para. 6.
611 *Jarass*, Charta der Grundrechte, 2010, Intro. 27.
612 B IV 1 b and B IV 2 b above.

are affected, but the Union's material interest in the free movement of goods is also encroached upon. This increases the requirements that apply to such justification.

The European Court of Justice carries out a strict assessment of proportionality with regard to fundamental freedoms, as compared to the areas of the right to property and professional or entrepreneurial freedom. Consequently, it is the responsibility of the legislator to always provide evidence of proportionality.[613] Scientific findings or international standards must be provided as comprehensible evidence of the necessity of an infringement.[614]

In the present context, it is therefore significant that the benefits of the prohibitions examined entail significant uncertainties for the protection of health, and that there are no practical indications of such protection.[615] On the other hand, as demonstrated, this not only concerns serious infringements upon fundamental rights,[616] but also a significant hindrance of the free movement of goods. This suggests that the legislator is restricted to measures that do not fully devalue the ability to use trademark rights since their utilisation is indispensable for manufacturers of tobacco products in other Member States.[617] If in the context of fundamental rights there is evidence that suggests that a prohibition of brand packaging does not observe the principle of proportionality,[618] then this must all the more be the case if the restriction of Art. 34 TFEU is additionally taken into account. The concerns regarding the proportionality of a prohibition of product display in retail sales facilities are also reinforced.[619] The requirements pertaining to the free movement of goods increase the protection of the fundamental rights concerned and vice versa.

---

613 *ECJ*, case ECR 174/82, ECR 1983, 2445 para. 22; case 13/91, ECR 1992, I-3617 para. 18; *Schroeder*, in: Streinz (ed.), EUV/EGV, 2003, Art. 30 para. 57.

614 *ECJ*, case 17/93, ECR 1994, I-3537 para. 17; case 473/98, ECR 2000, I-5681 para. 40 ff.; case 192/01, ECR 2003, I-9693 para. 46; case 150/00, ECR 2004, I-3887 para. 89.

615 Cf. B IV 1 b, B IV 2 b and B IV 3 b above.

616 B IV 1 a, B IV 2 a and B IV 3 a above.

617 The EFTA Court also deemed the following issue to be important: whether there are sufficient means which are less severe than prohibition of product display; EFTA Court, Case E-16/10 of 12.9.2011, para. 85 ff.

618 B IV 1 b above.

619 B IV 2 b above on these concerns.

D. Basic rights under German Basic Law

I. Principles and infringed basic rights

1. Parties bound by the Basic Law and those entitled to basic rights

a) Obligations of EU bodies under the basic rights

The last part of this examination will address the extent to which a prohibition of brand packaging, a prohibition of product display in retail sales facilities, and a prohibition of odorous substances and flavouring agents in tobacco products would be compatible with the Basic Law. This raises the question of whether, and if so to what extent, legal acts of the Union are bound by the basic rights of German Basic Law.[620]

The basic rights under the Basic Law are only binding for domestic public authorities. Bodies, institutions and agencies of the European Union are thus not bound by the basic rights.[621] The acknowledgement, transposition and application of EU Acts also do not depend on their compatibility with the basic rights pursuant to Art. 23 (1) Basic Law as long as the European Union, in particular the case law of the European Court of Justice, generally guarantee an effective level of protection for the basic rights vis-à-vis the Union which is to be considered essentially equal to the protection of basic rights afforded by the Basic Law.[622] To deem this requirement as unfulfilled, it is not sufficient if such protection of basic rights is not maintained in individual cases; to the contrary, this would require a general lack of protection.[623] That is a high hurdle that is hardly surmountable in practice.[624] Since and as long as EU law at least generally provides sufficient protection of basic rights, German basic rights do not apply with regard to legal acts of the Union.[625]

In the present context this means that legal acts of the European Union to regulate the production and sale of tobacco products, regardless of their nature, cannot be measured against the basic rights of the Basic Law. They are only bound by

---

620 The view of German constitutional law is used as a basis.
621 *Kunig*, in: v.Münch/Kunig, GG-Kommentar, Vol.I, 5th ed. 2000, Art. 1 para. 52; *Jarass*, in: Jarass/Pieroth, Grundgesetz, 11th ed. 2011, Art. 1 para. 46; probably also *BVerfGE* (Decisions of the Federal Constitutional Court) 118, 79/95; unclear Decisions of the Federal Constitutional Court 89, 155/174 f
622 *BVerfGE* 118, 79/95; 73, 339/387; 102, 147/162 ff; 123, 267/335.
623 *BVerfGE* 102, 147/164; BVerfG, NVwZ 07, 942.
624 *Streinz*, in: Sachs (ed.), Grundgesetz, 5th ed. 2009, Art. 23 para. 41.
625 *BVerfGE* 73, 339/378, 387; 102, 147/164; *BVerwGE* (Decisions of the Federal Administrative Court) 85, 24/29 f; *Classen*, in: v.Mangoldt/Klein/Starck, Grundgesetz, 6th ed., Vol.II 2010, Art. 23 para. 50.

b) Obligation of German institutions based on basic rights

To the contrary, activities of German institutions are to be measured against the basic rights of the Basic Law regardless of whether such activities are purely domestic, or include a foreign element.[626] This also applies to activities of German institutions issued to implement or execute EU law if, and to the extent that, EU law allows leeway.[627] In general, national institutions must fully observe the basic rights of the Basic Law if they are not bound by EU law.[628] That, within the leeway allowed by EU law, the fundamental rights of the EU must also be observed does, in general, not contradict application of the basic rights under German Basic Law since the fundamental rights of the European Union do not exclude further-reaching national basic rights.[629] Naturally, the priority of other Union law has to be observed.[630] Only where EU law does "not allow any leeway in implementation, but stipulates mandatory requirements", is it not possible to measure acts to implement EU law carried out by German institutions against German basic rights.[631]

In the present context, this means that when the German legislator drafts regulations on the production or sale of tobacco products without being obliged to do so under EU law, the basic rights of the Basic Law are fully binding. Even if the legislator acts to implement requirements of EU law, the German basic rights apply to the extent that EU law allows leeway.

c) Those entitled to basic rights

Pursuant to Art. 19 (3) Basic Law the basic rights concerned here, the freedom of profession under Art. 12 Basic Law, the protection of property under Art. 14 Basic Law and the freedom of expression under Art. 5 Basic Law, apply to natural persons as well as legal entities, as long as they are domestic legal entitles. This requirement

---

[626] BVerfGE 6, 290/295; 57, 9/23; *Herdegen*, in: Maunz/Dürig, Grundgesetz, as of 2010, 71; *Höfling*, in: Sachs (ed.), Grundgesetz, 5th ed. 2009, Art. 1 para. 86; *Badura*, in: Merten/Papier (ed.), Handbuch der Grundrechte, Vol.II, 2006, §47 para. 4.

[627] BVerfGE 113, 273/300; 118, 79/96

[628] *Dreier*, in: Dreier (ed.), Grundgesetz, Vol.I, 2nd ed. 2004, Art. 19 III para. 13; *Pieroth/Schlink*, Grundrechte, 26th ed. 2010, para. 191.

[629] On the relationship of the two levels of basic rights *Jarass*, Charta der Grundrechte, 2010, Art. 53 para. 10 ff.

[630] *Jarass*, in: Jarass/Pieroth, Grundgesetz, 11th ed. 2011, Art. 23 para. 27.

[631] BVerfGE 118, 79/95; BVerfG, NJW 01, 1267.

is satisfied if the legal entity is based in Germany, meaning the actual centre of its activities operate within German territory;[632] the citizenship or place of residence of the shareholders is not decisive for basic rights which apply to anybody, and therefore not for the basic rights concerned here.[633] Under EU law, legal entities and bodies of persons from the EU-area are to be treated as domestic associations, as the Federal Constitutional Court has just recently ascertained.[634]

2. Freedom of profession

a) Scope of protection

The freedom of profession under Art. 12 Basic Law protects "any gainful activity which is not exhausted through a one-time gain".[635] This requirement is regularly fulfilled by legal entities if carrying out business operations is among the purposes set out in its statutes.[636] In addition to the choice of profession, exercise thereof, meaning the entire professional activity, in particular form, means, and scope, as well as its structure, are protected.[637] The basic right also includes the right to individually determine the manner and quality of goods and services offered.[638] The professional external presentation or image also falls under the scope of protection,[639] and professional advertising as well.[640] Finally, operational and business secrets are also protected.[641]

In this light, there is no doubt in the present context that the use of brand packaging falls within the scope of the protection of freedom of profession. The same

---

632 BVerfG, NJW 09, 2519; *Huber*, in: v.Mangoldt/Klein/Starck, Grundgesetz, Vol. 1, 6th ed. 2010, 299; *Tettinger*, in: Merten/Papier (ed.), Handbuch der Grundrechte, Vol.II, §51 para. 45

633 BVerfGE, NVwZ 00, 1282; NVwZ 08, 671; *Enders*, in: Epping/Hillgruber (ed.), Grundgesetz, 2009, 36.

634 BVerfG, 1 BvR 1916/09 of 19.7.2011; *Dreier*, in: Dreier (ed.), Grundgesetz, Vol.I, 2nd ed. 2004, Art. para. 83; *Tettinger*, in: Merten/Papier (ed.), Handbuch der Grundrechte, Vol. HGR II §51 para. 49.

635 *BVerfGE* 97, 228/253.

636 *BVerfGE* 97, 228/253 with evidence.

637 *Breuer*, in: Isensee/Kirchhof (ed.), Handbuch des Staatsrechts, 3rd ed. 2009, Vol.VIII §170 para. 82; *Manssen*, in: v.Mangoldt/Klein/Starck, Grundgesetz, Vol. 1, 6th ed. 2010, Art. 12 para. 66; *Gubelt*, in: v.Münch/Kunig, GG-Kommentar, Vol.I, 5th ed. 2000, Art. 12 para. 38.

638 *BVerfGE* 106, 275/299; 121, 317/345.

639 *BVerfGE* 106, 181/192; 112, 255/262.

640 *BVerfGE* 94, 372/389; 105, 252/266; 111, 366/373; BGHZ 147, 71/74; BVerwGE 124, 26/28.

641 *BVerfGE* 115, 205/229.

applies to displaying tobacco products in retail sales facilities.[642] Use of odorous substances and flavouring agents during the manufacturing of tobacco products is protected by the freedom of profession as well.

b) Infringement

The prohibition of brand packaging, the prohibition of product display in retail facilities and the prohibition of odorous substances and flavouring agents in tobacco products qualify as encroachments of the freedom of profession under Art. 12 Basic Law.[643] These are binding requirements regarding the activities protected under Art. 12 Basic Law.[644] Moreover, the prohibitions indicate a tendency to regulate professions since they pertain to activities that are typically exercised professionally.[645]

Ultimately, a prohibition of product display in retail facilities does not only infringe the freedom of profession of the retailer. Since the measure has massive implications for the *manufacturers* of tobacco products, it is also infringement of the freedom of profession of the manufacturer even though the burden is only of an indirect nature. The manufacturer is affected to a far greater extent than the retailer if tobacco products only comprise a minor portion of the assortment offered by the retailer. It is an indirect restriction that is the equivalent of an infringement with regard to purpose and effect.[646] Additionally, this is an intended effect.[647]

3. Right to property

a) Positions worthy of protection

The basic right of Art. 14 Basic Law not only protects property within the meaning of the German Civil Code, but every right which qualifies as an asset granted by

---

642 See D I 2 b below with regard to the issue of whether only the retailer is affected in its freedom of profession.
643 Also, on the prohibition of brand packaging, *Stein/Rauber*, Rechtliche Grenzen der Bekämpfung des Tabakkonsums im Mehrebenensystem, 2011, 44; *Schwarz*, in: Pache/ Schwarz/Sosnitza, Aktuelle Rechtsfragen der Tabakregulierung in Europa, 2012, 121.
644 Cf. *Jarass*, in: Jarass/Pieroth, Grundgesetz, 11th ed. 2011, Art. 12 para. 14.
645 *BVerfGE* 97, 228/254; similarly *BVerfGE* 111, 191/213.
646 This is crucial for the assumption of an encroachment of basic rights; *BVerfGE* 105, 252/273; 110, 177/191; 116, 202/222.
647 On the relevance of this *BVerwGE* 71, 183/193 f; 90, 112/121 f.

the legislator,⁶⁴⁸ at least if it is subject to private law.⁶⁴⁹ This includes, in particular, the right to brand names or to trademarks as stated by the Federal Constitutional Court and the Federal Court of Justice⁶⁵⁰ and supported by legal commentary.⁶⁵¹ In addition, independent business secrets that qualify as assets are also protected.⁶⁵²

Whether Art. 14 Basic Law also protects established and practised business operations as a whole ("Recht am eingerichteten und ausgeübten Gewerbebetrieb") is unclear. This could be significant in the present case. The Federal Constitutional Court has expressly left open the applicability of Art. 14 Basic Law,⁶⁵³ whereby other courts and the literature affirms it,⁶⁵⁴ at least where the substance of this right is concerned.⁶⁵⁵ This issue does not have to be addressed in the present context. The prohibition of brand packaging concerns trademark law which, as demonstrated, is an area worthy of protection within the meaning of Art. 14 Basic Law. The same applies to the prohibition of product display in retail sales facilities since trademark law is significant with regard to product display. Finally, the prohibition of odorous substances and flavouring agents constitutes an encroachment on the right to property if the substances are a business secret.

b) Infringement

Art. 14 Basic Law protects, in particular, the use of property.⁶⁵⁶ If, therefore, the use of the trademark is subject to restrictions then this constitutes an infringement of Art. 14 Basic Law. That applies to the prohibition of brand packaging and the

---

648 Decisions of the *BVerfGE* 24, 367/396; 53, 257/290; 58, 300/336; *Papier*, in: Maunz/Dürig, Grundgesetz, as of 2010, Art. 14 para. 55; *Bryde*, in: v.Münch/Kunig, GG-Kommentar, Vol.I, 5th ed. 2000, Art. 14 para. 59.

649 On the situation with positions under public law see *Jarass*, in: Jarass/Pieroth, Grundgesetz, 11th ed. 2011, Art. 14 para. 11ff.

650 Decisions of the *BVerfGE* 51, 193/217; 78, 58/71; 95, 173/188; BGH, GRUR 2009, 678ff.

651 *Wieland*, in: Dreier (ed.), Grundgesetz, Vol.I, 2nd ed. 2004, Art. 14 para. 60; *Jarass*, in: Jarass/Pieroth, Grundgesetz, 11th ed. 2011, Art. 14 para. 9; *Depenheuer*, in: v.Mangoldt/Klein/Starck, Grundgesetz, Vol. 1, 6th ed. 2010, Art. 14 para. 15.

652 *Breuer*, in: Isensee/Kirchhof (ed.), Handbuch des Staatsrechts, 3rd ed. 2009, Vol.VIII, § 171 para. 38; cf. *BVerfGE* 77, 1/46; *BVerwGE* 115, 319/325 f; 125, 40 para. 7.

653 Decisions of the *BVerfGE* 77, 84/118; 81, 208/227 f; 96, 375/397; 105, 252/278; also *BVerwGE* 118, 226/241.

654 BGHZ 92, 34/37; FCJ, DVBl 2001, 1671; *Papier*, in: Maunz/Dürig, Grundgesetz, as of 2010, Art. 14 para. 95 ff; *Dietlein*, in: Stern, Staatsrecht, Vol.IV/1, 2191; against protection *Wieland*, in: Dreier (ed.), Grundgesetz, Vol.I, 2nd ed. 2004, Art. 14 para. 52

655 BGHZ 161, 305/312.

656 *BVerfGE* 88, 366/377; 98, 17/35; 101, 54/75; BGHZ 157, 144/147; *Axer*, in: Epping/Hillgruber (ed.), Grundgesetz, 2009, 64.

prohibition of product display in retail facilities. The situation differs considerably in this respect from a case in which warnings are required without restricting the function of the trademark as a guarantee related to the individual manufacturer.[657] Furthermore, a prohibition against using certain business secrets that are valued as assets, such as the formula for tobacco products, constitutes an infringement of the right to property since it makes it impossible to exercise the right.

4. Freedom of expression

Finally, the freedom of expression under Art. 5 (1) Basic Law could also be affected to the extent that it involves the prohibition of brand packaging and product display in retail facilities since it hinders the transmission of information to the consumer. The Basic Law also protects the expression of an opinion even if its expected result is to produce economic advantages.[658] Commercial advertising is included, accordingly, to the extent that it contains "judgemental opinion forming content or information, which serves to form opinions".[659] However, it must be pointed out that, in the view of the Federal Constitutional Court, the obligation to have warnings on packages affects manufacturers and distributors of tobacco products in the distribution of their goods, but not in the procedure of expressing and communicating their opinions, with the consequence that the labelling requirements must be assessed on the basis of the freedom of profession and not the freedom of expression.[660] This suggests that a prohibition of brand packaging and of product display in retail sales facilities does not affect Art. 5 (1) Basic Law.

On the other hand, it cannot be overlooked that in its opinion the Federal Constitutional Court essentially emphasised that the warnings are designed to imply that they do not express the manufacturer's opinion.[661] As regards the restrictions on brand packaging and product display there is no such indication. This could suggest that the freedom of expression is relevant in the present context.[662] Moreo-

---

657 The Decisions of the Federal Constitutional Court 95, 173/188 made significant reference to this.
658 *BVerfGE* 30, 336/352.
659 *BVerfGE* 95, 173/182; 102, 347/359; BGHZ 130, 196/203; *Starck*, in: v.Mangoldt/Klein/Starck, Grundgesetz, Vol. 1, 6th ed. 2010, Art. 5 para. 25; *Wendt*, in: v.Münch/Kunig, GG-Kommentar, Vol. I, 5th ed. 2000, Art. 5 para. 11.
660 Decisions of the Federal Constitutional Court 95, 173/181.
661 Decisions of the *BVerfGE* 95, 173 (182) The warnings contained such an indication.
662 *Stein/Rauber*, Rechtliche Grenzen der Bekämpfung des Tabakkonsums im Mehrebenensystem, 2011, 41 f.; also on warnings without mention of author *Hardach/Ludwigs*, DÖV 2007, 292; *Wachovius*, BayVBl 2005, 618. It is interesting that on 7.11.2011 the U.S. District Court in Washington issued an order against warnings on cigarette packages and referred to the freedom of expression.

ver, the legal commentary correctly asserts that Art. 5 Basic Law also protects the transmission of others' opinions.[663]

This issue will not be addressed here in further detail and in the following it will be assumed that the freedom of expression is not relevant. Both the prohibition on brand packaging and on product display in retail sales facilities contain, as demonstrated, an encroachment on the freedom of profession under Art. 12 Basic Law and of the right to property under Art. 14 Basic Law.[664] The freedom of expression is not likely to convey further-reaching protection with regard to these basic rights.[665] Unlike the right to property and entrepreneurial freedom at the European level, both the freedom of profession under Art. 12 Basic Law and the right to property under Art. 14 Basic Law demonstrate a far-reaching protective effect. In particular, according to the case law of the Federal Constitutional Court, these basic rights are also effectively reviewed with regard to proportionality.

II. Justification of the infringements

1. Freedom of profession

a) *Statutory basis and level of regulation*

aa) Any infringement of the freedom of profession requires a legal basis, however it does not necessarily have to be of a formal statutory nature.[666] Nonetheless, the parliament itself has to regulate all *issues* that are *essential* for the exercise of basic rights, in particular intensive infringements.[667] Furthermore, the law restricting the use of basic rights must be sufficiently specific, and the "scope and limits of the infringement have to be clearly recognisable".[668] The requirements on the specificity of the law are even greater the more intense the infringement upon the freedom of profession.[669]

---

663 *Kloepfer*, Produkthinweispflichten bei Tabakwaren als Verfassungsfrage, 1991, 28 ff.; *Kirchhof/Frick*, AfP 1991, 679; *Merten*, DÖV 1990, 768; see also *Koenig/Kühling*, EWS 2002, 14.
664 D I 2 b, D I 3 b above.
665 Cf. on protection through the freedom of expression *Hardach/Ludwigs*, DÖV 2007, 293 f.
666 Dietlein, in: Stern, Staatsrecht, Vol.IV/1, 2006, 1884 f.
667 *BVerfGE* 38, 373/381; 94, 372/390; *Manssen*, in: v.Mangoldt/Klein/Starck, Grundgesetz, Vol. 1, 6th ed. 2010, Art. 12 para. 119; *Wieland*, in: Dreier (ed.), Grundgesetz, Vol.I, 2nd ed. 2004, Art. 12 para. 98.
668 *BVerfGE* 86, 28/40.
669 *BVerfGE* 87, 287/317 f; 98, 49/60; 101, 312/323.

bb) The requirements for justification of the infringement upon the freedom of profession essentially depend on the level to which the encroachment takes place. A distinction is made between regulations governing professional practice and subjective and objective regulations regarding the choice of profession.[670] Regulations governing professional practice do not influence the choice of profession. If a regulation regarding professional activity is so severe that it makes it impossible to reasonably carry out the profession (not only in isolated cases),[671] it is regarded as restricting the choice of profession.[672] Despite the serious burden of a prohibition of brand packaging, of a prohibition of product display in retail sales facilities or a prohibition of odorous substances and flavouring agents, it is unlikely that these measures would be regarded as regulating the choice of profession.[673] Therefore, the requirements for regulations regarding the exercise of activities apply. This is still a borderline case considering the weight of the infringement of the basic rights, which has to be taken into account for the assessment of proportionality.[674]

b) Proportionality

aa) Infringements in practicing a profession must reflect the principle of proportionality.[675] This means that the infringement in question must be *suitable* to achieve the aims pursued.[676] A means is "suitable when it helps to achieve the aim being pursued".[677] Furthermore, the infringement must be *necessary*; that means it cannot be possible to achieve the aim through other means that are less of a burden on the party entitled to the basic rights.[678] This also applies to regulations governing professional practice as the findings of the Federal Constitutional Court repeatedly

---

[670] Cf. the evidence in *Jarass*, in: Jarass/Pieroth, Grundgesetz, 11th ed. 2011, Art. 12 para. 45 ff.

[671] *BVerfGE* 30, 292/315 f; 31, 8/29; 68, 155/170 f; Decisions of the Federal Administrative Court 120, 311/334.

[672] *BVerfGE* 123, 186/239; *Dietlein*, in: Stern, Staatsrecht, Vol. IV/1, 2006, 1901; *Manssen*, in: v. Mangoldt/Klein/Starck, Grundgesetz, Vol. 1, 6th ed. 2010, Art. 12 para. 142.

[673] Also, on the prohibition of brand packaging, *Stein/Rauber*, Rechtliche Grenzen der Bekämpfung des Tabakkonsums im Mehrebenensystem, 2011, 45.

[674] *Jarass*, in: Jarass/Pieroth, Grundgesetz, 11th ed. 2011, Art. 12 para. 37.

[675] *BVerfGE* 117, 163 (182).

[676] *BVerfGE* 46, 120/145 f; 68, 193/218.

[677] *BVerfGE* 115, 276/308; also *BVerfGE* 80, 1/24 f; 117, 163/188.

[678] *BVerfGE* 30, 292/316; 53, 135/145; 69, 209/218 f.

confirm.[679] An infringement is "only necessary if there is no other means with equivalent effect which is a less tangible restriction of the freedom of profession".[680]

An infringement of basic rights cannot be disproportionate to the aim pursued; it must be "appropriate".[681] The "limits of reasonableness" must be maintained in the overall evaluation of the weight of the encroachment and the "weight of the grounds which justify it".[682] In particular, the greater the infringement of the freedom of profession, the greater the weight of the aim pursued must be. Generally, the infringement is regarded as less severe for regulations governing professional practice than for those regarding the choice of a profession. Therefore, the legislator is given considerable leeway in its assessment.[683] On the other hand, it must be noted that when the freedom to *exercise* a profession is severely impaired, the interests that justify such an infringement must be particularly significant.[684]

bb) Ultimately, the specific burden on subgroups must be taken into account. Even if a regulation is reasonable for the majority of those affected, it can still infringe Art. 12 (1) Basic Law as read with Art. 3 (1) Basis Law if a subgroup is typically impacted to a far greater extent and thus requires special treatment.[685] Conversely, identical risks arising in a law cannot be weighted differently.[686]

2. Right to property

a) Determining content and limits, legal basis, other constitutional law

aa) Since Art. 14 Basic Law contains two different types of restrictions, the justification for restrictions on property differs depending on whether it involves the regulation of the content and limits ("Inhalts- und Schrankenbestimmung") of property or if it is a case of *expropriation*. Whereby justification of expropriation is based on the strict requirements of Art. 14 (3) Basic Law, determining the content and limits of property is measured against Art. 14 (1) (2) Basic Law and Art. 14 (2) Basic Law. This raises the issue of whether the measures to be examined here can be considered as an expropriation. The prohibition of brand packaging and the

---

679 *BVerfGE* 101, 331/347; 104, 357/364; 106, 216/219.
680 *BVerfGE* 80, 1/30; 30, 292/316; also *BVerfGE* 75, 246/269; 117, 163/189.
681 *BVerfGE* 117, 163/192 f.
682 *BVerfGE* 102, 197/220; also *BVerfGE* 51, 193/208.
683 *BVerfGE* 116, 202/224 ff; 117, 163/182 f, 189; 121, 317/356.
684 *BVerfGE* 61, 291/311; 77, 84/106; 103, 1/10; 121, 317/355; BSGE 60, 76/78.
685 *BVerfGE* 30, 292/327; 59, 336/355 f; 65, 116/126 f; 68, 155/173; *BVerwG*, DVBl 01, 743.
686 *BVerfGE* 121, 317/362.

prohibition of product display in retail sales facilities results in a significant loss of importance of trademark rights and thus a legal position protected by Art. 14 Basic Law.[687]

The definition of expropriation within the meaning of Art. 14 (3) Basic Law has been limited in the recent case law of the Federal Constitutional Court. Expropriation "is complete or partial deprivation of specific subjective property within the meaning of Art. 14 (1) (1) Basic Law to satisfy certain public functions".[688] In the present context, one could possibly speak of a partial deprivation of trademark rights. However, the requirement that the right must be intended to fulfill a public function is not satisfied. Therefore, the prohibitions addressed here are to be considered as the determination of the content and limits of property, at least if one follows the case law of the Federal Constitutional Court.

bb) A regulation regarding the content and limits of property can occur through any legal norm. The prerequisite, therefore, is formal legal authorization.[689] The law must respect the competency order set out in the Basic Law.[690] However, a regulation on content and limits must also satisfy all other constitutional norms.[691] In particular, the requirements of the principle of equality under Art. 3 (1) Basic Law must be observed.[692]

b) Proportionality

Any provision on the content and limits of property must observe the principle of proportionality.[693] The relevant provision must also be suitable for, and support, the aim pursued.[694] The provision on content and limits cannot restrict the owner more than required by the legislative aim;[695] no less severe alternative can

---

687 Legal commentaries also assume expropriation; *Kunz-Hallstein*, in: Bender/Schülke/Winterfeldt (ed.), 50 Jahre Bundespatentgericht, 2011, 668.
688 *BVerfGE* 70, 191/199 f; 72, 66/76; 102, 1/15; similarly *BVerfGE* 104, 1/9; BGHZ 99, 24/28; *BVerwGE* 77, 295/297; *Papier*, in: Maunz/Dürig, Grundgesetz, as of 2010, Art. 14 para. 527.
689 *Depenheuer*, in: v.Mangoldt/Klein/Starck, Grundgesetz, Vol. 1, 6th ed. 2010, Art. 14 para. 220; a. A. *Papier*, in: Maunz/Dürig, Grundgesetz, as of 2010, Art. 14 para. 339.
690 *BVerfGE* 34, 139/146; 58, 137/145.
691 *BVerfGE* 62, 169/183; 102, 1/17; 110, 1/28; *Wieland*, in: Dreier (ed.), Grundgesetz, Vol.I, 2nd ed. 2004, Art. 14 para. 129; *Papier*, in: Maunz/Dürig, Grundgesetz, as of 2010, Art. 14 para. 326.
692 *BVerfGE* 79, 174/198; 87, 114/139; 102, 1/17; 126, 331/360.
693 *BVerfGE* 75, 78/97 f; 76, 220/238; 92, 262/273; 110, 1/28; *Dietlein*, in: Stern, Staatsrecht, Vol.IV/1, 2247; *Bryde*, in: v.Münch/Kunig, GG-Kommentar, Vol.I, 5th ed. 2000, Art. 14 para. 63.
694 *BVerfGE* 70, 278/286; 76, 220/238.
695 *BVerfGE* 75, 78/97 f; 79, 179/198; 100, 226/241; 110, 1/28.

be available.[696] Ultimately, the burden on the owner must be proportionate to the aims pursued by the regulation and therefore appropriate and reasonable.[697] There must be a balance between the "interests of the owner worthy of protection and the interests of the common good".[698] Finally, the acknowledgement of private property in Basic Law through Art. 14 (1) (1) and the precept of common good of Art. 14 (2) must be observed.[699]

In the context of the assessment of proportionality, it is of significance that the legislator may have considerable leeway in its assessment and prognosis.[700] Whether this is the case, and the extent of such leeway, depends on various factors. The intensity, severity and scope of the encroachment on property are of particular relevance and, in the context of appropriateness, are of central importance.[701]

c) Factual and financial compensation

To avoid a disproportionate regulation on the content and limitation of property, it may be necessary to take the interest of the owners concerned into account through suitable compensatory measures. These may be transitional regulations, derogatory provisions, exemption clauses or other compensation arrangements.[702] Transitional regulations may be necessary, particularly to protect legitimate trust or expectations, which are in the context of infringements on property directly protected by Art. 14 Basic Law.[703] Exceptions may be appropriate if subgroups are impaired to a far greater extent than the majority of those affected by the regulation.[704]

If factual compensation is not possible or not compatible with the aim pursued, *financial compensation,* or even the acquisition of the property by the authorities (at market value), may be necessary.[705] This is often the case if the effects of a regu-

---

696 *Jarass,* in: drs./Pieroth, Grundgesetz, 11th ed. 2011, Art. 14 para. 38b.
697 *BVerfGE* 74, 203/214 f; BGHZ 81, 152/175.
698 *BVerfGE* 110, 1/28; 98, 17/37; 100, 226/240; *BVerwGE* 88, 191/194 f; *Papier,* in: Maunz/Dürig, Grundgesetz, as of 2010, Art. 14 para. 310.
699 *BVerfGE* 52, 1/29; 71, 230/246 f; 81, 208/220.
700 *BVerfGE* 53, 257/293; *Papier,* in: Maunz/Dürig, Grundgesetz, as of 2010, Art. 14 para. 321 ff.
701 *BVerfGE* 31, 229/243; ; 79, 29/41; 126, 331/363; *Jarass,* in: Drs./Pieroth, Grundgesetz, 11th ed. 2011, Art. 14 para. 40.
702 *BVerfGE* 100, 226/245 f; *BVerwG,* DVBl 03, 1075; DVBl 09, 1454; *Becker,* in: Stern/Becker, Grundrechte-Kommentar, 2010, Art. 14 para. 191.
703 *BVerfGE* 75, 78/104 f; 76, 220/244 f; 95, 64/82; 101, 239/257.
704 Cf. *BVerfGE* 30, 292/327; 59, 336/355 f; 65, 116/126 f; 68, 155/173; *BVerwG,* DVBl 01, 743 each on the freedom of profession.
705 *BVerfGE* 100, 226/245 f; *BVerwGE* 87, 332/383; 94, 1/12; *Becker,* in: Stern/ Becker, Grundrechte-Kommentar, 2010, Art. 14 para. 186.

lation on content are equivalent to expropriation.[706] Financial compensation may also be necessary in the case of less severe measures. This is an option primarily where an otherwise harmless statutory regulation has grave consequences in an individual case.[707]

III. Proportionality in the present context

1. Prohibition of brand packaging

a) Fundamental rights affected and severity of the infringement

The prohibition of brand packaging for tobacco products entails, as demonstrated, an infringement of the freedom of profession of Art. 12 Basic Law,[708] which (only) qualifies as a provision on the exercise of a profession.[709] On the other hand, it is a severe infringement of this right since the use of brand packaging is essential, and even indispensable for the sale of tobacco products. Tobacco products lacking a brand play a limited role in the market. Without brand packaging it is very difficult to sell tobacco products.

Furthermore, a prohibition of brand packaging also entails an encroachment of the use of trademark rights and thus a position which is protected under the guaranteed property of Art. 14 Basic Law.[710] This has a serious impact on the trademark rights. Specifically with tobacco products, the utilisation of brand packaging is the most important utilisation of trademark rights. If brand packaging is no longer permitted, the trademark rights of the tobacco products are essentially devalued.

b) The proportionality of the measures

aa) With regard to the *suitability* of a prohibition of brand packaging to protect health, reference can be made to the comments on the fundamental rights of the European Union.[711] The suitability of the measure is also assumed regarding the

---

706 Cf. *BVerfGE* 83, 201/212 f; 100, 226/245 f; 126, 331/363 f.; *BVerwGE* 88, 191/197.

707 *Wieland*, in: Dreier (ed.), Grundgesetz, Vol.I, 2nd ed. 2004, Art. 14 para. 133; *Jarass*, in: Jarass/Pieroth, Grundgesetz, 11th ed. 2011, Art. 14 para. 46.

708 D I 2 b above.

709 D II 1 a above.

710 D I 3 b above.

711 B IV 1 b aa above.

infringement of the freedom of profession pursuant to Art. 12 Basic Law and the right to property pursuant to Art. 14 Basic Law.[712]

bb) With regard to the *necessity* of the prohibition of brand packaging, there are serious doubts. An encroachment on the freedom to pursue a profession, as demonstrated, is only permissible if there is no other means with equivalent effect that is a less tangible restriction of the freedom of profession.[713] An alternative would be to consider enlarging the warnings on the package without (considerably) impairing the function of the package to make the brand sufficiently clear.[714] Such a measure could be just as effective to protect health, maybe even more effective.

cc) But even if, for this reason, one grants the legislator considerable leeway, and thus affirms the necessity, the third element of proportionality is still missing. This is the *appropriateness* of the measure. In comparison with the alternative described, a prohibition on brand packaging could only yield minor advantages for the protection of health. However, this minimal advantage cannot legitimize the severe infringement of the freedom of profession and the trademark right, which is protected through Art. 14 Basic Law. The severity of the infringement is not commensurate with the advantages that may be gained.[715]

In particular with regard to freedom of profession, the prohibition on brand packaging burdens the sale of tobacco products in a very sensitive way and creates a particularly high hurdle for the freedom to pursue a profession, especially for manufacturers of tobacco products. Such a prohibition will most certainly mean that it will be extremely difficult for changes in the market positions between different varieties of tobacco products. A prohibition on brand packaging would make the market situation much less flexible.[716] The measure thus also impairs the function of the freedom of profession to promote competition within the market.[717]

Furthermore, as illustrated, a prohibition of brand packaging results in a far-reaching devaluation of trademark rights.[718] Such an infringement of Art. 14 Basic Law can only be appropriate if it pursues a high-ranking aim, and the advantage

---

[712] Contrary *Schwarz*, in: Pache/Schwarz/Sosnitza, Aktuelle Rechtsfragen der Tabakregulierung in Europa, 2012, 124f.

[713] D II 1 b above.

[714] Cf B IV 1 b bb above.

[715] *Schwarz*, in: Pache/Schwarz/Sosnitza, Aktuelle Rechtsfragen der Tabakregulierung in Europa, 2012, 126f.

[716] Stein/Rauber, Rechtliche Grenzen der Bekämpfung des Tabakkonsums im Mehrebenensystem, 2011, 46.

[717] On this function *Jarass*, in: drs./Pieroth, Grundgesetz, 11th ed. 2011, Art. 12 para. 2; *Ruffert*, in: Epping/Hillgruber (ed.), Grundgesetz, 2009 Art. 12 para. 159; *Manssen*, in: v.Mangoldt/Klein/Starck, Grundgesetz, Vol. 1, 6th ed. 2010, Art. 12 para. 70.

[718] D III 1 a above.

must be provable and very important. The former is affirmative in the present context since it involves the protection of health. However, in comparison to the alternative measure described, the advantage is disproportionate to such a severe infringement of the basic rights.[719] As stated with regard to the fundamental rights of the European Union, there are measures that are less severe and protect health just as well while at the same time taking into account trademark rights.[720]

Overall, a prohibition of brand packaging has to be viewed as unreasonable. The leeway afforded to the legislator for regulations governing professional practice and provisions on the content and limits of property does not change the severity of the infringement. This applies, at any rate, to manufacturers who offer a large number of varieties and thus, for the reasons stated, are particularly reliant on using brand packaging.[721]

2. Prohibition of product display in retail facilities

a) Basic rights affected and severity of the infringement

The prohibition of product display in retail sales facilities entails an infringement of the freedom of profession pursuant to Art. 12 Basic Law.[722] This is a regulation governing professional practice. With regard to the severity of the encroachment, it is less severe than a prohibition of brand packaging. However, for the reasons stated with regard to the fundamental rights of the European Union, the severity is still significant.[723]

b) The proportionality of the measure

The leeway of the legislator for an assessment and prognosis will likely be more important with regard to the proportionality of these measures. Nevertheless, it needs to be examined more closely whether the protection of health cannot be sufficiently achieved through limiting advertising for tobacco products in retail sales facilities. As stated with regard to the fundamental rights of the European Union, there are strong arguments that the legislator should proceed in an incremental step-by-step manner, starting with less harsh measures before resorting to more

---

719 Also Stein/Rauber, Rechtliche Grenzen der Bekämpfung des Tabakkonsums im Mehrebenensystem, 2011, 49.
720 B IV 1 b bb above.
721 B IV 1 c above.
722 D I 2 b above.
723 B IV 2 b above.

severe measures if the lesser measures prove insufficient.⁷²⁴ Therefore, at the present time, one must view a complete prohibition of product display in retail sales facilities as unreasonable despite the leeway granted to the legislator. These findings are clear, at least with regard to those manufacturers who are particularly reliant on product display due to their variety of products.⁷²⁵

3. Prohibition of odorous substances and flavouring agents

a) Fundamental rights affected and severity of the infringement

The prohibition of odorous substances and flavouring agents in tobacco products impairs the freedom of profession expressed in Art. 12 Basic Law.⁷²⁶ Under certain circumstances this may also constitute an infringement of the right to property pursuant to Art. 14 Basic Law.⁷²⁷ For manufacturers of tobacco products containing odorous substances and flavouring agents, such a measure is inevitably a serious burden. In this respect reference can be made to the relevant comments on the EU basic rights.⁷²⁸

b) The proportionality of the measure

aa) For the assessment of the proportionality of a prohibition of odorous substances and flavouring agents, it is necessary to distinguish between substances which pose health risks and those that do not. In the first case, proportionality can be affirmed if the risks are not totally remote. This is the case according to the official justification of odorous substances and flavouring agents listed under Sec. 2 of the Tobacco Regulation.⁷²⁹

bb) However, if this is not the case, then there are serious doubts with regard to proportionality even though the leeway for assessment by the legislator is substantial. Upon closer examination, the situation is very similar to the situation at the EU law level. There are many reasons that suggest the measure is not suitable to support the protection of health.⁷³⁰ In any event, the infringement does not comply with the requirement of appropriateness. In this respect, the comparison with manufacturers

---

724 B IV 2 b above.
725 Cf. B IV 1 c above.
726 D 1 2 b above.
727 D I 3 b above.
728 B IV 3 b above.
729 BR-Drs. 479/77, p. 23 f. On the tobacco regulation A I 1 a above.
730 Cf. B IV 3 b above.

of tobacco products who produce tobacco products without odorous substances and flavouring agents is of significance; with regard to the freedom of profession, it is of relevance whether the burden on subgroups is particularly severe.[731] With regard to the right to property, it must be reviewed whether the infringing measure violates the general principle of equality.[732] It can hardly be fair if a measure disadvantages some manufacturers of tobacco products and leaves others unaffected. There are no sufficient grounds for such unequal treatment insofar as the odorous substances and flavouring agents do not entail any additional health risks.

4. The relevance of cumulative infringements of basic rights

a) *Principles*

As demonstrated, for the proportionality of infringements of basic rights, it is important to examine how much of a burden the measure imposes on the party entitled to the basic rights. If a party entitled to basic rights is burdened by a statute in several ways in parallel, then it is usually not sufficient to examine each infringement separately; instead, it may be necessary to assess the overall burden. This has recently been referred to as a "cumulative" infringement of basic rights: in the view of the Federal Constitutional Court, it is "possible that the overall effect of different infringements of areas protected by basic rights, which are minor when viewed individually, result in a serious infringement which exceeds the bounds of what is constitutionally acceptable."[733] The Federal Court of Justice and the Federal Social Court also maintain this view.[734] This view was further upheld by legal commentaries.[735] A cumulative burden must be taken into account if the infringements affect the same addressee, occur during the same period, pursue the same aim and

---

731 D II 1 b bb above.

732 D II 2 above.

733 *BVerfGE* 123, 186/265; similarly *BVerfGE* 112, 304/319 f.; 114, 196/247; here the court uses the term "additive" (cumulative) encroachment.

734 *BGH*, NJW 2009, 3448/3458 Rn. 99; *BSG*, GesR 2010 554/558 para. 26.

735 *Peine*, in: Merten/Papier (ed.), Handbuch der Grundrechte, Vol. III, 2009, § 57 para. 53; *Lücke*, DVBl 2001, 1469 ff.; *Kirchhof*, NJW 2006, 732; *Jarass*, in: Jarass/Pieroth, Grundgesetz, 11th ed. 2011, Preliminary remark 47 before Art. 1.

concern the same basic right.⁷³⁶ If this is the case then the burdens must be viewed cumulatively in the assessment of proportionality.⁷³⁷

b) Applicability in the present context

In the present context, if several of the prohibitions examined are to be introduced, their effective burden on the manufacturers of tobacco products must be assessed cumulatively.⁷³⁸ The prohibition of brand packaging burdens the manufacturers of the respective tobacco products just like the prohibition of product display in retail facilities and the prohibition of odorous substances and flavouring agents. The burdens also occur during the same period. In the end, the prohibitions all pursue the same aim and affect the same basic legally protected rights of exercising a profession, on the one hand, and the right to property, on the other. To the extent that the individual analysis has already shown that the measure does not observe proportionality, or if there are at least doubts with regard to proportionality, these findings will be significantly strengthened through the cumulative application of the instruments. In this respect reference can be made to the respective comments on the fundamental rights of the European Union.⁷³⁹

Moreover, at the level of domestic basic rights, it must be noted that the valid law already contains far-reaching restrictions to the detriment of manufacturers of tobacco products.⁷⁴⁰ This must be taken into account when assessing new and additional burdens.⁷⁴¹

---

736 E.g. *Peine*, in: Merten/Papier (ed.), Handbuch der Grundrechte, Vol.III, 2009, § 57 para. 53; *Hillgruber*, in: Isensee/Kirchhof (ed.), Handbuch des Staatsrechts, Vol.IX, 2011, § 200 para. 97; *Lücke*, DVBl 2001, 1470; somewhat broader *Kirchhof*, NJW 2006, 734.

737 *Hofmann*, AöR (public sector agency) 133 (2008), 540 ff.; *Lücke*, DVBl 2001, 1477 f.; *Peine*, in: Merten/Papier (ed.), Handbuch der Grundrechte, Vol.III, 2009, § 57 para. 54.

738 Also, in the same context, *Schwarz*, in: Pache/Schwarz/Sosnitza, Aktuelle Rechtsfragen der Tabakregulierung in Europa, 2012, 109 f.

739 B IV 4 b above.

740 A I 1 a above.

741 In this respect reference can also be made to the comments on the fundamental rights of the European Union, B IV 4b above.

E. Summary

I. Initial situation

1. *The subject of the study* is three far-reaching proposed regulations which lead to a drastic intensification of the requirements for the production and sale of tobacco products: the obligation to use uniform packaging without brand-specific design (prohibition of brand packaging), the prohibition of presenting tobacco products in retail sales facilities (including advertising for such products), and the prohibition of odorous substances and flavouring agents in tobacco products (pp. 85–87 above).
2. The use of *trademark rights* plays a major role in the present context. It is therefore significant that due to their legal and factual functions, the brands or trademarks are of monumental importance in a market economy. They are integral and indispensable components of a system of fair competition (pp. 87–89 above).

II. Fundamental Rights of the European Union

3. The primary law basis of the fundamental rights of the European Union is the (legally binding) Charter of Fundamental Rights of the European Union and the fundamental rights developed by the ECJ as general legal principles. The ECHR and the explanations of the Praesidium on the Charter of Fundamental Rights are significant sources of legal knowledge (pp. 92–93 above).
4. The fundamental rights comprehensively *oblige* all bodies of the Union. The Member States are bound to the extent that they implement EU law, in particular if they execute or enforce EU law (pp. 93–94 above).
5. The *Freedom of expression and information* under Art. 11 CFR also protects all statements and information conveyed in an economic context. This includes the use of product trademarks. Thus, the prohibition of brand packaging and the prohibition of product display in retail sales facilities interfere with the fundamental right (pp. 95–97 above).
6. The *right to property* under Art. 17 CFR protects the right to a trademark as well as business secrets. Consequently, the prohibition of brand packaging and the prohibition of product display in retail facilities entail infringements of the right to property. This applies especially with regard to a prohibition of odorous substances and flavouring agents if it is no longer permissible to use a business secret (pp. 97–99 above).

7. The *freedom to conduct a business* under Art. 16 CFR includes a special provision concerning the entrepreneurial freedom. The prohibition of brand packaging impairs this fundamental right just as the prohibition of product display in retail facilities and the prohibition of odorous substances and flavouring agents do (pp. 99–101 above).
8. *Restrictions* on the freedom of expression and information are only possible under the conditions of Art. 10 (2) ECHR. In particular the principle of proportionality must be observed. Restrictions on the right to property must observe the conditions set out under Art. 17 (1) (3) CFR and also observe Art. 1 ECHR Additional Protocol. In this respect the principle of proportionality also applies. With regard to restrictions on the freedom to conduct a business, this principle must also be observed, despite the reference to EU law and the legal provisions of the national laws in Art. 16 CFR (pp. 101–105 above).
9. The principle of proportionality plays a role in primary EU law beyond measuring restrictions on fundamental rights. In current case law, the ECJ observes an independent *general requirement of proportionality* which is identical to proportionality based on the fundamental rights, the definition of which can (also) be used in the area of basic rights (pp. 105–106 above).
10. A proportionality assessment evaluates the *suitability* of the measure with regard to the aim pursued. The further requirement of *necessity* initially indicates that the means which is the least invasive but equally effective must be used. Moreover, the interests concerned must be *balanced*, which is interpreted in Germany as an independent, third element of proportionality, the appropriateness. Under certain circumstances, proportionality may make transitional provisions and exceptions or compensation necessary, even in the area of the freedom to conduct a business or the freedom of expression and information (pp. 106–108 above).
11. In the case law of the European Court of Justice, the *intensity of judicial control* in the area of the freedom of expression and information is higher than in the area of the right to property and the freedom to conduct a business, in particular with regard to serious infringements of basic rights (pp. 108–109 above).
12. The *prohibition of brand packaging* may likely be seen as suitable. By contrast, there are serious doubts pertaining to the necessity and the obligation to balance interests with respect to these measures since less severe measures are available which serve to protect health almost as well. At the same time, they do a much better job observing trademark law. This applies particularly to manufacturers with a wide assortment of products. These findings should also apply to excessive labelling requirements on packaging that make it impossible for consumers to recognize their brand on first sight (pp. 110–112 above).

Summary | 143

13. There are fewer doubts with regard to the *prohibition of product display* in retail sales facilities. With regard to the requirement of necessity, there are, however, strong indications that less severe measures must be taken first, and that their effects must then be assessed (pp. 113–114 above).
14. The *prohibition of odorous substances and flavouring agents* may observe the principle of proportionality when there are health risks associated with the substances themselves. If this is not the case, then there are already serious doubts as to whether the prohibition is suitable to promote health (by reducing tobacco consumption). At any rate, despite the leeway afforded to the legislator, a prohibition of such substances does not satisfy the obligation to properly balance the interests affected. Further, it only affects a portion of manufacturers and thus infringes upon fair competition (pp. 114–115 above).
15. Ultimately, infringements of fundamental rights borne by the same party, occurring at the same time, and which essentially pursue the same aim and affect the same legal interests, must be viewed cumulatively in the context of proportionality (*cumulative infringements*). In the present context, this increases the doubts regarding proportionality (p. 116 above).

III. Free movement of goods

16. The prohibition of measures having equivalent effect under Art. 34 TFEU *obliges* the Member States as well as the Union (pp. 117–118 above).
17. With non-discriminatory provisions, a *measure has equivalent effect* as a quantitative restriction if it legally or effectively obstructs or strongly hinders access to the market for products from another Member State more than it obstructs or hinders access for domestic products. This condition is fulfilled with regard to the prohibition of brand packaging and the prohibition of product display in retail sales facilities even if the Union issues such regulations. These prohibitions lead to a far-reaching devaluation of trademark rights and thereby make access to the market more difficult for manufacturers of tobacco products from other Member States as compared to domestic manufacturers (pp. 118–120 above).
18. Restrictions on the prohibition of measures having equivalent effect may be *justified*. This depends on the proportionality of the restriction. In this respect the Court of Justice applies strict standards of control, also in the area of health and consumer protection. In the context of proportionality it is necessary to consider whether the restriction of the free movement of goods simultaneously infringes basic rights (pp. 120–122 above).
19. In view of the fact that trademark rights are, on the one hand, an important instrument of cross-border trade but, on the other hand, essentially depleted through the prohibition of brand packaging and product display in retail sales

facilities, *in the present context*, there are strong arguments against the proportionality of the restriction of Art. 34 TFEU (pp. 122–123 above).

IV. Basic rights under German Basic Constitutional Law

20. The basic rights under German Basic Law do not *oblige* the Union, in particular, not if the Union adopts legislative acts. In contrast, the German legislator is bound insofar as EU law has not enacted regulations or if it allows the Member States leeway. This applies particularly to the transposition and execution of EU law. This is of significance in the present context for the transposition of directives on tobacco production and the sale of tobacco (pp. 124–126 above).
21. A prohibition of brand packaging, a prohibition of product display in retail sales facilities and a prohibition of odorous substances and flavouring agents in tobacco products infringe the *freedom of profession* pursuant to Art. 12 Basic Law; in particular, these are regulations relating to professions. Furthermore, a prohibition of brand packaging and of product display is an encroachment of the *right to property* pursuant to Art. 14 Basic Law since they significantly restrict the use of the trademark rights. This applies to the prohibition of odorous substances and flavouring agents to the extent that utilisation of a business secret is excluded. It is uncertain whether these two prohibitions must also be measured against the *freedom of opinion* pursuant to Art. 5 (1) Basic Law. Unlike at the European level, this basic right does not give further reaching protection than Art. 12 Basic Law and Art. 14 Basic Law; thus, the question of applicability can be left open (pp. 126–130 above).
22. With regard to the conditions for *justification,* the infringement of the freedom of profession must be considered like regulations governing professional practice (and not choice), albeit of a very serious nature. Similarly, there is much to suggest that the prohibitions constitute restrictions on the content and limits of property (and not expropriation). As such, they must observe the principles of proportionality and equality. Compensation may eventually be necessary (pp. 130–135 above).
23. The *prohibition of brand packaging* constitutes a very serious infringement of both the freedom of profession and the right to property. These infringements cannot be considered appropriate since less severe measures are available which support the protection of health almost as well but observe trademark rights much more effectively (pp. 135–137 above).
24. With regard to the *prohibition of product display* in retail sales facilities, the leeway of the legislator plays a greater role. However, there are strong indications that the principle of proportionality requires less severe measures to be taken first and their effectiveness subsequently assessed (pp. 137–138 above).

25. As for the *prohibition of odorous substances and flavouring agents*, it depends whether there are health risks associated with the substances themselves. If so, one has to affirm proportionality. Otherwise, proportionality may fail due to a lack of necessity. At any rate, the requirement of appropriateness is not satisfied despite the significant legislative leeway (pp. 138–139 above).
26. According to the case law of the Federal Constitutional Court, it is necessary to consider the overall burden in cases of *cumulative infringements* of basic rights. This applies when the burdens affect the same party entitled to basic rights at the same time, whilst pursuing essentially the same aim and affecting the same legal interest. In the present connection, this increases the doubts concerning the proportionality of the prohibitions examined (pp. 139–140 above).